MW00344804

TURNING BACK

TURNING BACK

The Personal Journey of a "Born-Again" Jew

A Memoir

MICHAEL LESHER

LINCOLN SQUARE BOOKS

Turning Back: The Personal Journey of a "Born-Again" Jew
Copyright © 2020 by Michael Lesher
New York, New York

Lincoln Square Books supports the right of free expression and the value of copyright. The purpose of copyright is to encourage writers and artists to produce creative work that enriches our culture.

All rights reserved.

A Lincoln Square Book
Published by Lincoln Square Books
www.lincolnsquarebooks.com

ISBN (paperback): 978-1-947187-05-4
Library of Congress Control #: 2019949470

WHAT THE CRITICS SAY ABOUT ...
TURNING BACK

"In recent years, a number of memoirs have been published by people who . . . made the journey away from ultra-Orthodox Jewish communities. Michael Lesher's beautifully written book explores that trajectory in reverse, offering a deeply personal account of what religious Jews would call his 'return' to Judaism.

"[His] story . . . renders vividly that necessarily eccentric corner of the religious world that exists to bring formerly non-Orthodox Jews back into the fold, [and] does not involve a 'neat' path to conversion . . .

"Instead, Lesher grapples honestly with a process that can result in isolation from one's family of origin and prior Jewish community, while also providing a richly rewarding . . . and a highly circumscribed way of life that 'makes more precious the experience of what's left inside.'

"Indeed, Lesher's powerful intellect and relentlessly questioning nature bring him to the realization that in undergoing such a transformation, he is bound to disappoint people from both his past and 'new' lives, failing to meet the expectations of either— and very likely the rest of us who may think we know why someone would undertake such a journey."

—Hella Winston, sociologist, investigative journalist and book author (*Unchosen: The Hidden Lives of Hasidic Rebels*)

"Michael Lesher is a man of questions. His questioning of the secular Jewish life of his youth led him as an adult to a lifestyle of Orthodox, religious observance. His questioning of what he considered sexual improprieties committed by people who identified as Torah-observant Jews led him to become an outspoken advocate on behalf of young victims—and to use his legal training, in addition to his writing skills, in order to better represent the victims. In *Turning Back*, Lesher, searingly honest and unapologetically iconoclastic ... , describes the ... risks he took that have often put him at odds with ... Orthodox Judaism ... As befits his personality, his book is full of questions; his answers are a guide to what made him successful."

—Steve Lipman, staff writer at the
Jewish Week (NY), and author of two books.

"Michael Lesher takes the reader with him on his personal, fascinating journey into the world of Orthodox Judaism. "*Turning Back* is informative, well-written and deeply moving."

—Norton Mezvinsky, Distinguished Professor Emeritus
at Connecticut State University and President of the
International Council for Middle East Studies

WHAT THE CRITICS SAY ABOUT OTHER WORKS BY MICHAEL LESHER...

Sexual Abuse, Shonda and Concealment in Orthodox Jewish Communities (McFarland & Co.)

"Michael Lesher is a radical, a rebel, a hero. He has stood up against an unjust system by speaking terrible truths, and with these truths he might just manage to shatter one of the modern-day religious fundamentalist forms of oppression in our midst."

—Christopher Ketcham, contributing editor, *Harper's, Vanity Fair, GQ, The Nation, Mother Jones*, and other magazines.

"Michael Lesher has written an exhaustively researched analysis of why the Orthodox Jewish community, as a whole, goes to great and damaging lengths to cover up sexual abuse of its children. Perhaps the most valuable aspect of Lesher's book is his cogent analysis of the interplay of a complex set of Orthodox norms and values. He maps out their historical and psychological underpinnings, sketching a clear picture of how the community's growing obsession with women's modesty and children's purity is deeply tied to its emphasis on authority and the suppression of sexuality. With deep appreciation for the nuances of Orthodox culture, he explains why anyone who threatens this carefully constructed fortress of fear is expelled, with the result, all too often, of re-victimizing the people who were abused in the first place

—Debra Nussbaum Cohen, contributing editor for *The Forward*, and New York correspondent for *Ha'aretz.*

"If you buy one book this year, whether you are a member of the Jewish faith or not, this compelling book will force you to finish it in one sitting"

—*theunorthodoxjew.blogspot.com.*

"*Sexual Abuse, Shonda and Concealment in Orthodox Jewish Communities* is a call to the media, politicians, and governmental agencies charged with protecting children from abuse to refuse to appease powerful rabbis who try to prevent child sexual abuse cases from being reported and investigated. The book serves as a wakeup call to mainstream Jewish leaders and congregants to demand that more conservative and authoritarian branches do more to protect the youngest and most vulnerable members."

—Janet Heimlich, author of *Breaking Their Will: Shedding Light on Religious Child Maltreatment and founder of the Child-Friendly Faith Project*

For *Surfaces* (a collection of poems published 2019):

"Lesher's poems are possessed, as Rilke's and Rothko's works are, by a heightening spirituality that is inseparable from their formal beauty. They relate our human bodies, our physical relationships, our lust and love and fear."

—Jonathan Rapp, poet

The error of modern representatives of religion is that they promise their congregants the solution to all the problems of life, an expectation that religion does not fill. Religion, on the contrary, deepens the problems, but never intends to solve them.... The religious man endures constantly, mental upheaval, psychic collision.

— Rabbi Joseph B. Soloveitchik

Tradition ... cannot be inherited, and if you want it you must obtain it by great labour.

— T.S. Eliot

AUTHOR'S NOTE

In order to protect friends and acquaintances from any needless embarrassment, I have changed the names of most of the people who appear in this book. One consistent exception I have made is for immediate family members, concerning whom such a device would be pointless. Occasionally, where a figure is so well known that a name change would serve no purpose, I have identified that person accordingly.

This book was largely written relatively early in my journey into Orthodox Judaism. Inevitably, some things have changed between the time I wrote the book and the time I managed to have it published. I have gone through a divorce. My brother Rob has experienced major events in his private life that influenced his own religious attitudes. In August 2019, my father died. Nevertheless, whatever its limitations, the book still seems to me a complete representation of what I wanted to write at the time I wrote it.

I am indebted to so many people for the material that makes up this book that any effort to list them would be both pedantic and inadequate.

TABLE OF CONTENTS

INTRODUCTION

This is a book about life—about my life, to be specific—and not about movements, statistics or trends. Its subject is my choice to reroute my life into an Orthodox Judaism in which I was not raised, and that is a personal story for which I alone bear responsibility.

There are many other Jews who, like me, have moved back toward traditional religion. (There's even a popular phrase for us among the Orthodox: "B.T.s," short for the Hebrew phrase *ba'alei t'shuvah*, or "those who return.") And this pattern is probably part of a general religious trend rightward in today's United States.

But I'm not a statistic, and my life has had to be lived one day and one choice at a time. I didn't choose a religious life as part of a social trend. Nor is my story as simple as a steady movement in one direction. Yes, I've moved into the framework of Orthodox Judaism, but my questions haven't stopped there. They have only evolved. And I've evolved with them.

So I am not writing in order to preach Orthodox Judaism to the reader, nor am I offering an exposé of my coreligionists' failings or shortcomings. This is my own story, and for better or worse it's more about transformation than certainty. If I am successful in communicating that story, I hope it will help to show how excavating one's religious past, with all its values, influences and limitations, carries its own rewards.

And I hope in particular that a reader may take from this book some of the excitements that go along with that process: of trying to extend the continuity of life backward as well as forward; of loosening the knot of time by playing out the lines that connect us to the history of our beliefs; of digging always deeper by turning back.

PART 1: TRANSITIONS

Suppose the trip gives me absolutely nothing, still won't the whole journey yield at least two or three days that I shall remember all my life, with rapture or with bitterness?
— Anton Chekhov

God offers to every mind its choice between truth and repose. Take which you please—you can never have both.
— Ralph Waldo Emerson

CHAPTER ONE

When my oldest friend's uncle died suddenly in 1975, I went to his funeral without knowing quite what to expect. True, I'd known Martin since the first grade—I came as close to having grown up with him as I came with anyone, after a childhood spent following the roving career of my reporter-father.

But I had known Martin's uncle Sidney only slightly. I knew that Sidney's funeral would take place outside a synagogue. But that didn't mean much to me. Or to Martin either, since his mother was not Jewish, and his father (who, like Sidney, had been trained as a mathematician and a scientist) had no interest in religion. The only reference to anything Jewish I had ever heard from Martin's father was a recollection of the first time his mother had tied phylacteries, the leather straps and boxes religious Jews wear during morning prayers, on his head and his left arm. Back then he'd been a boy in Boston, and his mother was a Yiddish-speaking immigrant trying to plant her family's customs in a strange new land.

"She was tying me up with these straps," he'd said, raising a bushy eyebrow at us across the dinner china and brisket—"and I remember thinking, 'Boy, what a lot of nonsense.'"

And now his brother—my friend's uncle—was to be eulogized outside a synagogue, by a rabbi who'd become his close friend in the last years of his life. Why? We all knew Sidney hadn't expected to die. He hadn't come to the rabbi for solace, as some people do. In his fifties, with a long academic pedigree trailing behind him, Sidney had decided to learn about Judaism.

On the few occasions when I'd seen Sidney at my friend's house, I'd been tempted to ask him about that. But I never quite dared. Sidney's round body and short neck, sheathed in a double chin, always made me think of a turtle cased inside an unpretentious gray suit—but there was nothing disarming about his abrupt manners or his chilly, intelligent eyes. Once he had snapped at my friend, who was having difficulty grasping the mathematical theorem known as Euler's formula, that anyone who couldn't understand its proof on inspection had no right to call himself educated.

Being just seventeen at the time, I decided to explain Sidney's interest in religion as an attack of nostalgia—a disease I associated with the old, and from which I thought I enjoyed a lifelong immunity. Judaism to me wasn't something one studied. It was just a feature of the landscape in which most of my friends had grown up, an old eyesore that nobody had got around to demolishing and that only visitors really noticed in the first place. It surfaced, occasionally, when grandparents and great-uncles used Yiddish phrases, or muttered gloomily about the appearance of a Jewish name in a scandalous headline. Or on the first night of Passover, when my mother cooked stuffed fish and soup with matzoh balls, and, seated around the dining room table, we read from slim gray volumes, used only once a year, about how the Jews were supposed to have escaped from Egyptian slavery some three thousand years earlier. I'm sure my friend Martin gave Judaism even less thought than that.

So I was unprepared for the way it surfaced at Sidney's funeral. On a hot, brilliant summer day, the rabbi described a man who had delighted in helping others, who had made a series of anonymous gifts to people who wanted to travel to Israel, who was self-effacing, generous, and forbearing "of everything but stupidity"—in short, a man I'd never known. The rabbi, wiping sweat from his forehead, told us how Sidney had eventually come to look at each piece of knowledge gained, whether about mathematics or about the laws of Jewish ritual, as nothing less than a way of approaching God.

Under the circumstances, this was baffling to me. Sidney had died in a freak car accident, the result of the careless positioning of a seat belt. It was exactly the sort of death that seemed to me to cry aloud the randomness of the world. Life, I thought then, couldn't be about knowing God—unless you meant by that knowing about his arbitrariness. And who already knew that better than the Jews? Less than four decades earlier, nearly an entire Jewish generation had gone the way Sidney went. Yet here was the proof that even so great a shock hadn't unwound us from our past. Even Jews like Sidney still wanted to be Jews.

It was too late to ask him why—or to ask relatives I had lost during the war, or my immigrant ancestors, or their parents and grandparents who had kept the old tradition alive. But thinking of it—a question I'd never asked anyone—struck me through with a chill stronger than the summer heat, and made me for the first time so conscious of death that I could not handle the shovel the mourners passed around to cover Sidney's coffin with earth, spadeful by spadeful, according to old Jewish custom. As the rabbi wiped his eyes, as my friend Martin turned away from the grave, I had to let the shovel drop. And the question dropped with it.

But a few years later, I found myself asking my mother if she might be interested in following the traditional dietary laws.

"Never."

My mother is a woman of moderate views, so I was surprised at the conviction in her voice. "Why not?"

"Well, for one thing," she said, "because I did it before. It was a pain in the neck. A lot of nonsense." As I remember it, she was standing over the kitchen sink, scrubbing the freckles off a potato in a white stream of water.

"You *did*?" Somehow it seemed to me that she'd revealed something slightly shameful.

"It was when I was first married," she continued. "Steve hated the idea, of course. He hated anything that meant work." (My parents divorced when I was sixteen and have not had many kind words for each other since.) "But I tried. Separate dishes, meat and dairy, separate meals. The only *kosher* butcher was forty miles away. They didn't have those things in Columbus, Georgia, you know."

She snorted. "And for what? To act like the immigrants from Poland, right off the boat? I'm proud of being Jewish, but thank God, I wasn't raised *that* way."

I can understand her point of view. She had wanted the ancestral legacy to reach me, if at all, through *her*—as parents generally do. She'd figured that what seemed meaningless in Judaism to her would leave me just as unimpressed.

A few months later, my father's response was even blunter.

"I stopped doing that years ago," he said. We were in his new home at the time, a sparklingly clean Georgetown condominium he shared with his second wife (who was not Jewish).

"Not that I didn't try for a while. Oh, the awful meat we used to get. Your mother hated it. The only *kosher* butcher was—"

("I know, I know," I said.)

"And what's the point of it all? Surely," he wound up, "there are other ways to have a religious life."

That was jolting to me, coming at a certain stage in my own religious development. But after all, I had jolted *him*: my question had forced him back to a childhood Judaism that had made no sense to him, to old men with inexplicable customs from which he had gratefully escaped and toward which, without warning, his son seemed to be wandering back.

Without meaning to, I had started a quarrel about the real meaning of the past.

I began to write this book when it occurred to me that my children may one day have a similar quarrel with *me*. Not that they will have to ask about the details of Jewish observance. At three, my son and daughter were already learning Hebrew and reciting blessings. Traditional Judaism is something they take for granted.

But maybe that very fact will be the starting point for their accusations against me. Maybe they will resent me for narrowing their own range of religious choice. Or maybe they will resent my pre-religious past for implying other roads they could have followed, or at least explored, if only they'd been born into the circumstances their father inherited and contemned.

It won't be much of an answer to say that most of us level more or less the same accusation at our own parents. I suppose all that accusation can ever really show is the ironclad limits of what parents can teach their children. Too often the most valuable lessons in our own lives come at the most evanescent moments—when time seems just about to pull back the curtain on the Grand Prize. Such moments are beyond recapture. The gilt box hidden behind folds of velvet, which for the moment seems priceless, is reduced the next day to another item in life's yellowing inventory.

Nor will it be much of an answer to point out to my children that I have not remained in Orthodoxy complacently, that I have continued to change and to question. After all, I still live in Orthodox Judaism. How can I explain making a choice for them, any choice, before they had the chance to subject it to the same examination that I demanded for myself?

But maybe my children will understand more than I am giving them credit for. Maybe they'll realize that my greatest gift to them was a starting point from which to begin the chain of questions and answers that will define their own lives. And that I gave them that chance by turning back the course of my own life toward an older ideal—which was how I started the chain of questions that have defined *me*.

If they do understand that, then they may want to know, one day, how it was when I first entered the Orthodox Jewish world—that exotic destination which is their humdrum reality. And how it is whenever I'm reminded of just how far I've traveled along the way.

Or how little...

CHAPTER TWO

It is 1991. I am on the New York subway, squeezed against the side of the car in the commuter rush. A tallish, middle-aged stranger suddenly leans down and addresses me in Yiddish—a language I only vaguely understand.

"You don't talk Jewish?" he says next, in English. He has registered my confusion. And smiles in a way that seems at once superior and wistful. "What I said was, 'Have me in mind.'"

He points at the softback pamphlet from which I have been reading, the pages crammed with Hebrew text. I am thirty-three years old, married but childless, and I am on my way home to Monsey, New York—after that, to the Hasidic community of New Square to visit, with my wife, the resident holy man, the "Squarer Rebbe."

I know, now, what the stranger means. He has not called me back to the present for nothing. I represent something to him—hanging innocently on my metal "strap," reading my scholarly pamphlet.

According to Jewish tradition, the study of such a text qualifies as the fulfillment of a divine commandment—the study of the Torah, or ancient Jewish law. The specific subject matter is irrelevant to the commandment. (As it happens, this particular text comes from the *Mishnah*, the second-century compilation that forms the kernel of the Talmud; the passage in question has to do with the apportionment of damages among the victims of a rampaging ox.) What's more, the merit for the study can be bestowed on anyone who participates, or who merely wants to participate, even vicariously.

In other words, "Have me in mind."

"Haven't seen that stuff in a long time," he is saying now, over the subway-clatter. Advertisements for psychics and for bank-teller training programs have been glued to the curving metal wall of the subway car just above his head. The beatific face of a young, dark-eyed woman—a teller, I guess—smiles at me from atop this stranger's older, coarser one, a longish face under gray-fringed hair.

"I used to learn it but that was a different world, a long time ago. I figured there were other ways to be Jewish, and anyway like we say"—shrugging, he uses another Yiddish phrase, which he then translates for me as, "If you're eating pork, let it drip from the chin."

"I guess your generation doesn't speak much Jewish. You know, once you start on the other path, so to speak, the non-Jewish path, you might as well keep going farther off. My grandfather could never understand. It's a whole different world there." He shakes his head. Despite his age he is a healthy-looking man, ruddy and lean.

"You shouldn't know of it, like we say. But that's how it is. Once you start you just keep on going. I mean, who would I be fooling, learning this kind of stuff now, right?"—again gesturing at my pamphlet.

I'm starting to understand. He assumes, naturally, that I've always been an Orthodox Jew. And that sets up a paradox: I'm young enough to be his son—but apparently pious enough to be a stand-in for his grandfather. At least that's probably what he's thinking, looking at my scholarly softback, my *yarmulke*, the ritual tassels hanging out around my belt. That I was nearly thirty before I stood a chance of reading this text or of following his Yiddish phrases is a possibility that doesn't occur to him. Nor does the figure I will cut in a few hours, when, among the black-frocked Hasidim, I will resemble a piece of the *goyishe* modern world every bit as much as this man does to his own jaded eyes, standing next to me.

"So where do you live?" he asks.

"Monsey."

"Oh, Monsey. Yeah. Lots of religious types there. You know, uh, Rabbi Feuer? He used to live in Monsey."

"No, I'm afraid I don't."

"No? I thought everybody knew him. The Vizhnitzer Rebbe? You know *him*, don't you?"

"Not personally. I know of him."

"*N'vu denn!*" he shouts jovially. This phrase, at least, I know. It means—Well, of *course*!

"Anyway," he says, removing the swarthy hand he had momentarily clapped to my shoulder, "it's good to see some young people still studying Jewish law, somebody's got to be Jewish and I can't believe most of the young generation today. Doing everything they do, it's a disgrace. So have me in mind." With that, his thick eyebrows bunch together over a quick smile; then he pulls himself up again on his strap and heads for the door. We have reached his stop.

I've met older Jews like him before. In elevators, in subways, in train stations. It's odd to realize I'm a sort of a magnet to them. They see me and want, for a moment, to touch what they imagine my world to be. They hastily insert me into their own dusty family albums of bearded rabbis and bonnetted grandmothers, assuming all the while they've paid me a compliment.

And then they disappear.

Where? What shadowy place sustains them now, if the shadows from which they have emerged are still so alluring?

CHAPTER THREE

New Square, New York is only about fifteen minutes by car from Monsey, where my wife and I live. But on arrival we have stepped into another world. This is the demesne of the "Squarer Rebbe"—which, in Yiddish idiom, means simply "the Rebbe of New Square"—and like most of the others who crowd the place, Michelle and I are supplicants at his court.

Not that "court" implies opulence. Some Hasidic rebbes, I'm told, flaunt their eminence in high style—silver canes, elaborate retinue. But here at the Squarer Rebbe's residence the floor is green-and-white tile, rather like an old-fashioned hardware store. The walls could use a good cleaning. This is probably because of the hands of the busy Hasidim who are forever brushing it on their way around corners. They gesticulate, emphasizing a question (palms upward, shoulders hunched), driving home a point (forefinger stabbing the air), annotating a day's tale (a loop in the air with one hand, as the speaker describes the traffic that afternoon on the New York Thruway). Dozens of arms are pumping a flow of excited talk like Bernstein conducting the Philharmonic.

We are in the large outer room for people who want to ask the Rebbe's blessing in some personal matter. I would call this a waiting room, but most of the Hasidim are too restless to wait. Black-bearded men, in wide hats and side curls (*peyos*), they dart in and out of the room, talking loudly. It is nearly eleven o'clock at night, and I marvel at their energy.

Across from Michelle and me are the only two others in this crowd who are sitting down. They are local Hasidic women—pale, heavily covered up. Hardly more than girls, they are both obviously married: they wear the head scarves of Hasidic matrons. Like the other women here they use no makeup. Their long, plain cotton dresses reach from their collarbones to their wrists and ankles. They both stare stiffly in front of them. I wonder what trouble has brought them here.

Our own trouble is modest enough. Michelle and I have been married a year and she isn't pregnant. To me this doesn't seem to demand supernatural intervention, but Michelle wants a child badly and has other ideas. The Talmud records miracles said to have resulted from some righteous man's blessing. So, fifteen centuries later, religious Jews in places like Monsey are still asking for them.

Besides, we are "connected." The procedures of Orthodox social life are essentially unchanged since the days of the Russian Pale. You know someone who knows someone else, who is a big wheel with so-and-so, and strings are pulled. Strings were pulled for us the last time we came, and we waited until after midnight and never saw the Rebbe. But that was my fault. I came to the Squarer court without a suit or a hat. Even worse, I didn't throw any weight around.

"Why didn't you tell somebody you were Moishe Belkin's friend?" my connection to Moishe Belkin impatiently asked me the next day. "They would have made place for you."

"I can't behave like that," I said.

He gave me a Jewish wave of the hand, from the elbow, dismissing me from the ranks of creatures with enough sense to come in out of the rain. "You 'can't behave like that.' *You'll* never get anywhere."

Tonight I hope to do better. I'm properly dressed—Orthodox-fashion—in a coal-black suit and hat. Not that I resemble the Hasidim, in their knee-length coats and side curls. My parents are forever asking why, if I wear a *yarmulke* now, I don't have side curls and don't let my beard grow wild.

"Law and custom aren't the same," I tell them.

But here, as I sit chafing in my black Stetson, I am surrounded by people for whom the difference is negligible. Jewish life for them is not an abstraction gleaned from legal codes. It's the life they live. If that means speaking Yiddish, wearing jackets that brush their knees, growing side curls, or asking the Rebbe's blessing before every job interview or car purchase, then these things are Jewish, and only a gentile would ask niggling questions about them.

Tonight, at least, I'm determined to act as I'm expected to. And the strategy seems to work. After an hour and a half Michelle and I are finally admitted to the inner sanctum. It's a room very much like the other, outer room, only smaller. A tiled floor, walls with aging wooden veneer. The Rebbe has a large chair—the only rich-looking thing in the room—in which he rests, hunched amid the ornate upholstery. The air is close and a little stale. My wife is quickly motioned to a distant chair; the Rebbe does not look at women.

For several minutes he ponders the card handed to him when we were admitted, prepared for him by his middle-aged factotum, describing our situation in a few scrawled Yiddish sentences. (These were written in the antechamber, while I stammered and the facto-tum muttered, "I see. Oy, I see, uh *huh*.")

The Rebbe presses his palms together. He frowns for a moment. Then he speaks. In English, to my surprise.

"You haven't always been religious," he says to me.

I didn't tell the factotum that. How did the Rebbe know? Maybe he learned it from Moishe Belkin. In Orthodox communities every-body seems to hear everything about everybody, so I am not greatly surprised.

He looks at my card again and sighs. His large hands work an obscure pattern on the wide, scuffed desk before him. "No child yet."

People have told me remarkable stories about the Rebbe. About couples barren for years who conceived promptly after receiving the Rebbe's blessing, *et cetera*. Well, whatever else is true about him, he seems a kind man. Our tiny problem has touched him.

He switches to resonant, formal Yiddish. "May you soon have a child who will be a source of joy, who will grow up for Torah, mar-riage and good deeds," he says.

I respond, "Amen."

And now what? I'm unfamiliar with the rules at court, but it seems proper to wait for the Rebbe's dismissal. Michelle is sitting tensely in her chair, as confused about the proceedings as I am.

Outside, beyond the portals to the sanctum, I can hear querulous voices interrogating the factotum, asking when the Rebbe will be free. By now the hour's late even for them. "*A groisse sach*," I hear one of them saying, his voice rising—"a very important matter!" But the Rebbe's mind is turning around a *groisse sach* of his own.

"You know, everybody always wants to ask someone who becomes religious, what made him change?" the Rebbe says. He strokes his beard, smiling. "But really, that's not the question. Imagine, if a person got lost, and found his way home, people wouldn't ask, 'How did you get home?' It's the same thing with a Jew. When a Jew comes back, it's no big surprise. The surprise is that he can get lost in the first place."

The Rebbe stands up—an imposing business, for he is a large man, with heavy cheekbones, a white avalanche of beard.

"That's all it is when a Jew becomes religious," he says—and at his gesture, Michelle and I are on our way back into the antechamber, into the tiled room with its swarm of Hasidim, and then out into the busy night of study halls and *kosher* pizza shops and roads streaked with car lights and crowded with caftan-wearing men. "It's no big deal for him to come home."

Home was never like this.

CHAPTER FOUR

In September 1982, Palestinians in the Lebanese refugee camps of Sabra and Shatila near Beirut were massacred.

I was eating supper with the rest of my family when my youngest brother, Joe, came in with a sober face to say we should all look at the television, something was happening.

At first the images on the screen looked so bizarre they were almost funny. Scores of people lying down in the bright sun, twisted up like mock drunks, striking impossible poses. You kept expecting them all to jump up: no one could really rest in such positions. Then you saw the insects investigating their eyes, saw the motionlessness that wasn't repose but something that stuck to you.

I had never looked at dead bodies before. Now the television newsmen were determined that I would. That we all would.

It was Rosh ha-Shana, the Jewish New Year and traditional day of judgment.

We had just returned from services at Rodef Shalom ("pursuer of peace" in Hebrew)—the Reform Jewish temple in northern Virginia to which my mother had belonged since I was a child. Rosh ha-Shana had once been a day of family gatherings. That year, the holiday gathering at my mother's house was as close to a family as we could muster. My twelve-year-old sister was away—on one of her periodic rebellions, as I remember. My brother Rob was elsewhere too. And nine years before, my father had moved out to marry the woman he'd met after traveling to Washington from Los Angeles to buy the new family house. So he was absent, too.

It wasn't yet clear what the murders in Lebanon were going to mean for us. But already Israeli complicity was suspected and tongues were starting to cluck. I was Jewish enough to know about that. Tongues had clucked in the Georgia elementary school cafeteria whenever the subject of Jews and money arose; tongues had clucked when I had refused to sing Christmas carols. Jewish tongues clucked, too, throughout my childhood—whenever a Jewish-sounding name showed up in a report about corporate fraud, say, or a case of medical malpractice.

"No good for the Jews," Grandpa Phil would say from a couch, behind an everpresent Camel.

On a bus one day in Washington, a young Pakistani who wanted to talk politics had asked me, "Why do you Jews always have problems with other people?"—and I had been torn between wanting to punch him in the nose, to apologize, or to say, "Look, I'm not a Jew, I just happen to have Jewish parents, for God's sake!"

That Rosh ha-Shana I took shelter in my old bedroom. Very little had been moved since I first went away to college, so the room had that awkward feeling of a place that belongs to an earlier time in one's life. It suggested a world I knew to the last corner and crevice, but an alien world nevertheless, seen through a hole somehow too narrow for me to squeeze through. This room had housed my first erotic fantasies. And somewhere, buried in an old dresser drawer, there was still the fragment of a diary I had started when I was sixteen, when my parents' divorce was new. "How can I confess what I don't understand?" I had written there. The pang that had made me write those words seemed to hold back a storm—but tears never came, and nothing I wrote in that placid room ever quite seemed to take their place.

A whole Greek chorus of tongues were clucking by night's end. Possible Israeli responsibility for the killings was the theme of all the broadcasts. After all, Israel's invading army had occupied Beirut and surrounding territories, putting Israel's government effectively in charge. (Ultimately, responsibility for the massacre was officially pinned on the Lebanese Christian Phalange, though the Israelis had assisted them in the killing.) Late that night, an Israeli diplomat appeared on ABC's *Nightline* to tell Ted Koppel—another Jew, my mother was quick to point out—how Israel was going to determine who had really been at fault in the matter.

"I don't understand," my mother said sadly, as the polished diplomat and the implacable Koppel pointed fingers at each other on the T.V. screen—lying on her back in the old queen-sized bed as, with a puzzled gesture I had first seen after my father moved out, she pushed the hair back from her forehead.

"Why are they blaming *us*?" she asked. "Arabs killed Arabs. Look at that Koppel, a Jewish man. Why he is putting it all on us? *We* have to figure out what happened to *them*?"

I didn't like the provincial narrowness of the "us." But I knew what she meant. For months Israel's army had been clawing its way northward toward Beirut, desperately trying to dislodge the Palestine Liberation Organization from where it had massed itself just north of Galilee, over months of Jewish alarm and international indifference.[1]

"Now what?" my mother said. "The only story is that some Arabs got killed? That's what Ted Koppel wants? He's going to give all the anti-Semites an excuse to say we planned the whole thing?"

Not knowing how to respond, I asked, "Have you heard from Dad?"

"Sh," she said. "Next you'll be asking about Rob."

Rob, the eldest son after me, had become an evangelical Christian while a college student at Virginia Polytechnic Institute in Blacksburg, Virginia. Now he spent most nights with his religious friends.

I was glad that at least we didn't have to contend with *them*. "They're gonna legalize the homos in France," one of Rob's overalls-wearing coreligionists once said to me, shaking his shaggy head

---

1   That was how I understood matters at the time. Today I know that the Israeli attack was a premeditated crime that killed between 17,000 and 20,000 people, overwhelmingly civilians.

with an outrage that had a sort of relish in it. His clothing ran to faded denim, he drove a pickup truck, and he liked to slap dollops of mayonnaise on his sandwiches: "A real *goy*," as my mother said. He also seemed to enjoy talking about the world's depravity and the eschatological consequences, his disordered black hair bouncing in a sort of halo around his head as he jerked a thumb at heaven (actually, our kitchen ceiling) for emphasis.

"God's watchin'," he said. "Folks don't think he is, but he's watchin'. And you know what that means? France is gonna get zapped for that." He snapped his fingers. "I mean, *zapped*."

When the group dropped into my mother's home, they used to hold conclaves lasting late into the night, squatting around the kitchen in their denims like farmers, and fuming about devils and Democrats at such a pitch that my mother would probably have thrown them all out—except that the door had already closed forever on her husband, and she wasn't ready to see it close again on a son.

"I'm sure he knows how to be fair," my mother said diplomatically, when I wondered aloud whether Rob the Christian would join with the other "anti-Semites" on this latest issue.

I recalled a conversation with Rob that had challenged all my own ideas about his ability to be "fair."

It had happened over a year earlier. We'd been on an overheated bus from Charlottesville to Washington, plowing along an Interstate through cold, quiet countryside on our way home together for winter vacation from our respective Virginia colleges. Rob had just told me he'd become a Christian.

It was absolutely the last thing I had expected to hear from anyone in my family, and at first I thought he couldn't be serious. But he just looked at me out of his thin face and earnest, deep-set eyes, without a hint of wildness or excitement in him, and assured me that he wasn't joking.

"I'm more sure of this than of anything in my life," he said.

"How?" I asked.

"Because it's true."

I didn't know what to say to that, so I fell silent, helpless in my half of our vibrating seat. I kept turning over images of past years with my brother—how many of them were there?—trying to bring this scene into line with what had gone before.

During our shared childhood in North Carolina, Virginia and Georgia (wherever the peregrinations of my father's career had taken us), Rob and I had done plenty of Baptist-dodging. We'd been accosted so often by missionaries that we'd learned to be wryly humorous about them: serious, wide-lapeled young men standing on our porch, or outside school, asking earnestly whether we wanted to burn.

"When the Lord touches you, you know it," Rob went on. He still *looked* the same. No one I ever knew kept his dark hair in a neater helmet around his high-domed cranium. The neatness was a family joke: no one was permitted to touch Rob's hairbrush. The trip we were on was familiar, too: the bus rattled up the same highway we'd traveled on the way home many times before, threading the same cow pastures and castoff Virginia towns between Charlottesville and the Washington suburbs, stuffily oblivious to the sermon going on inside.

"Doubts are Satan's territory," Rob said.

As I tried to get a grip on what he was saying, the only thing that rose out of my memory was a voice I'd tried to forget a long time earlier—a disembodied voice pulsing in the warped magic of the same phrases Rob was using now. But the voice wasn't my brother's. It belonged to a preacher whose radio broadcasts I used to intercept on Sunday afternoons in Atlanta, when I was just twelve or thirteen. I had started playing with the tuning dial on that radio in the hope of finding something funny to while away the summer afternoons.

"Burn!" it shouted out of the cracked Zenith on the end table next to my bed. "Think you're better than God? There's nothing for you but *fire* in *Hell*!"

19

Every Sunday it was more of the same. I never told anyone I was listening to the preacher. I assumed my parents would disapprove. I myself disapproved of him, yet a horrified fascination made me keep coming back to the preacher's Sunday afternoon sermons during a breathlessly hot summer vacation. Or rather to his voice—for that's what I remember best: soggy and guttural as it worked its way into a passion, insanely sure of itself. What if God really did sympathize with that voice? I'd think of mayflies that died in midair by the hundreds over a lake near our house, their flimsy bodies choking the water's surface. I'd think of the rudimentary astronomy I had learned, according to which the earth was born in one fiery orgasm and was doomed to perish in another. And my ears would ring with: *Burn* in *Hell!*

But now it was my own brother's voice I had to contend with.

"Let me make sure I understand." I was trying to be reasonable. "Are you saying you've become interested in Christianity? Because there's nothing wrong with —"

"Not 'interested,'" he said shortly. "I'm a Christian. I believe in the Bible. That means literally. I had a real baptism. Immersion, not this sprinkling the left-wing churches do. And I believe in a personal God. I can talk to him and, if I'm fortunate, he can talk to me too."

On my bedstand the night of the Sabra and Shatila massacre was an oddity: an old Jewish prayer book. Almost small enough to hold in my palm, it had a smudged white plastic cover secured with a little clasp across the page ends, so that the book could actually be snapped shut—for what purpose I could imagine only with difficulty. The pages themselves were so yellow and brittle they threatened to crack when fingered. In fact, that's what they eventually did.

By the end of that week I was to read that book several times through. At the time I had hardly looked at it. When my old friend's uncle Sidney had died seven years earlier, he had left behind a large collection of books. I was the only person interested in a palm-sized Hebrew-English prayer book printed in 1926.

It had occurred to me that Sidney must have used this book in the course of his religious development. I wanted to see what the words it contained might have had to do with Sidney's change of life. So now I lay back in my old bed, framed by the beige walls that had once been so familiar, and started to read.

Curiosity quickly gave way to confusion. The English, often quaint and vague, did next to nothing to diminish the strangeness of the mounds of thick, printed Hebrew. I could read it with difficulty—I'd had some Hebrew training in Jewish Sunday schools over the years—but what was I to make of it all? It read like the sort of pious toadying I had always associated with my mind's vague image of medieval Christianity: "Please, in Thy mercy, accept our prayers as if they were the sacrifices of bullocks.... Let not loose upon us the entire measure of Thy wrath..." To my imagination the words brought on sight and smell, invasively vivid: the sweat of penitents; tiny stained glass windows high overhead in a narrow gloom, the very embodiment of stinginess, putting a price even on the inpouring of the saving light.

How could this have appealed to an orderly mind like Sidney's? And what could it tell me about something like Sabra and Shatila?

True, one had to say *something.* Hours before the first pictures of corpses appeared on television from the Palestinian refugee camps, the Reform rabbi at Rodef Shalom hadn't been any more helpful than Sidney's prayer book.

He was smallish, normally a jolly sort of man—neatly groomed, pleasantly rounded, clean-shaven. I had known him since I was a child. He had the sort of olive skin that made some people think he was Israeli by birth. In fact, he was a farm lad from a Carpathian village. As an adult he had learned fastidiousness—he had excellent manners and a carefully-arranged little bald spot, like a tonsure, at the crown of smooth, fine brown hair. Also a good baritone singing voice, of which he was a little vain. At a swimming party he hosted for graduating tenth graders, he had pushed one of his students into the pool as a practical joke. You wouldn't have guessed that this optimistic man had passed through the gates of Auschwitz at the age of fourteen. He and a few of his friends had dodged the gas chambers by claiming they knew how to repair automobiles, which resulted in their being placed on a train bound for a military factory in Berlin. In the chaos of those days the train never made it to the capital. The future Rabbi Berkowitz had weighed so little that Red Cross doctors were later amazed that he could walk.

What was his message that Rosh ha-Shana? The world's view of us was unfair, he said. We were blamed for other people's misdeeds. Or else, we were held to a higher standard than everyone else. Which amounted to the same thing.

"Yes, I heard the news," a Jewish friend had told me angrily over the telephone, after the sermon and before the television reports from the refugee camps. "Chancellor on NBC already called the attack on Beirut a 'blitzkrieg.' Did you hear that? They don't call us Christ-killers any more, so they've come up with another way of saying it, haven't they?"

Rabbi Berkowitz was not so extreme. Still, he spoke angrily about "a long, hot summer for the Jewish people," and went on to suggest that every critical news report about Israel was aimed cynically at easing non-Jewish guilt. This was a familiar message, and comforting in its way—a ready-made defense against malicious blame by outsiders.

But for that very reason, I felt betrayed by it somehow—-as if the rabbi had owed me something I *didn't* know. You didn't have to invoke memories of gas chambers to realize that something had gone hideously wrong in Beirut. And whatever you chose to believe about what had happened there, you certainly knew that Jews and Jewishness had something to do with one's response to it. In the shock of the sight of bloody corpses at Sabra and Shatila, I realized that I hadn't been ready to face my identity's implications. I had been calling myself a Jew without giving any thought to what the word might mean.

"But after all," my Jewish girlfriend, Janet, said to me over the phone—"after all, other people have been killed, and other people have been responsible. Just because you've come from a particular culture, or ethnic group, doesn't mean you have to share some part of its every deed."

"But I don't *want* to," I told her. I'm sure I was being more theatrical than clear. "Isn't that just the *point?*"

"The point of what?"

"The point of constantly worrying what people are going to say about me. The point of not exactly knowing whether I should be accusing or apologizing. Or even to *whom.* Do you understand?"

Maybe she did. Since early childhood, her parents had brought her to a synagogue in their New Jersey town exactly twice a year. The occasions were the end of services for New Year and the Day of Atonement. At the very end of the prayers, congregants who had paid for their seats on those days began to file out and a free berth could be snagged for fifteen minutes or so. The reason her parents went, and brought young Janet in her white holiday dress, was so that they could tell their own parents that they had been "in *shul*" on the High Holy days. So year after year, on Judaism's holiest days, Janet arrived late with her parents, hovered with them near the outside of a synagogue exit, and then slipped into an unpurchased folding chair at the synagogue rear—a perch rarely lasting more than ten minutes—while the people around them were either getting up to leave or were muttering prayers in a language that, to her, had remained completely incomprehensible. Janet had once confided to me that the sight of a synagogue through a car window could still make her feel like a thief.

So maybe she could understand my own welter of ambivalence. Still, I hung up unsatisfied. We'd been arguing somehow, I suddenly noticed—demanding things from each other we knew we couldn't deliver and didn't expect to receive.

❧ ❧ ❧

I learned from Sidney's prayer book that the story of Abraham's near-sacrifice of Isaac in the book of Genesis is recited by Orthodox Jews as part of the daily liturgy. The text rose readily to my memory, as it will for most people. But to repeat it, with all its implications, every single day?

On my back in bed, prayer book in hand, I read it through once again.

God, having miraculously arranged Isaac's birth to enliven his parents' old age, and having promised Abraham that a great nation would issue from the boy, suddenly orders Abraham to kill his son.

Abraham uncomplainingly saddles his donkey, takes Isaac with him to a designated spot atop a mountain, a journey of three days, and binds Isaac for the fatal sacrifice. (We are left to imagine the scene: the father's violence, the boy's protests or resignation or hysteria. All this is assumed, it seems, in the Bible's silence: it's as though the text had drawn all the outrage of the scene into a kind of wordless stare.)

Abraham raises the sacrificial knife to the boy's throat. At the last moment an angel orders Abraham to desist. "For now I know you are a fearer of God," the angel says, "and have not withheld your only son." Isaac is unbound. Father and son prepare a ram as a substitute sacrifice, Abraham is promised a great reward—and the story ends.

Alone in my room, I tried to imagine what this weird passage was meant to teach my ancestors. Obedience to God under any and all circumstances? Faith that God will not ultimately demand human sacrifice? (But then, why require Abraham to attempt bloodshed in the first place?)

Of course, I wasn't the first to ask these questions. Critics have found in the passage plenty of things to dislike: the image of God as hateful and capricious; violence as a test of faith; Abraham (or God) as the prototype of the hyperdemanding father who sees his children as possessions to be sacrificed to his own hopes.

But the Talmud says simply: "Love is irrational." Apart from softening the tale's implications by insisting that Isaac was a willing participant in the planned sacrifice, the Talmud is eager to stress that Abraham isn't praised for his faith or piety or obedience, but for his *love*—a love intense enough to defy reason. Which means that the murderous and intimate moment on the hilltop, the point that virtually disappears under the delicacy of the Bible's narrative restraint, might actually *be* a moment of love, indescribable as any such moment.

Looking at it that way, I could begin to see Abraham as a strangely sympathetic figure, human even in his violence and submission. Certainly he was a generous lover; just how generous is already implied shortly before the story of Isaac's sacrifice, when Abraham pleads for the lives of the wicked people of Sodom.

But how can you love God—*especially* the God of justice—when God stands ready to annihilate the very qualities his name stands for? Obviously you can't—not if God is an abstraction for you, a tyrannical principle demanding a gift of bloody swaddling clothes. But there is another way to look at the story. You can focus on Abraham's passionate attachment to life itself, a life that he, as a prophet, would have described in terms of divine blessing. The point then, maybe, is that such a passion can reach its highest pitch in the absence of any mediating object: child, lover, idol.

Of course there is danger in that. Surely it's a moment of sublime comedy when, at the end, an angel actually has to urge Abraham, not once but twice, *not* to murder his own son. (To remind him that he may be tempted to sacrifice too much to his religious ardor?) There's even the hint, through the angel's appearance, that God himself fumbled the rescue, forgetting to give the restraining message the angel rushed in to issue instead—in God's name, of course, but at the last possible moment. Is this a darkly wry reminder that religion sometimes seems preoccupied with the temperature of our faith and neglects the weak vessels that are the subjects of its passions?

❧ ❧ ❧

For me, at least, the Abraham story hung like a fog over a strange, sorrowful assembly that took place a few nights after my conversation with Janet. I was listening to Elie Wiesel, in a seat suspended somewhere in the huge cavity of Washington's Constitution Hall, the opulence of which was jolting, considering the purpose of the event—a memorial for the thirty thousand Jews killed at Babi Yar during the German advance of 1941.

I didn't yet know how the Orthodox world looked down its nose at this Nobel laureate, who had watched his father die in a concentration camp, who had written in *Night* how the flames that loomed over the Auschwitz crematoria in the dark sky seemed to threaten heaven itself.

("He's one of those people who say, 'This mustn't happen again,'" one of my American-born Orthodox acquaintances would later say. "But God punishes us all for the sins of the assimilated Jews—Jews like him. So because of him, it *can* happen again.")[2]

All I know is that something remarkable happened when that small figure, with its wave of hair lumped awkwardly on the narrow head, looked out at us and quoted from, of all things, the Talmud: "'The only complete heart is the broken heart.'

"All of you," Wiesel added, looking around the packed auditorium, "know what that means tonight."

I shifted in my seat. Was this another reading of the Abraham story? That the only complete lover of God must suffer the loss of something precious? My moral sense rebelled against the idea, but there it was.

"I don't know what happened in Lebanon," Wiesel went on. "But something went wrong. I only know it shouldn't happen as long as there are Jews."

---

2   I see Wiesel very differently today from the way I did then, though not for the reasons given by most Orthodox Jews. I describe him here the way he figures in my memory of that night's events.

The next moment Wiesel was telling us of a Jew in Kiev, taken with thousands of others to the shallow gorge of Babi Yar when the Germans occupied the city. The SS soldiers, assisted by local Ukrainians, did their work with alacrity. Stripped naked, knocked down by the human rain of bodies during the machine-gunning, this Jewish man had been forced into the mass grave while still alive. Somehow he had managed to find enough air, under the corpses, to go on breathing until dark, when he was able to dig his way out. He found his way to a house where a Christian widow lived alone. At the door, he begged her to let him in.

"Who are you?" she asked the mud-caked naked man through the crack of the door.

"I am Christ, your Lord," he intoned.

"And she believed him," said Wiesel, "and he survived the war."

Suddenly there was a new dimension in the place. Breathing at once seemed deeper and more difficult, as if the oxygen were flowing to capillaries and muscles never quite reached before. *I am Christ, your Lord.* To a woman who probably believed the Jews killed Christ. But who saw Christ himself, not his murderers, in the filthy Jewish body.

Next we were all repeating the *kaddish*, words traditionally recited for the dead. I had heard them before—dozens of times. But now they weren't the mumbo-jumbo they had seemed in the past. What was obscure in the language before seemed like just a natural hesitance—a way of holding onto a little silence in front of a chasm of time.

Magnified and sanctified be His great name...

I actually caught myself shaking. This is an emotional effect, I thought. Brought on by circumstances and the size of the crowd. Get a grip on yourself.

But I couldn't.

... in the world He created according to His will—and may He reign in our lifetimes and in our days and in the lifetimes of all Israel, speedily and soon...May there be abundant peace from Heaven—and life for us, and for all Israel...

It seemed presumptuous to put myself into the world this survivor had just painted. But at that moment I felt that, somehow, I
was part of the message. True, my loss was impossibly small when
compared to the Nazi genocide. But now it seemed big enough to
drown in, and I sensed this was because the words had reminded
me that this too—the loss of fathers by sons who had expected
more from them—was a reality as old as life itself. The few years I
had been on the planet didn't give me enough voice to express the
timelessness of the grief. But now, by linking up with the *kaddish*, I
was expressing it. My ancestors had joined their voices with mine to
help me find the words.

And I knew something else, too. My particular geography of
loss made up only a part of what mattered. Everyone lost much
more than a father as life moved ahead. Everyone always had. Time
was the thinnest of tissues. Every moment it tore in one's fingers,
yielding sacrifice or reprieve, only to tear again. And yet, somehow,
it had to hold together.

How?

*May there be abundant peace from heaven, and life for us and all
Israel—and let us say, Amen.*

"Amen," the voices around me echoed.

It was over. The mass grave of the past closed beneath me.

"What did you think?" my mother asked me when I'd returned
home.

I wasn't able to tell her. But whatever the step was that I'd taken
in that haunted room, I knew it left no place for turning back.

Chapter Five

L ater that year I was in New York—the city of my father's birth— inspired by what I called idealism, and driven by poverty.

I had just received a Masters degree and I was finished forever with school. (Or so I thought. Law school, and then a stint in a *yeshiva,* were both actually nearer than I would have dreamed possible at the time.)

Obviously, I needed a job. But doing what? I was clearly unsuited for any sort of money-making I'd been familiar with. My grand idea was to go to work for a liberal activist organization, Income and Purpose working together in lofty harmony. I naïvely assumed New York City would be the perfect place for that sort of thing.

But 1982 was the wrong year for liberal activism. Ronald Reagan was in the White House; wealthy America was busy preening, not looking for Noble Causes to invest in. Interviewer after interviewer told me that he'd love to have me work for him, but given the political climate, I surely understood that I'd have to contribute on a volunteer basis. Or there was always fundraising— did I own a car?

I didn't own a thing. Worse, I had to repay student loans in addition to earning a living. So, as my money ran out, my only suit got stained, the landlord more insistent, and my store of resumes embarrassingly depleted, Noble Causes had to yield to more basic necessities. By 1984, after breaking up irrevocably with Janet, I found myself at work in a narrow turkey pen of an office in a legal publishing house in New York City, behind a synthetic slab the company called a desk, typing and copyediting footnotes for treatises with names like *Weinstein's Evidence* and *Federal Litigation Practice Guide*. And because the idea of continuing to do nothing but that for years ahead seemed intolerable, and because I didn't know a better way out, pretty soon, at night, I was toiling away once again as a student—this time at Brooklyn Law School. (The tuition, miraculously, was paid by my employer.)

Law school had been my mother's idea. ("My son the law student" was much better than "My son the editorial assistant who earns less than the neighbor's maid.") As for me, I had no real idea whether the study would, as Mom put it, "lift" me to any professional opportunities. I'm not sure I really cared.

Where I chose to live in New York, once the regular salary started coming in, came closer to reflecting my own preferences. The apartment I shared with a young lawyer (just out of law school himself and struggling to make a living) was a little place with damp wallpaper, inadequate ventilation and aging brown carpeting in one central room, piled atop a Greek restaurant in the northernmost tip of Brooklyn. All in all, its charms were about what you'd expect—considering my income and that this was New York City. My bedroom, the smaller of the two, was barely large enough for a cot wedged between an old mahogany chest of drawers (once my grandparents') and my battered, spindly-legged writing desk. My bedroom floor was made of cracking tiles, and despite one window-mounted air conditioner in the kitchen, the entire apartment sweltered in the summer.

But I loved it. It was as far from suburbia as I'd ever been; that alone was worth the cramping. The city roared and buzzed all around us. The great arch of the Brooklyn Bridge over the East River was only a short walk away. And directly across the street stood an especially intriguing sight: the multistoried, fence-ringed white slab that was the local prison. It floated inescapably above our busy intersection at night, when searchlights washed it to the color and texture of marble, like a giant's tombstone. All night long, trucks clanged their invisible way below my window, and the unnatural roar of the subway forced itself through the gratings down below—to my romantic mind, the sound of New York's phantoms prowling the limits of their subterranean cages.

On the landing halfway up the stairs to our apartment was something else that commanded attention. God wasn't the only thing on my mind in those days. Up against the wall was a large, framed photograph of a naked woman. (I assume it belonged to the landlord, who also ran the restaurant downstairs.) The setting she stood in was a rather dark room. The woman was half-way and almost translucently shown, but poignantly close-up, her back against a gray wall, her brownish skin glowing through a crisscross of shadows that lay over her body like a tightly-curved net.

She seemed to have chosen not to struggle against the net. Her face, behind the faint veil of the photographer's obscuring technique, held no clue to her feelings. If her pose communicated anything, it was an air of waiting. Not submission. Just the suggestion of some very delicate mystery, the rainbow in a soap bubble, that might or might not be held by the web of light and shadow as she waited there. Longings only half identified with anything I'd experienced seemed deepened, rather than stirred, by the touch of that brown, shadow-ribbed skin on the surface of my daydreams. What would it mean for that woman's eyes to search for *me*?

Meanwhile, there was Sam Lehrman—Shmuel, as he preferred to be called, since he insisted that Jews were properly known by Hebrew names. Shmuel worked in a cubicle near mine at the publishing company, where both of us did glorified secretarial tricks for what was charitably called a living.

Shmuel was a newly Orthodox Jew—the first Orthodox Jew I had ever really known. I don't remember how or when he discovered my own ethnicity. But he soon attached himself to me like a stinging fly.

"I used to be as confused as you are," he told me. "Until I got my act together."

He had recently studied at two *yeshivas* specifically designed for newly-religious adults. Whatever else they taught him there, they certainly removed his social inhibitions. When I told him Janet and I had finally broken up, all he said was, "Good. She'd just lead you wrong."

He was determined to lead me right. He wore a knitted white-and-blue skullcap. Under his oversized shirts (he had the build of a linebacker) was the extra, tasselled garment required by Jewish law. He brought his own food to work in order to observe the dietary laws. He didn't appear on the Jewish holidays—including holidays I'd never heard of. His zeal intrigued me. Once I saw that there was no danger of offending him with questions, I pumped him for as much information as I could.

"I studied Russian history in college," he told me. "Because I wanted to learn about my grandparents. I didn't even know that my grandparents weren't Russians. You know that, don't you? Jews in Russia weren't Russians?"

"I know they weren't supposed to be," I said.

Shmuel once rowed crew at Rutgers. A beard, and some affectations of Yiddish phrasing, stood out oddly against the linebacker body. ("In Virginia your mother lives?" he would say.) Intelligent, curious eyes. Over six feet of bulk—the middle softening a bit. He was fond of those awful sugary cakes in wrappers (assuming he could find a *kosher* insignia printed on the outside). He was what my mother calls "nervy." Always late somewhere, he generally had a dark stubble-shadow along his generously-sized neck, and at close range he conveyed to me a faint trace of hygienic carelessness.

"A liberal's answer," he snorted at my ignorance. "It doesn't mean anything, Russia or America. Jews in America aren't Americans either."

While a college student, Shmuel had wandered one day into the university's Chabad House—one of many such campus centers created by Lubavitch Hasidim, who were particularly active in intra-Jewish missionary work. Sam, as he was known then, was an athlete, living high off a Social Security pension since the early death of

his father. He drove a BMW and chased girls. Despite his build
and good looks he was too naive to be really successful in that
line. (Once, he confided to me, he nearly made it with an Italian
Catholic girl—only to have her murmur at a crucial moment, "I
want you to know that I intend to be a virgin when I get married."
Not knowing how to proceed under the circumstances, he gave up.)

But something in the texts they showed him at Chabad roused
his dormant mind. "I used to think all that Talmudic stuff was
for old people, devotional things, like reciting Psalms. But those
books were *hard*. I mean, you had to *think*."

He had read a lot since then, though he rarely tackled whole
books from beginning to end. He was too restless to finish a long
run of reading. He was more at home with thousand-word columns
in newspapers like *Ma'ariv, Israel Shelanu,* or *The Jewish Press.* He was
enthusiastic about Meir Kahane, the Brooklyn rabble-rouser who
had gone to Israel to campaign on a platform calling for the expul-
sion of the country's entire Palestinian Arab population. That was
the subject that touched off our first major argument.

"*Kahane?*" I demanded.

"Why not?"

"That fascist?"

"You're talking in phrases," Shmuel told me. "Like all the liberals. The question is, What does the Torah say? That's the question
Kahane asks. If you don't like the answer, don't blame him."

"Well, what *does* the Torah say?"

"For one thing, that you can't eat *that,*" he retorted, his right
hand now pointing at the falafel I had bought from a Greek street
vendor.

I winced. Then I fired up. Even I knew that vegetables and fruits
are *kosher.* Did everything have to be cooked by a Jewish matron in
apron and shawl? With a rabbi standing over her to make sure she
didn't grease the pans with lard?

"Look," he told me. "If you want to invent your own religion,
fine. But inventions won't get you any closer to God. Give me a little
credit—I've spent two years in *yeshivas.*"

Well, that was true. The fact that he was virtually bounced out of both of them—for being quarrelsome and for sleeping late—may have weakened his case in point of scholarship, but to me it only emphasized his devotion to the Law being taught there, since he clearly hadn't reaped what psychologists call "secondary benefits" from his course of study.

But what about Kahane?

"Kahane isn't the point. It comes down to this," he said. "The Torah is either true or not true. It says it was a revelation from God. So either it is or it isn't. If it isn't, if God didn't reveal it, then Moses *lied*. And what you call 'Jewish morality' will have to make room for deceit, fraud and superstition, which is more than I can swallow."

There was dignity in so much such loyalty to the text. But what had convinced Shmuel it *was* true? He never exactly said. "I don't claim to be a great representative. But that doesn't matter. It isn't about me. It's about Torah. You'll find out for yourself, if you're any good."

My first Talmud sessions were with Shmuel. He was hardly the sort of person I would have chosen to introduce me to the Talmud. But he insisted on doing it, I could not refuse, and so the choice was made for me. Our company had several unused offices, and I ate lunch during the fifteen-minute coffee break, leaving lunch hour free. How Shmuel got away I don't know. One day he took me into a vacant office, a dusty folio volume with a Hebrew title under his arm, grumbling something like, "We've been talking long enough."

"Nervy" as always, Shmuel didn't want to turn the light on, which would have been visible under the door and might have called attention to us. There was some weak light from a window. The half-darkness seemed appropriate to me as we opened the volume, Shmuel swaying back and forth from the waist, the way he'd learned to do in the *yeshivas*, though he wore a green knit shirt, not the black suit and white shirt preferred in those places. As always, he had on a knitted skullcap. Before we could start he insisted that I, too, cover my head. But as neither of us had a hat and there was no spare *yarmulke* to hand, this presented me with a quandary. In the end I folded a large paper towel from the bathroom into a kind of bonnet, and sort of wore that, sitting at the one desk in the room, prompting Shmuel to laugh at me. That did nothing to improve the atmosphere or to make the task before us any more enticing.

But I soon forgot about that. The text itself was like a step into a cloister. It took a while for my eyes to adjust, so to speak. I had to get used to the Talmud's dimmer light. But I'll never forget the moment I did get used to it and started to look around in earnest. It was as if a whole new world had unrolled in front of me.

I can still sympathize with those Enlightenment Jews who condemned the Talmud's disciplines as stuffy, narrow, baroque. It *is* a peculiar text, full of idiosyncratic questions, distinctions and convictions. It requires a specialized sort of study, which is why reading it cold, even in translation, is generally a waste of time. That may be why so many have given up on it before uncovering its treasures.

Yet the treasures are real. The world of the Talmud—a "sea," it has been traditionally called, and the comparison is apt, both for size and mystery—is uniquely intriguing. I quote Herman Wouk: "Under the opaque Aramaic surface the Talmud is a magnificent structure of subtle legal brilliancies, all interwoven with legend, mysticism, the color of ancient times, and the cut-and-thrust of powerful minds in sharp clash." Not a bad description of the moment the text sucks you in for the first time.

Studying the Talmud, even in those early sessions with Shmuel, reminded me of something else, too. Or rather, I was more and more reminded of Talmud study as something else happened at the same time that study was ripening—I mean, as I began to change my life. Like studying the Talmud, that process was rather like wandering around a maze of unfamiliar streets until, suddenly, some detail jumped out that seemed to hold a key toward making sense out of the whole scene. Then everything suddenly looked as sunlit and inviting as if I'd lived there all my life. That is what a deep change feels like, I guess: everything goes from being the jumbled details in a bad dream to the sudden focus of a familiar view; you can navigate the neighborhood, or block of text, or group of ideas, as if they had always been yours. And you can almost convince yourself that they really *were* always yours. Partly, I suppose, because the act of discovering them, the lifting of the fog, is such a keen and liberating pleasure.

But just now I was taking the first steps. No one spoke my language, the streets were long and crooked, and there was no end in sight.

Though I began spending Jewish Sabbaths with Shmuel—where we continued our Talmud study—my progress into Orthodoxy was slow. Of course I was participating in Sabbath rituals, and others too, while I was in Shmuel's neighborhood, but I didn't bring the rituals home with me. It was one thing to read an interesting old text or to spend one day a week in traditional observance. It was something else to join a community and embrace its way of life. From almost any non-religious Jew in New York I could quickly learn of the assorted evils attributed to the pious Orthodox Jews. Their narrow-mindedness and greed. Their contempt for women.

Actually, I first learned of many of these claims from Shmuel himself. He had the New Yorker's habit of assuming that everyone knows what New Yorkers know. I didn't, but after listening for a while to his storms and sneers, I began to get an idea.

He himself took an oscillating view of the charges against the Orthodox. On his high horse, he would dismiss them as petty calumnies, excuses given by "the liberals" for not observing the commandments.

"Girls have no business reading from the Torah in the middle of the synagogue," he told me, one Sabbath afternoon in his slovenly apartment. "They only want to show off."

"Why isn't it showing off when boys do it?" I wanted to know.

"Because they're commanded to. Girls who really care about what's right do what's right for them, not what they think makes a good impression."

Still, at times his temper pushed him to the other side of the question. Then he'd say he hated the "frummies," as he called most Orthodox Jews" ("*frum*" is Yiddish for "religious"), for the way they forced their mores upon him without actually opening their lives to him.

"These people drive me crazy," he said. We were in the cluttered bedroom where he spent most of his time while in the apartment. On that particular day he hadn't managed to get out in time for morning prayers.

"They're always after me for missing prayers. Or not wearing the right sort of suit. Or hat. Yadda yadda yadda. Well," he said, "I can't help missing prayers. During the week the morning prayers are at impossible hours. Do you get up at 5:45? But the frummies are always there."

"And if you're not there," he went on, "where were you? And all their gossip about where they eat and don't eat. Their what's-not-kosher-enough-for-me-and-my-daughter crap. The father is descended from a famous rabbi. And you don't marry your daughter to somebody who didn't grow up religious, because he doesn't know how to wear a hat properly. Or he may want to have a television."

Shmuel was in a particularly gloomy mood that day: he had been dating. As usual on our Sabbath afternoons together, he was lying on his back on the still unmade bed, his hands under his *yarmulke* on the back of his head, though the posture in his case did not denote relaxation. By this time he was in slacks and an undershirt, which showed a little staining under the arms. The television set—off for the Sabbath—was partly hidden under the white shirt, blue blazer and conservative silk tie Shmuel had worn on Friday.

"See, the girl said to me, 'Shmuel, why can't you dress in a black suit and wear a hat, like everybody else?'" He pursed his lips and did a wickedly accurate impersonation of the girl's Brooklyn whine. "'I mean, *really!*'"

I said nothing.

He snorted in disgust. "At least it wasn't the usual question: '*So-ow*, what do you *do*?'" Again the Brooklyn whine from the bed.

Then in his normal voice: "Which means, How much are you worth? Arabs are killing us in Israel, and this is what they care about. Money and hats. They don't even read the newspapers. That's what I like about Kahane. You may call him a nut…"

"I do call him a nut."

"Well, he knows some things. He knows they're going to build a Mormon temple in Jerusalem. And what do they say here? 'Oh, it's those wicked Zionists, they're as bad as the wicked Americans.' And then back to the strudel. Nobody does anything. And *I'm* a nut, too? I guess that's what they all think. At this rate I'll never get married."

Shmuel had chosen to live in Far Rockaway, in one of New York's most intensely Orthodox enclaves. The neighborhood included a large proportion of observant Jews who, like Shmuel, had not been raised Orthodox. But he couldn't, or wouldn't, fit in. "Nu-, nu-, nee-, nee-land," he called the community, mimicking the dinner-table Yiddishisms with which parents scolded their children. He never did like wearing dark suits. Or hats. Some of the newly religious Jews in Far Rockaway had gone still farther, donning the long frock coats of Eastern European tradition, teaching their children Yiddish. "And these are people I went to *high school* with. I remember competing with one of them for the same Catholic cheerleader, oh God, oh God."

His dating history in the Jewish community was as erratic and unlikely as his way of careening into Orthodoxy. He was rejected by any number of young women because of community reports that he had difficulty holding a job and did not always show up for prayers. Then he almost became engaged to a woman much younger than he was, whose religious mother, a divorcee, cherished a hatred of men beside which the diatribes of a Germaine Greer (detested by the Far Rockaway frummies) were mere whining.

I used to hear about it regularly on Mondays. The mother and Shmuel both liked to argue. So they did argue—about men, about marriage, about God—until Shmuel came to work hoarse after each weekend. He'd rail bitterly to me against the mother, but I got the impression that Shmuel paid rather more attention to her than to her daughter. Fortunately for everyone, the engagement fell through.

Then Shmuel somehow hooked up with a half-Orthodox Jewish *femme fatale* (his description). They met, went for a drive somewhere, then ended up at her apartment. She let him argue late into the night, not saying much while he assailed her with an attack on "modernism," but watching his expressive eyes until she finally said, "Shmuel, I'd go to bed with you, but I'm afraid you'd like me too much."

He grieved for days about that.

Shmuel is married now, with three children. I was a minor honoree at his wedding. He married a woman newly arrived from communist Hungary, almost as tall as he was, who told him she didn't believe in God but was willing to accept Orthodox practices. How he found such a woman, and why she married him, I'll never know. Some of his old *yeshiva* friends tried to talk him out of the marriage. Failing at that, one of them actually tried talking to *me*.

"He doesn't know what he's getting into spiritually," he argued. (Does anyone? I thought.)

Shmuel called me shortly after the wedding ("I just *know* she's pregnant," he groused over the phone)—to tell me she had taken away all his credit cards when she found out the extent of his debt. He sounded relieved.

"We have to pay everything back. 'No more *meenoos*,' she said. And no more Entenmann's cakes. Or Empire hot dogs, uncooked, out of the package. So she does want *meenoos* on the weight, I guess. Oh, and the place is so neat you won't recognize it."

Once I had spent ten minutes with him trying to locate a telephone, which we reeled in by its cord like a hooked marlin, through the heaps of clothes, empty tuna cans, paper plates and hot dog blister packs that littered the floor of the room.

He named his second son after Meir Kahane, who was murdered shortly before the boy was born. "Oh, how my mother is going to hate that," he told me over the phone.

We no longer worked together and rarely saw each other. As a married man, he got less sleep than before, worked harder, detested his new job. But he sounded galvanized by the idea of his mother hating his son's name.

"Oh, the sermon I'll get. Oh, those people with their little Reform temples and their little lectures about 'Judaism.' I can argue circles around them. Well, what do you think, Meir Dovid?" I heard him turn to the infant. His rough voice sort of softened. "You want to go live in Israel? You want to grow up to be strong and kill Arabs?"

CHAPTER SIX

My mother was aghast when she learned I was attending regular classes in Orthodox Judaism in a daily after-work program held in a suite of offices in the Empire State Building. To her, it must have sounded as though séances were being conducted in a classroom at M.I.T.

Even I was taken aback my first afternoon (it was summer, no night classes at Brooklyn Law School for a while, and the throng in the lobby of the great building was the rush-hour crowd) when the door opened and there stood a pale, narrow-faced, bearded Hasid in what a Monsey friend of mine calls "full battle dress": long frock coat, wide-brimmed black hat, side curls, white shirt buttoned up to the Adam's apple, a fringed ritual garment visible between shirt and caftan.

I was game for almost anything, but the comedy thickened as the Hasid looked me over as if *I* had fallen from another planet. (I later learned that he had only just arrived in New York. He had lived for years in the ultra-Orthodox enclave of Meah Shearim, in the old city of Jerusalem, where the most exotic creature he had probably seen, from his point of view, was an Orthodox Jew without side curls.) His Rebbe—that is, the dynastic leader of his Hasidic community, in this case known as "Belz," after the Polish town where it had originated—had ordered him back to America to aid in the education of assimilated Jews like me because he could speak English. By Hasidic standards, that is.

I don't think he was older than I was. It's hard to tell under a dense beard. The eldest of his five children was only about nine;

assuming marriage at eighteen, he was probably twenty-seven or twenty-eight. But closeness in age was our nearest point of contact. His walk, his handshake, the lilting cadences of his speech, even the mobile way he held his face, were all alien. He sang when he talked—and grimaced, yawned, or rubbed his shaved head rapidly with his large velvet *yarmulke*.

After a few moments of basic question-and-answer, we sat down in his office.

"How did you hear about our program?" His full lips made unconscious mouths as he wrote my answer onto a piece of paper.

I told him Shmuel Lehrman had sent me. Of course, he had never heard of Shmuel. The program was brand new, he said. That was fine, I told him; I was brand new myself.

He stared at me open-mouthed, a reaction I often elicited from him, though all it meant in this case, evidently, was mild surprise. His face quickly collected itself and he introduced himself as Rabbi Rosen. He hoped I would come often. Could I read Hebrew?

Somewhat, I told him.

What did I want to study?

"The Talmud."

I got my second open-mouthed look. I suppose he was amazed at my audacity. Here I was, confessing I could hardly read Hebrew, and demanding to study—in the original Hebrew-Aramaic jargon—what may be the most elaborately demanding text ever composed.

But circumstances were on my side. Rabbi Rosen's program was so new there were only two regular students. I was to be the third. Under these conditions the students could dictate the curriculum.

I know this isn't the way everyone would have set about pursuing my goals. I had come to the Empire State Building to study "my heritage," as Rabbi Rosen quaintly but correctly put it. It did seem a little strange to find myself in a room on the 60th floor of a New York City office building, analyzing in detail with two other students and a Hasidic rabbi exactly what, if anything, a Jewish congregation in ancient Babylonia could legally buy with the proceeds of the sale of a scroll containing the Five Books of Moses.

On the other hand, my teachers saw nothing eccentric about this. To Rabbi Rosen, nothing could have seemed more natural than that I should begin my studies where his children had begun theirs.

But I wasn't one of his children. That much was obvious the first time he took me to visit his own synagogue deep in Brooklyn, where he argued in Yiddish with his nine-year-old son about the implication of a passage dealing with the marriage rights of the sons of two brothers married to two sisters. Meanwhile, other kids with side curls eagerly investigated the leather bag with the shoulder strap in which I'd carried my books down to their part of Brooklyn. They laughed out loud when they realized a man and not a woman had carried it. Nothing bashful about those kids: they pointed at me while they laughed. (I was also taken aback when, at Rabbi Rosen's home, the same nine-year-old son gleefully told me a "true" story about an anti-Semitic Polish bishop whose neck gets chicken-wrung in a noose of tree branches through the magic of the local rabbi. The boy's version of the Big Bad Wolf, I suppose, but rather less innocent.)

My fellow students at the Empire State Building weren't Rabbi Rosen's children either. There was a young, shy, studious fellow I never got to know well. And there was a nervous young mathematician named Aaron who worked at the New York Public Library, cooked every night for his two cats ("I wouldn't give them the poison they sell in the stores"), and was struggling to extricate himself from debts even worse than Shmuel Lehrman's.

"I can't figure out credit cards," he told me. "My calculus is good, but my arithmetic stinks."

Aaron worried about looking too much like a gentile because he had not yet grown a beard. On the other hand, he worried about losing his job if he attempted to let one grow. In one summer, he started three of them, and shaved off each one.

"I think they were looking at me funny," he said of his co-workers. "And I already get enough of that when I leave early for the Sabbath during the winter."

If his co-workers eyed Aaron, it may have been because he dressed ten years out of date and constantly fidgeted with his hair. This latter trait was not the product of vanity but of nerves. Aaron was a chronic worrier. He worried so much about the sort of clothes he should wear that he was never actually able to buy new ones, which was why he kept wearing ten-year-old shirts. He worried about commercially sold cat food. Then he worried if the food he made for his cats was nutritious enough for them. He worried that he didn't earn enough money to marry an Orthodox woman: "We'll be sending our children to *yeshivas*, and how will I pay for it?" He worried about growing beards. On himself, that is. And about not growing them. ("Do you think people notice the stubble?")

But most of all, he worried about Christian missionaries.

"They're all over the place," he muttered to me one day between Talmudic passages. "Like vultures. Well, if they tried that stuff on me, I'd show them a thing or two."

He returned to the subject again and again, in brief intervals during our Talmud study. One night, after our session, we both rode the same subway downtown with Rabbi Rosen, heading for Brooklyn. We sat together in the stuffy metal car, and he griped about the missionaries who sometimes rode the subway too.

After Rabbi Rosen got off to change trains, Aaron leaned over to me and said, over the train noise, "I envy him. Nobody will ever try to convert *him*."

"But even if someone did try, he wouldn't succeed. So what's the difference?"

"I saw one today," Aaron said, blinking, as if a bright light had flashed in his eyes. "At the corner of Fifth and 40th. I stopped and told him off."

"What did he say?"

"Nothing. He just stared at me. But I told him Jesus was an imposter. That he was nothing but a dead Jew. That he, the missionary I mean, was promoting a religion about a dead Jew. He stared at me. That was telling him, don't you think?"

I didn't say anything.

"It's the fault of the American Jew!" he flared up suddenly. "Nobody taught me anything. I almost believed those people, don't you see? I could have been a Christian. I guess I almost was."

He dropped his head into his hands. "Yeah, once they almost had me convinced. I really could have ended up just like them. One of those."

I winced. I had never told Aaron that one of my brothers was also one of "those."

"That's why Rabbi Rosen is so lucky," he said. "His children will never have to face that problem."

Yet that same night he had stared at me in disbelief when Rabbi Rosen had blandly suggested that a Jew was obligated to hate gentiles, because one must always hate those who hate God. Aaron had looked stricken, and he had blinked more than usual during the rest of the Talmud class. I had avoided his gaze, thinking then, too, of my brother, and not wanting to broach the subject.

I had had a taste of another side of Rabbi Rosen's teaching when, during the study of some law or other—I don't remember which—the subject of masturbation somehow arose.

"A sin a person commits with a part of the body that he uses to go to the bathroom," murmured Rabbi Rosen between tensed lips, without the least trace of humor. "You know what I mean?"

I knew.

He exhaled windily through his nose. His stare held me. "It's one of the worst sins in the world. As bad as murder. Doctors"—he pronounced the word with indescribable contempt—"*doctors*, they say it's normal. That's a complete lie. If you put someone in a room with nothing but the Talmud, such a thing would *never* happen. It's only living with the *goyim* that makes it happen, because here we have to see their impurity wherever we look!"

Now Aaron turned defeated eyes on the floor of the subway car, blinked, and said morosely about our teacher, "But his life is a damned funny way to live, isn't it?"

One of the Talmudic stories I learned in those days was of a young man, deathly ill, who seemed actually to die. Then he spontaneously recovered—much like the cases recorded in Raymond Moody's twentieth-century book, *Life After Life*. And like the people whose stories are recorded there, this young man is supposed to have had a taste of another world.

"I saw an upside-down world," he tells his rabbi-father in the story.

"What do you mean?"

"Everything esteemed in this world was lowly in that one."

"You did not see an upside-down world," the father explains. "You saw the true world. This one is the upside-down world."

The Talmud's point, of course, is the familiar one that money, prestige, etc. mean something only according to the standards of an imperfect society. But I also like the implication that the world we live in, apparently so solid and reliable, may not in fact teach us anything about permanent realities. That instead of resting solidly on its base—a perfect model of conservatism—our world may be quivering, barely balanced, on its nose, while a truer and larger conservatism threatens any moment to knock it all over into a jumble of exploded conventions.

Life in New York could raise such thoughts, too, especially in someone not hardened to it. I remember being jammed on a crowded subway against a pretty young woman who stood with her eyes downcast, avoiding mine—a posture that would have struck me as graceful in such circumstances, if the direction her gaze took hadn't been that of my groin. (Where would the swooning imagination fall in a New York subway? Too many hands reach out to catch it—peeling ads posted to the walls, the crush of bodies, the greedy silence of other imaginations.) The fact that such conflicting impressions were stirred in me by a stranger—a girl who could pierce my world so intimately, and then disappear forever—was just another typical taste in the brew. Rabbi Rosen would have given this a simple and contemptuous name. I couldn't, but I admitted (silently) that the daily pressure was unsettling.

Later that particular day, I was waiting for a rush-hour train on a shabby bench in Penn Station. From somewhere out of the crowd another stranger, a pale but vigorous middle-aged woman, dropped down next to me. She asked me earnestly what I was besides American. Italian? Spanish?

"I'm just American," I told her.

"Are you Swedish?"

I shook my head, volunteering nothing. This was New York City, remember, at six o'clock.

"Are you Jewish?"

"Yes, I'm Jewish," I said. And instantly regretted it. This woman was showing some signs of age—she had pasty cheeks and crow's feet around her eyes. But the blue eyes themselves had the obstinate serenity of a child's, or a lunatic's.

"You're Jewish?" she repeated.

I nodded.

"Well," she said brightly, "you've got to remember that, and brush up on it, because everybody in this country's going to the dogs because they don't know who they are any more, and we're all run by a bunch of nitwits."

Nodding, evidently very pleased, she got up and left me.

CHAPTER SEVEN

Memory is notorious for its sleights of hand. I didn't discover how busy my own illusionist had been over the years—rewriting the incidents of my religious pilgrimage—until I reread entries in a journal I fortunately kept during those confusing years in New York.

On my first bus trip home from the Orthodox enclave of Monsey, New York (where I would live one day) I glibly told a middle-aged Hasid, in response to a surprisingly serious question, that I had become religious to find "a meaning in life."

Even at the time, that way of putting things sounded a bit strange in my own ears. The setting was poorly chosen for such a tidy summary. It was at night during the holiday of *Sukkos*, or "Tabernacles." By that time I had been genuinely Orthodox about six months. A friend had recommended spending the holiday in Monsey, and I had no difficulty securing hospitality through one of the local *yeshivas*. Now I was on my way back to New York City, and so was everyone else, it seemed. The bus—Monsey's own "Jewish" bus—was so jammed with Hasidim for the return trip that I literally had to bend over backwards, my feet braced on the floor of the aisle, my hips wedged against the arm of one of the seats. Even worse, the bus was divided between women and men by a dusty blue curtain down the center of the aisle. To preserve "modesty," I'd been told. Billowing waves in the curtain marked the progress of large-hipped women maneuvering their trunks and hat boxes up and down the invisible side of the aisle, and spelling disaster for me if I didn't suck in my breath at the right moment.

On my side of the curtain, the Hasidic men were dressed in holiday finery—fur hats, long brocaded caftans of black silk. They carried the plastic cases in which they kept the ritual palm branches, citrons, myrtle leaves and willows used throughout the holiday. The fruity aroma was fascinating, but some of the Hasidim could have used a bath.

"Very nice," said my Hasid (whom I had met about two minutes earlier) in answer to my pious phrase. His accent told me that he was Israeli. I was impressed with his dignity, under the circumstances. The pressure of the other standees had me practically on my back in his lap. All around us chaos reigned. The driver wasn't sure of the exact route through Manhattan to Williamsburg. So dozens of the Hasidim were shouting advice at him—all of it different, of course. The driver wasn't used to this, and was in a lather.

"Why can't they shut their mouths and let me drive the lousy bus wherever I good and well want to?" he fumed. That didn't bother the Hasidim. The good-natured shouting went on.

"A good crowd," said my Hasid in his dignified way. Yet I couldn't be sure he wasn't joking. "Lots of people coming to Monsey for *Sukkos*, thanks God."

What was so special about Monsey? I asked him.

He deliberated for a moment before answering, still with polite ambiguity: "Ah, well, you know, it isn't Brooklyn," he said.

I didn't ask for clarification. He smiled at me. Rather an enigmatic smile, behind a full beard.

"You'll pardon me, my English isn't too good. But I'm, how do you say, impressed. A young man like you finding the meaning in life."

Maybe he *was* joking. Anyway, my journal from earlier years tells a much less tidy story about my progress.

By the fall of 1984 I had broken up with Janet and entered night classes at Brooklyn Law School. I shared my apartment, the under-ventilated place over the Greek restaurant, with a lawyer for the Securities and Exchange Commission who was extraordinarily tolerant of my religious vagaries, which had started to include some, though not all, Jewish dietary restrictions. When I came home, there was a bright purple *yarmulke* I had fished out of God knows where that would often end up on my head. I would read Hebrew texts out loud, at all hours of the night, trying to get used to the sound of the language. Bit by bit, my life began to change. I began tentatively observing the Sabbath. I was relieved that my roommate never objected to any of this.

I was less lucky with a high school chum named Steve Hamill who decided one day to convince me of the value of wealth.

"I'm taking you out to dinner," he said carelessly one evening, calling me at my turkey pen in the legal publishing house. For some reason there were no law classes that night.

"All right," I said.

Steve had known me during my Zionist period which led, unexpectedly, to the shock of Sabra and Shatila and then to the haunting antidotes of Elie Wiesel. One summer, between grades in high school, I had worked for the American-Israel Public Affairs Committee, the major pro-Israel lobby in the United States. All I did was help reorganize the filing system so that donor information could be typed into a computer, but Steve had never stopped ribbing me about it. He believed my support for the Jewish State was obsessively one-sided (a charge I denied at the time) and that it reflected, in any case, a mixed-up sort of nationalism in someone with no other Jewish commitments (a charge I soon had to admit).

Anyway, that night Steve had bigger fish to fry, as I found out when I met him at the office and he led me to a restaurant of his choosing. He knew that I was a law student, and he'd somehow or other got wind of the tenor of my religious aspirations. He did not beat about the bush.

"I'm taking you out to demonstrate to you the pleasures of the good life," he said.

I should mention that Steve long ago developed a conviction in my naiveté. From time to time he had taken it on himself to educate me. It was he, for instance, who gave me pointers on the mating rituals he assumed I would encounter in college. (We were at a hamburger joint, late one summer night, both of us in our first year of college—and I couldn't help blushing, not only because I had done so little of what he described, but because of the huge gulf fixed between my actual world and the overripe region of my fantasy.)

"First you get her into your room," he'd said then. "On *your* turf, she knows she can't be too uppity. Then find some excuse to touch her. Any excuse will do. Any amount of touching, no matter how small, to start with. See? Hold her finger if you can't hold her hand. Use humor. You can make a joke out of *that*, holding her finger, you see? And look: don't take the whole thing so damned seriously."

This time we were at some very expensive restaurant, as it turned out. Maybe I was supposed to recognize it by name, but I didn't. The interior was dim; the walls were reddish, it seems to me now, hung maybe with some sort of damask. The decor had an unmistakably rich gloss, but what I mostly remember was the seemingly interminable series of waiters who came to serve us. The second or third of these, a middle-aged man with a nurse's obsequious fussiness, hovered near our table as we talked—or rather, as Steve talked, since I felt too embarrassed by the setting to say much of anything. A different waiter had taken our order. Somehow the waiters' way of casting their eyes downward made them all appear interchangeable, as if they were soldiers in uniform and we were their generals, concerned only with their rank, not their identities.

"You are now in law school," Steve said, in what sounded suspiciously like a rehearsed speech, "and presumably will do as well as you have in past academic endeavors. Your value on the market has dropped lately, due to your delay in finding a real job, and the inexplicable choice of that legal publishing company, where the salary is about on a level with that cheap tie you've got on."

Which I had been fingering as he spoke.

"What exactly are you earning now?"

I told him.

"And what do you plan to be earning in, say, five years?"

I said I didn't know.

"I see." Steve was considered a little funny-looking in high school. Largely, I think, due to his habit of running everywhere, with his head thrust forward and his arms stiffly at his sides, clutching books. The posture made one think of a high-speed tortoise. Time had done a lot to smooth that out. His features were good. He had made a lot of money, too, writing complicated software for some financial applications connected with securities trading. But there was still something reptilian in the quick movements of his head, and the flatness imparted to his eyes by thick, black-rimmed eyeglasses. Now he jerked his head slightly to one side to regard me closely.

"I have a proposal for you," he said. "I know your problem. You have ideals. It's the same problem you have in your love life. Now that woman—what was her name?"

"Janet."

"You went at that all wrong. Religion first. Why couldn't you just say, Look, let's get married, have some good sex, and we'll work this Jewish stuff out later?"

Why not, indeed? Steve's Catholicism, which was a good deal more than a pose, was a good deal less than a cold shower.

"Really, I don't want to dwell on that," he said. "I just don't like seeing you get short-changed. So here's the idea."

At that moment our food arrived.

The restaurant was not *kosher*. In those days I assumed that *kosher* spots would be full of Orthodox Jews, and supposing most Orthodox Jews to be like Shmuel Lehrman I thought it better for my digestion if I avoided them. Meanwhile I dodged the religious issue, more or less, by eating a vegetarian diet. It hadn't occurred to me to tell that to Steve. And when we'd picked up our menus and I started looking for something meatless, only one entree seemed to hold out any promise. Steve said it was a sort of fish soup. I had never heard of it, but Steve seemed to know what he was talking about. So I went ahead and ordered the "bouillabaise."

But what came to our table—delivered by yet another waiter— was not what I mean by "fish soup." It looked, to me, like a museum's worth of mollusks.

Shellfish are not *kosher*. My grandparents, and their parents before them, did not eat lobster, shrimp or clams. True, my own parents had not observed the old proscriptions within my memory. But tradition had survived longer than religious scruples. In my mother's kitchen we sometimes saw fried shrimp, occasionally lobster meat, but seldom things in real shells except as decorative drawings on plastic place mats.

But now, out of the waiter's ladle, dropped—what? Several types of mussel; a rounded, hard lump I took to be an oyster; a striped bivalve that seemed to contain nothing at all within a capacious shell; and a pink crustacean, complete with legs and eye-stalks. All unavoidably real. Even worse, around all this was a thin, shimmery, yellow-greenish broth that a horrible fantasy almost persuaded me was the very seawater in which all these creatures had once lived and had just been scalded to death. So freshly, they might have been at the bottom of an aquarium, while I goggled at them through the few limp strands of vegetation that completed my "fish soup."

When the waiter had finally gone I whispered to Steve, "I don't think I can eat this."

He didn't ask why, but he turned his head to one side, lizard-like, again. "So just drink the broth. It's just fish, anyway."

A complex odor had reached my nostrils. One of the few food smells that have ever had the power to revolt me. (Another is the stale, greasy stink of fried bacon in the halls of Grand Central Station at six in the morning. The old grills heating up under their load of oil, oozing a scent timeless as despair.) Steve and I sat under lights obscenely low, over the carcasses of sea creatures. Among bankers and stockbrokers. Talking about the good life.

"When you get out of law school," Steve was saying, "here's what you do. Once a week you can put on some jeans and hop over to Hell's Kitchen to do some good old *pro bono* law. Like, represent some dude who just raped his mother. Won't that do enough for your social conscience? The rest of the time you can make the money you ought to be making, and putting it to some good use, for a change. To begin with, some new clothes."

"Sure," I said. I was trying to figure out what to do with the soup. "Now, as to this Jewish stuff."

He sat back and assumed his most magisterial manner. Largely a failure, I'm afraid. But his determination in that direction was impressive in its own way.

"I'm not going to talk about the ethical side of this, because ethics aren't objectionable. But I've heard of ghettos and such. Fundamentalism. Does this—well, all *this*—mean you're going to ignore the rest of the world?"

I wish I could have given him a good answer. I did my best, such as it was. I told him that I couldn't yet predict the outcome of my exploration of Judaism, but that I believed whatever I could contribute to "the world," as he called it, would have to descend from my own stuffy little identity, whatever that turned out to be. And, of course, much of that identity turned on the fact that I was Jewish.

I half expected peals of laughter from the dim walls of the restaurant that had given me bouillabaise and could now hear me talking piously about "Judaism" and my traditional "identity." Not far from us still another waiter, half-visible in the moneyed gloom, bowed and scraped. Steve, meanwhile, gave me as troubled a glance as a reptilian eye can give.

"Well, all I can say is I hope this won't make you end up ignoring life. That would be a shame. That's another thing I wanted to show you tonight."

I could not, of course, ignore the soup. There it bubbled before me, a noxious message from a world already foreign. The mollusks were at rest in their sea, staring up at me with the maddening solemnity of the dead.

And then, in another moment, I was eating it. What else could I do? I couldn't interpose a religious scruple, I told myself—or what was I doing there in the first place? Besides, Steve was paying for it. I knew my position exactly. The poor relation, shamed with bounty. Oh, Steve had made a stronger argument than even he knew, in a way. I nearly choked on his "good life."

I have thought about that episode since, sitting in places like the apartment in Monsey where my wife and I began our married (Orthodox) life together. With separate dishes for meat and dairy, a list of *kosher* supervisors taped to the refrigerator. I think of many of my visits to my mother's house. Our pots and pans rattling in the trunk, brought along for the trip, Michelle and I racing to the local supermarket in Mclean, Virginia to do our own shopping (hunting for *kosher* symbols on each item) rather than relying on food my mother had bought for us and our children. I'm sure this was irritating to my mother. Yet I will not do for her what I did for Steve Hamill. I won't set my objection down to squeamishness and favor her feelings over my ritual.

Consistency is my defense, of course. The unraveled private life ought to spell *something*, and if not one's commitments, then what? Tell me I was a clown at Steve's shellfish party and I'll agree with you. But try telling that to my mother. Between her divorce, my brother's conversion to Christianity, and my own Orthodoxy, her personal life has been torn to shreds by other people's "consistency."

And I know how she feels. Years ago, I awoke one night in a very different world from the Monsey one. The place was Bloomfield, New Jersey. It was too dark to see the familiar things around me: a sleeping cat, a notebook full of bad poetry, Sidney's prayer book, a girlfriend who was probably tiring of me.

I was only conscious of spinning. It must have been my weak sense of balance acting up. As a child I was exempted from tumbling exercises because I couldn't stand up after a simple somersault. Now, for a panicky, nauseated moment, I didn't know if I was lying flat or sliding off the bed. Centrifugal forces took hold of me, strained me to the breaking point—and spinning with me was the question, *What am I doing here?*

It all made no sense. Here I was with the makings of a life assorted around me. But there was no life. I wasn't yet actively Orthodox. But even then I had gone too far to turn around. And Janet had little interest in making the trip with me. Was I a Jew? A writer? A lover? Was there any way to explain what I was doing in this ethnic-Italian New Jersey town in the middle of the night, sick as a dog, with a Riverside Shakespeare on the shelf, a Hebrew prayer book stuffed inside a drawer, Janet breathing beside me? *What was I doing there?*

I can remember another such dizzy spell. This one struck just before the Sabbath, years after that. I was living on the Lower East Side. I was by then fully Orthodox. There was just enough time left to shave before sundown. I'd come home feeling tired—I was a night student with a full-time day job, sleeping five or six hours a night, getting up every morning for six-fifteen prayers—but otherwise all right. The level afternoon sun struck the gray Williamsburg Bridge, visible from my window, meaning the Sabbath had almost arrived. No Orthodox Jews were on the streets at that special hour. Even in New York, I thought I could hear the world quiet down for the Sabbath's approach.

I was shaving and humming to myself. Then, suddenly, I was on the floor. For a moment I smiled, as if at someone who'd just played a practical joke on me. The bathroom floor couldn't really be crawling in a circle around my ear. There was no one else in the apartment; my roommate, a young rabbi, was in Canada. The electric shaver was buzzing in my hand. But I had lost sight of my hand.

Then the nausea hit. The bathroom swung in violent rings, like the guys at a wedding once who, not knowing my infirmity, grabbed my hands and spun me around in a wild merry-go-round dance until I blacked out.

But now I was still conscious as I crawled for the toilet, the electric shaver buzzing somewhere on the floor behind me. Today when I am sick I can be put to bed. Friends can call or drop by to say the ritual *"r'fuah sh'leimah"*—"a complete recovery." My prayer shawl can be fetched from the synagogue where it usually resides, I can recite prayers at home, read a page of Talmud, keep up the precious rhythms of life. I can do everything, that is, that helps me pretend I'm not alone.

But that afternoon the beginning of the Sabbath sped by me without any sort of acknowledgment; a toilet was all I had for company; and during the feverish night that followed—God or no God—I lay as naked as I have ever been.

PART 2: LOVE AND PAIN

He [Deronda] wanted some way of keeping emotion and its progeny of sentiments—which make the savours of life—substantial and strong in the face of a reflectiveness that threatened to nullify all differences. To pound the objects of sentiment into small dust, yet keep sentiment alive and active, was something like the famous recipe for making cannon—to first take a round hole and then enclose it with iron; whatever you do keeping fast hold of your round hole. Yet how distinguish what our will may wisely save in its completeness, from the heaping of cat-mummies and the expensive cult of enshrined putrefactions?

— George Eliot, *Daniel Deronda*

Love does not go too well with weakness; for it requires a stout vessel to resist the pressure of its workings.

—Jean-Joseph Surin

CHAPTER EIGHT

In one of his quieter moments, Shmuel Lehrman told me about some friends who gathered in a secret conclave one night in the basement of a religious school. According to Shmuel, the group recited a mystical formula, raised hands together, and, with appropriate gestures and incantations, made one of their number float off the floor.

When they later told a rabbi about this exploit, he reacted not with disbelief but with worry. He told them that what they had done "could be dangerous," and cautioned them sternly not to try it again.

Over the years, I would hear about such things on other occasions. *Yeshivas* (that is, traditional Jewish schools) abound with tales of the occult. Although not officially sanctioned where I studied, kabbalistic hocus-pocus was talked about not only by isolated old rabbis but by young, college-educated American Jews. I saw, for instance, young men with backgrounds not much different from mine eagerly line up to consult a visiting *m'qubal*, or mystical sage, to try to learn the names of their future mates. The *m'qubal* claimed that he could predict this by means of complicated acrostics involving the men's names. I watched for an hour as he scribbled and frowned, scribbled and frowned, gripping a ball point pen with his old fingers and coarsely-cut nails, forming Hebrew characters on a piece of notebook paper and from time to time pronouncing a woman's name, while the line of bachelors inched past.

I am not Shmuel Lehrman, and for better or worse I don't believe those Talmud students really levitated one of their classmates. Yet I don't write about Jewish magic as a pure skeptic. I'm not attracted to the occult *per se*. But something about the principles and language of magic is intriguing. In its own way the religious approach to magic is a kind of poetry, with its emphasis on the power of the word to define reality, its insistence that language can pierce the barrier that divides thought from fulfillment. That's what fascinated and charmed me about the old man I met on the Lower East Side and soon learned, however disharmonious the conjunction of our lives might seem to strangers, to call "Reb Baruch."

In the late spring of 1986 I moved into a part of New York City that, owing to an old pier-naming convention later hallowed by a century of ethnic legend, is still referred to as the Lower East Side. My religious observance had reached the point where it made sense to me to live in an Orthodox neighborhood. From my apartment I could walk to a synagogue, find a place to study Talmud, and wear a *yarmulke* without embarrassment.

It didn't much matter that I didn't know anyone there. I strained my shyness to the limit to talk to people in synagogues after morning prayers, but I really needn't have worked so hard. The Jews there were eager to seize a newcomer, and when they learned I was single and newly Orthodox, well, the red carpet rolled. It soon seemed that everyone had invited me to his home at least once, and some of them many times. On the Sabbath, I almost never ate at home.

Still, one old man among my hosts stood out as extraordinary. I didn't even know his name, though I had seen his frail figure collecting guests up and down East Broadway, the busy, shabby street through the center of the Jewish neighborhood of the Lower East Side, shepherding one stranger from here, another there— until I described him to a new acquaintance of mine, who casually remarked, "Oh, Reb Baruch. Of course I know him. Everyone knows him." He added, "Reb Baruch is a man who attracts miracles."

He laughed, looking at my expression. Rain was beginning to spatter the street corner where we stood. It was a Sabbath afternoon. My interlocutor started to worry for his hat, put up one hand over it in a vaguely protective way, and made to hurry off. "I forgot, you haven't lived with religious people before," he said. "You'll see."

I know the words "Lower East Side" have *cachet*—summoning up nostalgia-blurred images of trolleys, the Yiddish theater, pushcarts and delicatessens. But by the time I moved in, the Jewish community of the East Side was hardly more than a collection of remnants shoehorned into low-rent apartment cooperatives and crumbling storefronts between Chinatown and Manhattan's East River. The only reason I ever met "Reb Baruch" was that one of those remnants was his synagogue.

I should mention at once that Baruch Epstein wasn't actually a rabbi. He was only responsible for the synagogue on the Sabbath, when the rabbi and the other old men who studied Talmud there during the week were at home in Brooklyn, on the other side of the Williamsburg Bridge. Nor was his synagogue really even a synagogue. It was just a large upstairs room. Heaven only knows how long Baruch had been in charge of it on Saturdays. It had walls that had once been white, and a cracking wooden floor, up one flight from an abandoned apartment where a famous Hasidic rabbi had once lived and, many years before, had died. Doubtless at one time the "synagogue" had had its regular crowd of Sabbath worshipers, but by the time I knew him, Reb Baruch was reduced to borrowing some men from neighboring synagogues to round out the quorum of ten men required for formal prayers. He was a short, stooped old man whose narrow ruin of a face was crowned with big, startled-looking eyes, the intensity of which was heightened by his skin's pallor. Parkinson's disease gave his hands a continual tremor, but the moment Baruch saw me standing unattached on the sidewalk one Sabbath morning he pulled me off the street as handily as a stevedore, shepherded me along with other guests up the long, dark flight of stairs and shoved a prayer book into my hands. I'd guess the average age of the other worshipers there was above seventy.

After that first experience, I became a regular worshiper myself. That is, Reb Baruch expected me to be a regular there, and I could never figure out how to elude or refuse him. I had barely learned his name when Baruch began pulling me up the same stairs each Saturday morning, toward the same group of old men.

"Well, Goldberg, still alive?" an eighty-year-old epileptic who sat in the back of the synagogue, wearing a dusty black suit, would cackle when I arrived with (as it usually happened) an even older man in tow. "Goldberg" was a neighbor of the epileptic. Cruelly wrinkled, sunk into his own disorganized bulk as if he were a sack of spoiled cotton, he used to wait for me at the bottom of the stairs just after I was dumped there by Reb Baruch, who, after nabbing me on the sidewalk and bringing me far enough inside the door to be sure I wouldn't turn back, was on his way out to the sidewalk to find yet another young worshiper to add to the crowd. I have no idea how the old man used to get up those stairs before I began to pray there. Whenever I came he was waiting for me. He'd impatiently grab my arm for the ascent, grunt, and up we'd go together. One slow step at a time.

He and the epileptic evidently disliked each other, so when the epileptic would cackle, "Still alive?" Goldberg would purse his lips at him as if about to spit.

Everything about that place—its mousetraps, its disorder, the pockmarked wooden floor cluttered with slivers of yellowing paper from ancient prayer books, quivering in the breezes caused by anyone walking near them—made me ache for some miracle of deliverance, but despite my acquaintance's comment linking Reb Baruch with the supernatural, I can't say I ever saw a miracle occur around the old man. The nearest approach to one occurred one Jewish New Year's Day, when the Bible requires the blowing of a ram's horn, or *shofar*, during the prayer service.

In my new guise as observant Jew, I had volunteered to help the old men round out their quorum for prayers on that day. Naturally, Baruch considered it important, and the day's requirements were stricter than usual. For one thing, there was the *shofar* itself. Baruch had found a "young fellow" (that is, someone only middle-aged) willing to do the blowing of the ram's horn. But when I entered the synagogue that morning the place was in an uproar.

"That young fellow—he went away to be with his father," Mr. Birnbaum, an immigrant from Poland back in the Thirties, was saying. "He says his father has a cold, and his father's blowing *shofar* too, only now his father's not sure he can blow. So the young man, he has to go help him blow somewhere else. In case the old man can't manage it."

"Imagine, imagine!" some voices chimed in.

Others were clucking their tongues, or (sparing old throats) waving their arms in dismay. "What do we do now, eh, Baruch?" someone asked. "We don't have a *shofar*!"

Baruch quieted the uprising by insisting, in his thin, nasal voice, that the "young man" would come back. The other regulars accepted his prophecy and set about their prayers. Baruch's decision meant that two hours or more would have to be expended on the prayers, in the blank hope that the *shofar* and its blower would return on time—and the "young man" clearly had made no promise. If he didn't return, we'd have to scurry somewhere else at the last minute, and might miss the required *shofar* blowing altogether.

But no one besides me seemed to think of this. Baruch's orders were followed; prayers marched slowly ahead. And my private agony of frustration over the next two hours showed itself unnecessary when, at precisely the right moment in the service, as the long prayers gathered up to the climax that could only be broken by the *shofar* blasts, a door opened downstairs and a scuffling of shoes up the old staircase marked the return of the stocky "young" fellow with the ram's horn.

If that was a miracle, it passed without comment. Reb Baruch himself was too absorbed in his prayers to notice how close we had come to trouble as the blower rushed in and started the ritual noise-making. Or maybe he just didn't care. On the annual Day of Judgment, I suppose he may have had graver matters on his mind.

Baruch lived in a stuffy apartment a few blocks from his synagogue. Bookshelves lined the walls there, loaded with Hebrew books whose cracked bindings and dog-eared pages showed that Baruch had studied them thoroughly and often. Long ago, as a young bull of a man, Baruch had served ten or fifteen guests at every Sabbath meal in this apartment, which had been a newer, cleaner replica of its present self. Now, because of the constant tremors, he couldn't even peel an orange by himself, and his wife, an invalid, wasn't often out of bed. His only guests now were a handful of acquaintances from far back, and a few down-and-out Jews too poor to refuse Baruch's standing invitation. (Whenever he saw a stranger, he'd buttonhole him, hiding his shaking hands in the pockets of his loose-fitting black jacket, and say: "You have to eat by my house. Everybody eats there.")

I will always remember a tiny green throw rug on which Baruch would meticulously wipe his shoes, regardless of the weather, before entering the simple dining room with its one long table. That, and the smell of overcooked chicken that spread itself from his kitchen on Sabbath afternoons. It was one of his daughters (he told me) who put the food on the stove every Friday afternoon before the Sabbath began. She had married a judge and had a family of her own, but apparently she came to Baruch's apartment every Friday to enable him to continue entertaining his guests.

One old regular had once been a *yeshiva* student in Poland, and he told me how the students had hoped, from day to day, they might be able to eat something between long courses of study. Another was a dreamy, middle-aged American-born bachelor named Sam, who seemed almost desperate to talk but, once a conversation started, would invariably embarrass himself with some trivial comment he seemed to find too revealing, and then would retreat, with stammering shyness, back into silence. During the week, Sam used to fill his need to talk simply by talking to himself. To conceal the long monologues, he held them on public pay telephones, acting as if there were a listener at the other end of the line. (It didn't fool anybody. "He just likes to talk," old Mr. Birnbaum told me loudly, smack in front of Sam, who pretended not to hear. "He don't hurt nobody. And this way, he don't even have to pay the quarter!") On the Sabbath, forbidden by religious law to use a telephone, Sam was denied even his own ear.

The oddest regular of all was a rumpled, pear-shaped man named David. He was hardly over thirty—-very young in that crowd. But his face had a set, bitter expression that made him look much older than he really was and which, together with his bleary red eyes, stained trousers and shaking hands, told a pretty clear story of the way he spent the remainder of the week.

But what really stood out about him was his surliness. He refused to appear at the same time as the other guests, always turning up half an hour late. He never apologized; he glared with the stubbornness of someone with nothing to lose. Stolidly eating his bread and chicken, he made no effort to ingratiate himself with anyone else. (The others said, with disgust, that he traveled on the Sabbath if he thought he'd get a free meal out of it. Of course, they themselves would mooch a meal wherever they could, but they wouldn't drive or ride a subway on the Sabbath in order to get one.)

Not surprisingly, all the old-timers among Baruch's guests disliked him, but they hesitated to say so in front of Baruch, who extended his open invitations to David as well as the others.

David did not reciprocate the courtesy. I knew David used to harass one of Baruch's guests (an old bore who ran a junk business) with late-night, drunken phone calls, word of which must have reached Baruch himself. But if David felt any embarrassment about that while he ate Baruch's chicken, he never showed it. Even in Baruch's presence, David would infuriate his stodgy victim by addressing him as "Skippy."

Knowing, I suppose, that Baruch wouldn't have the heart to turn him out, David had devised a particularly ingenious torture for Baruch himself. While the old man, with his shaking hands and diseased face, tried to expound the week's Scriptural reading, David would needle him with the remnants of what must once have been a thorough Talmudic education.

"So Joseph took care of the Egyptians," Baruch would say. (I sat next to him, trying to steady the book he held, usually a mystical commentary on the Pentateuch.) His way of talking was a mix of old-world phrasing and Brooklyn colloquialisms.

"He put up grain in the storehouses in the bad years. You know what means bad years? When they didn't have what to eat. Why did he do so? So the Egyptians couldn't point at him and say, 'Oh, those Jews, see, they're greedy.'"

"Sure they could," David would put in. The guests ignored him, but he knew full well that Baruch couldn't. "He made them his slaves before he would feed them," David pressed on. "They had to sell themselves to him for grain to eat. It's all in the Bible."

The old book jumped up and down, up and down, in Baruch's hands. "According to you, it would have been better for 'em all to starve?"

"You're missing the point, Baruch. Didn't he make them sell themselves as slaves?"

"Answer my question," Baruch said.

"Answer mine."

David's dogged comments were proof against Baruch's rising irritation. Finally someone would say, "Go on to the next part."

"What would *you* rather do, David?" I asked, hoping to distract him. "Be a slave or starve?"

"I'm already a slave," he said, expressionlessly.

"But he won't starve," put in Birnbaum. "He gets Social Security."

"I get enough to eat and too much to drink. I've told you all about it before. All right?"

"Not enough to get married," Birnbaum persisted.

"Don't talk about marriage to me. Women are the bane of mankind," David said coarsely, but still without heat.

"That's not in the Bible," Baruch piped as loudly as he could in his frail voice. "It says a woman is a man's help."

"A helper *against* him. That's what the Hebrew says: *ezer k'negdo.* *Against* him, isn't it, Baruch?"

Baruch, his cheeks faintly flushed, with some difficulty half raised his small frame from his chair at the table, like a white-faced prairie dog emerging from its hole. "What does the Talmud say? If he's worthy, so, then she's a helper. If he's not worthy, then she's against him!"

David snorted and kept his stolid gaze on his plate. A few minutes later he pointed a surprisingly delicate finger at Baruch's curtainless window, beyond which two seagulls were descending toward the East River, and declared that seagulls shouldn't be admired, they were "rats with wings." He said it a few times to make sure everyone heard him. Poor Baruch was in agony, not because he loved seagulls but because he couldn't stand to hear the word "rats" spoken at his Sabbath table. Finally Baruch asked him to stop. Whereupon David fell silent, except for some raspy, adenoidal breathing.

I stayed after the other guests left to help Baruch put the dishes into the sink. The old man didn't complain about his age or his physical weakness. In fact, the only thing I ever heard him complain about was the tremor in his hands, because it made it hard for him to read his books. But David had bothered him.

"That young man," Baruch said after a while. "I wish he didn't come."

"Are you going to throw him out?" I asked.

Reb Baruch looked at the wall. "He's got nowhere to go. Other people don't want him by them. I think 'cause of how he acts. Father's dead, you know. He was some sort of rabbi, he used to say."

"David seems to know a lot."

Baruch hesitated a moment. "I don't know about that father. I think he had a problem. You know what means—uh, drinking too much?"

"And the son?"

Again Baruch was silent.

"So what are you going to do?" I persisted.

He made a tiny shrugging gesture. "It's the things he says. They bother me."

I tried for a moment to imagine precisely what troubled Baruch about David. Of course, I knew that Baruch's invalid wife was in bed not fifty feet from where we stood. I ended up visualizing the sort of woman David had had in mind when he'd uttered his passionless curse against the gender, which, to my distress, I found pretty easy to do. Nothing in the imagery of the pious Jewish housewife, whether gleaned from Talmudic texts or from Reb Baruch himself, seemed to leave much room for anyone who could understand a David.

"*Nu.* I'll tell you a little story," Baruch said, this time his way of thanking me for the dishes, I suppose. "I used to have a neighbor who always used to tell me, 'Baruch, when I'll be seventy, I'll be religious.' I used to say no, if you really believe, the right time to be religious is *now.* But he said, when I'll be seventy."

"So what happened?"

It seemed to me he was trying to grin, through the unresponsive muscles. "He didn't make it to seventy."

"And David?"

"How do you know you'll be around later? You don't know. You speak Jewish? *Vays nit.* You never know."

A few weeks later, one Sabbath morning, he wanted to know whether I could read the prescribed passage from the Torah that day.

"Are you a *ba'al qorei?*" he asked, using the Hebrew phrase for someone skilled in the techniques of the public reading.

"No, Reb Baruch, I'm a *ba'al t'shuvah*"—meaning one who is becoming more religious, or more generally, a penitent. I only meant to say that I hadn't ever been taught how to do the reading; but he jumped right over that.

"We're all penitents," he said, and though the crippled face was immobile, his voice danced—a strange accompaniment, I thought, to the words. "*Nu,* we're always penitents. Always returning. We gotta get a little closer to God every day. And," he said, hustling me along to my seat in his inglorious little arena, "we gotta do it *joyous.*"

I saw Baruch, off and on, until I moved away from the Lower East Side to attend a *yeshiva* full-time in Monsey, New York. His condition steadily worsened. But the guests still endured the readings in his apartment.

All except David. One day shortly before I left, a neighbor broke open his door and found him on the floor of his room. His head had been fatally injured in a fall against a corner of a heavy wooden desk. He had been there alone for almost two days. A few shirts and several empty whiskey bottles were scattered around the floor of the apartment.

CHAPTER NINE

"*M*arriages,*" says the Talmud, "*are as difficult as the splitting of the Red Sea.*"

The Talmudic method leads one to seize a question by the most accessible knot. So, what makes one miracle more "difficult" than another? Granting that splitting an ocean is a miracle—that is, an act only God can perform—what does it mean to call a given miracle "difficult" or "easy"?

Here is a Talmudic story: A very poor sage prayed for help from the angels for his straitened circumstances. Suddenly the heavens opened and the leg of a table fell to the earth before the sage. And not just any table leg, mind you, but a table leg made of gold, and studded along its entire length with priceless jewels. Stunned by such riches, the sage went home to share his treasure with his wife, who, instead of being overjoyed, immediately exclaimed: "Don't you see what this is? This is part of the table at which we are meant to feast in paradise after we leave this world. If you keep this, here on earth, we'll be laughingstocks up there: everyone else with four-legged tables while ours teeters on three! You must tell the angels to take it back again!" The sage did so. The table leg was taken by the angels back into heaven: and its retrieval into heaven was a greater miracle than the original giving of it, since, says the Talmud, "what is given is not taken back."

What is given is not taken back. So there is a hierarchy of Talmudic miracles, of the bending of nature; nature resists above all things the re-absorption of a part that has been severed from the whole. You can split an earthworm in two, and each half will grow into

70

a new earthworm. But no can sew two earthworms together and make them live again as a single organism. So, the table leg dropping from heaven wasn't just divided from the table; it was severed from another world. To go back, it had to give up this world and graft itself back to the world it had left.

Midrash, or rabbinic lore, has it that at the moment of the parting of the Red Sea, all bodies of water everywhere in the world divided into two walls. Water itself was altered at that particular moment. Every body of water suddenly divided itself naturally into two mutually resistant halves instead of merging into a single pool. So when God reversed the process—bringing the waters of the Red Sea on the heads of the Egyptians—he wasn't *releasing* the two walls of water he had been holding apart, but changing the water back, restoring it to the sort of nature that makes it form seas and lakes. A "greater" miracle than the splitting: two half-bodies grown foreign to one another, now becoming one all over again.

Midrash also says that human souls come from male-female pairs: units combining the male and female beings that later take on personal features. These pairs are broken in two and become distinct personalities, man and woman, as they enter this world. As such they separate, and become individuals, private worlds, strangers to their original partners. But then each half of the former whole seeks out its lost mate. And awaits the reunion of the two.

In those days in New York I shared an apartment with a young rabbi, which sounds edifying but wasn't. For one thing, the young rabbi, already twice divorced, was busy doing the same thing I was: trying to get dates. For another thing, he was much more successful at it than I was.

Women whose histories fascinated me—a former cult member, a mystic who lived on a houseboat, a blonde Jewish dancer from Texas—passed in and out of our rundown apartment, oblivious to me, doing their utmost to make themselves attractive to Moshe, for whom they were never quite good enough.

"She talks too much," was all he could say about one exquisite young bohemian who admired his singing.

"*So do you, Moshe,*" I thought, but all I said was, "Hm."

Moshe's first wife, as nearly as I could gather, had been the conventional Orthodox article. A wig. Two children. A Brooklyn address, from which the boys made sorties into local *yeshivas* Sunday through Friday. Why she had married Moshe in the first place I cannot imagine. I should explain at once that Moshe was not conventionally attractive. As a matter of fact, though a rabbi, he himself was not remotely the conventional Orthodox article. He was clever in a way but clumsy, a ne'er-do-well—-a wild-bearded, wide-eyed, carelessly dressed, perennially unemployed, guitar-playing fellow who collected free cheese and welfare benefits and had a nervous horror of being anywhere on time. He liked standing on his head as a method of relaxation. I could well understand why the first marriage hadn't lasted. That it had produced two children before it broke up was really the riddle.

Moshe's second wife was another story. Of course, I learned about her entirely from Moshe, and long after that marriage, too, had ended in divorce. But at least from Moshe's description, Number Two was a hot-tempered bohemian who was in the process of becoming Orthodox when she encountered Moshe, somewhere in Southern California. I don't know what Moshe was doing for money at the time. They had sung and hiked together, and so on—and she had agreed to marry him after an acquaintance of a few weeks. It all sounded very passionate, but the woman soon took a dislike to Moshe. Undisciplined herself, she may have expected more dependability in a husband, especially an Orthodox husband. Moshe told me that she had resented his slovenliness and his carelessness about money. On top of that, since by then Moshe was her one and only serious link to Orthodoxy, her dislike of him quickly spread to religion, so that she began to flout Jewish law at home—making phone calls on the Sabbath, for instance. At least, that was how Moshe explained the origin of their violent quarrels.

Nevertheless, he had wanted her to stay. When she stormed out to the car in a rage one day, he actually jumped onto the windshield as the car backed out of the driveway, thinking that this wild gesture would prevent her from driving off.

It didn't. She rammed down the accelerator and barreled out of the driveway with Moshe hanging on to the windshield wipers for dear life. Then she threw him off on the tarmac and roared away, into the palms and insipid distances of the Los Angeles highways. According to Moshe, a short time later he came home from a teaching job and found the little white stucco house entirely emptied of furniture. He had never seen her again.

What made him particularly irritating to me was that Moshe (Hebrew for "Moses") brought his dates to our apartment deliberately to let them observe his homemaking skills. But the skills weren't his; they were mine. Moshe didn't cook. He didn't clean. He didn't even own a mop when I moved in. If I so much as sprayed a commercial cleanser on a sink or toilet while he was there, he would run into the corridor outside the apartment yelling, "It pollutes the air!" After a few such experiences I learned to grin and bear the accumulated dirt as long as he was in the apartment. After he left, I'd go back to trying what Lysol could do in the bathroom against six months of carelessly directed urination.

Still, Moshe made himself almost tolerable by filling me in on a side of Orthodox Jewish life I hadn't discovered in my reading. Orthodox law, as I'd learned, is extremely strict on the subject of male-female contact.

"You mean," my friend Steve Hamill scoffed when he found out, "you people are supposed to go out on dates and never even hold hands?"

That's right, I told him.

"That's not strict, that's fantasy."

"You don't know," I protested.

The trouble was, neither did I. So Moshe's accounts of "pious necking," delivered in loving detail and with rabbinic thoroughness, considerably complicated my picture of Orthodox life.

"Does everybody do this?" I asked him.

"Not everybody. Those who have to, if you know what I mean."

"But how do—I mean, well, how do you know when to stop?"

He shrugged his rounded shoulders inside his old shirt, which was missing a button. (Moshe kept broken umbrellas piled against a closet wall, insisting cheerfully, against all evidence, that they'd be useful someday.)

"How do you *know*?" Moshe repeated my question with a patronizing smile. "You do your best. And if you can't, well —" he shrugged again—"are you familiar with the word 'concubine'? It's quite common in the Bible."

I stopped him there.

"Well, you're the one who asked," he said, still smiling.

But I was a newcomer and wanted to play by the rules—rules for which, all things considered, Moshe didn't seem like the most reliable authority. Then again, I was a reasonably normal thirty-year-old male, and unmarried Orthodox Jewish women, at least those who were willing to glance in my direction, seemed as rare as hummingbirds.

What to do?

I have never met anyone who can explain the origins of Orthodox matchmaking. Most religious Jews I know are under the vague impression that the system was entrusted by God to Moses at Mount Sinai. I have even heard it said that the Bible's description of Isaac's marriage to Rebecca is the model for Orthodox Jewish dating— though the comparison runs aground on a few obvious rough spots. For one thing, in the Bible's account Isaac and Rebecca never actually date at all: by the time they meet they are already engaged, so there's no time for Rebecca's family to grill Isaac about his income, or why he isn't a doctor or at least an accountant, or which part of Eastern Europe his family hails from, or which synagogues his relatives belong to, or how many siblings he has, and where all of *them*

pray, and why all of *them* aren't doctors or accountants, or married already, and so on, and so on. And then, no member of the Isaac party demands to examine Rebecca's mother's dresses for immodest hemlines or too-short sleeves. In fact, Isaac asks no questions at all about Rebecca's family. He doesn't even confirm that Rebecca is willing to wear a wig after marriage (since a peculiar Jewish law holds that married women must cover their hair in public, but are permitted to wear wigs to satisfy this requirement). Such an omission is unheard of in the Orthodox circles I know. All in all, if Isaac and Rebecca had married today, the Orthodox world would probably have pronounced them both sinfully impetuous.

So I don't know when or where contemporary Orthodox dating practices originated. The process is not really "match-making," as it is often called by outsiders—though the Hebrew word we use for dates, *shidduch*, does literally mean "match." ("I have a *shidduch* tonight" means "I have a date tonight," though it could be literally interpreted as "I'm getting married tonight.") The marriage broker, or *shadchan*, as Orthodox Jews generally call her, does not actually arrange a marriage. What she generally arranges is a meeting between two people, of opposite sexes, who are seeking marriage. Possibly with each other. But there is more to it than that.

For instance, after a first date has been arranged, the *shadchan* awaits responses from both parties about the advisability of a second date. If both are in favor, the *shadchan* will tell them so. If either one demurs, the *shadchan* will convey the news to the rejected party without—*point d'honneur!*—disclosing any comments that might hurt the rejected party's feelings.

Now, at this point in my summary, I have to admit that these services can be genuinely helpful. But there are other and less pleasant features obstinately ingrained in the system. For one thing, the rules require the man to pursue the woman, never vice versa; he must initiate contact, make all calls, pick her up at her door, pay all expenses, etc. He must also take the initiative concerning whether the relationship is to continue. Feminism doesn't exist for *shadchanim* except as a vague synonym for heresy. What is more, even

well-paid female professionals in the Orthodox community, when
dating, seem to prefer it the old-fashioned way. (It is a curious fact
that modern American women who join the Orthodox community
as adults seem quite comfortable with this gender-biased system, at
least in my experience.)

Now, this single anachronism inevitably affects the direction
the process is going to take. In my case, since it is my fortune to
be male, I was required by *shadchanim* to undertake extraordinary
efforts to meet, impress and entertain a large number of women I
had never seen before and who (if I had even *once* seen and spoken
to any one of them) I would not have troubled myself over long
enough to make a single phone call. I don't mean to gripe. My point
is just that the option of waiting for someone to try to impress *me*
was not available.

The inequality of the system extends beyond financial favoritism. A *shadchan* once reprimanded me for wanting to know what
the woman I had just driven all the way from New York to Baltimore
to date (once!) thought of me—before I committed to driving
another five hours, each way, to date her a second time. "But," I
protested, "her opinion makes a difference, and surely I have the
same right to it that she has to mine." The *shadchan* wouldn't budge.
It was a woman's prerogative to keep her opinions to herself until
the last possible minute. Thus it had always been, and thus it must
be in this case. The five-hour drive ahead, before I could find out
what the woman thought of me, was simply irrelevant to the priorities of matchmaking.

Another weakness in the system is the loss of spontaneity. I'm
not talking about a couple's sudden whim to go skinny-dipping
under the stars. The web of law and custom that defines Orthodox
courtship extends far beyond such indiscretions. In fact, any devia-
tion at all from the plodding and not very private progress that
marks the average *shidduch* involves a conflict with the rules. Much
of this occurs simply because the process is largely out of the hands
of the participants. The *shadchan*, by arrangement, knows all, so
she ultimately controls the pace and direction of what happens.

For instance, after a few dates between the same man and the same woman, she will stop arranging any meetings for the young man with someone new. He is no longer free to date as he pleases. For at that point he is supposed to be trying to "decide"— decide, that is, whether or not to propose marriage. (This is true for Orthodox *men*. For Orthodox women a different standard prevails, and one man I know claims that his wife dated another man on the very night he proposed to her.) After two months or so of steady dating, the question becomes not *whether* but *when*. At that point the young man is likely to be told, sternly, that he's trifling with the young woman's feelings unless he is prepared to solemnize the relationship. Yet during all this, the two are not permitted to touch, kiss or even to be completely alone together. This built-in dichotomy of speeds—slow in terms of physical contact and almost recklessly rapid in its required commitments—intensifies the pressure of an already difficult process.

Then there's the problem that marriage, in the Orthodox community, is a communal affair. *Shadchanim* arrange matches on the basis of what the community thinks goes together, not what couples may actually want for themselves. Elaborate hierarchies are employed to rule out all sorts of possible combinations. It is one's pull in a vaguely imagined marriage market, where values are fixed by convention, that determines who one is likely to meet. Or will never meet. If your family contains Talmudic scholars, or is very rich, your value goes up. If you are new to Orthodoxy, it goes down. If you are too poor, or too old, or if someone in your family suffers from a serious illness, you will not be matched with the "best." I know an Orthodox diabetic who was bluntly told by *shadchanim* that anyone he dated would have to have "something wrong with her." Otherwise, no date.

On top of this, I've found that it is rarely worth the effort to ask the *shadchan* to take into account the love you are prepared to give.

"Love?" one snapped at me, when I was foolish enough to mention the word in her presence. "Love is *two percent* of a marriage!" And she subjected me to a lecture about the foolish modern heresy of romantic love. (I was tempted to ask what the other ninety-eight percent of marriage might consist of, in her opinion, but considering my helplessness to date any Orthodox women without the aid of *shadchanim*, and knowing that *shadchanim* have a way of talking to one another, I refrained.) No wonder a friend of mine, also newly Orthodox, says, "They all say they want you to marry Jews, but in practice they make it very difficult and very unattractive... It's very, very hard for a Jewish man to marry a Jewish woman under the existing system, at least for someone not born to the Orthodox tribe." Under the circumstances we seem to impose on dating, there is very little room for a relationship to grow in the eccentric, unpredictable ways in which relationships often do grow.

And when the new flower refuses to be teased into line, what happens? Well, usually it dies. What else can be expected? It dies— and the old pressures grind on.

I am on the New York subway, on a part of a line that climbs into the air at one dramatic point to cross the East River along the Manhattan Bridge, suspended between Brooklyn and Manhattan. It's past midnight. I'm coming home from a date, alone in a rattling, fluorescent-lit car. I've got on a black pin-striped suit, in which I feel stiff and tired.

The air inside the car is sodden.

But the train itself is alive.

It has been a typical and depressing date, and the trip home, despite the hour, is the high point of the night. This train, when it leaves Brooklyn, rises high above the water before it dives back below ground, into the tunnels through which it will take me home to the Lower East Side, through painted-metal and concrete caverns, cage after cage.

If you don't live in New York, and you're ever in the city, you must take this night ride at least once in your life. Preferably very late at night.

It's best if you're alone in the car and can forget that you are on a commuter train ridden by millions. In the dark of summer it becomes something else: a hot, half-living thing, its hollow body groaning and echoing, the steel frame shaking like a crack addict as it crests the great bend of the bridge. Usually the heat and talk of a crowd would confuse the scene. Not now. Now it's just you and the train.

You are the creature's eyes as it races toward the city's heart from high up on the bridge.

You're peering through the bleary windows straight into the fantastic, fragmented swarm of neon that is New York's body heat and nervous energy rolled into one. There is no view in the world more impersonal. And yet even the anonymity it grants is strangely enticing, as a prostitute can be.

Tonight I've just been given a rather elegant cold shoulder. Not by a prostitute, of course. A date. Silk blouse, neat mascara, pale lipstick, etc. After I paid for her meal, I found, through desultory conversation, that my date disapproved of my "going to movies." What can you say to that? ("Are you referring to *Citizen Kane*, Miss, or to Olivier's *Othello*?") You say nothing. Fate's hand closes. Another one down, and another point against my religious scruples (for insisting on dating women likely to sneer at "movies"), or against my lack of them (for watching films anyway)—who knows?

I'm sick of so much seriousness. I'm glad to be away from the endless inquisitions of Orthodox families and their too-good-for-me daughters. It's pleasant to be hovering above the uncritical excitement of the city, even if (maybe especially if) I know that the excitement isn't meant for me personally. I feel overdressed for the summer night—Orthodox-dressed—and I'm glad of a moment's freedom and anonymity.

I feel angry, too. At my date? At myself?

I guess I resist being pegged as mere *homo sapiens*, as I was tonight, not *homo Orthodoxicus*, which is what I'd like to think I've become, after investing so much effort into the process. Certainly, whatever I was tonight in this woman's eyes, I wasn't Michael Lesher—though who he is, now that I've "changed," seems to be anybody's guess.

And if I don't know, can I even guess at what he wants? Can anyone?

Let me count the possibilities...

Maybe, a love that lets me hide myself from my animal commonness, as religion itself may be a way of deflecting the humiliating monotony of desire.

Or just the opposite? Maybe, after so much religious self-exposure, I'm fantasizing a marriage—baldly defined by the *shadchanim* as a mechanism for having children—that's just physical, a religiously-sanctioned counterweight to spiritual aspiration. This would mean using the religious community's dualism of flesh and spirit to license a less-than-spiritual union while allowing me to keep the "religious" side of myself free from sweaty personal details. Not a likely fantasy, you might think, but here in the guts of the subway I'm half seduced: after all, just keeping up conventional pretenses (the poker face of the straphanger in the crowd) could bring with it the freedom of anonymity. And then...

In such a world the individual might escape judgment, the complex qualms of self-examination. After all, his religion tells him, "You're only human."

A strange way to capsize the gnawing inadequacies of the flesh? Not really. Some people might give a lot for such an escape.

But if I'm half seduced by the idea, I'm also repelled. Isn't romance, in or out of spiritual union, supposed to work the other way—toward self-exposure? If religion seems like a way of dodging that goal, isn't it just a way of papering over the hungers that make us most human? In other words—a fraud?

I don't know.

We're leaving Brooklyn at last. The Hudson is a flat track below, prickled with city lights. The train has found its highest perch, the haunting point in its line of traveled tension, the apex of desire. And now it moves on, gathering speed as it descends...

Above a city whose hum of nighttime illumination upstages everything but beauty. The lights obscure the buildings but leave a tantalizingly abstract pattern of red and white in neon, fireworks accidental in their combinations and all the more astonishing for that. Everything imagination can synthesize out of light and power—everything in that enormous mass of wishes burning outward from its narrow island, filamented, glare-driven—is below me.

How the huge soul hungers and flares!

How appetite writes itself gorgeously over the depths of river and darkness.

The train goes down, accelerating, pours off a dip in the bridge, surges through a brief gasp of summer air, and the images below me pivot, collapse into swimming doldrums, come nearer, disintegrate. The exhilaration of the illusion dissolves into urban immediacy.

The train dives below ground.

I lose track of time as the cars grind on. A string of subterranean lights, arcing downward. Then relaxation, as the metallic collisions of track and wheels gradually soften.

Arrived at my stop, I get off and head through empty streets to my apartment on the Lower East Side. I'm feeling down now, depressed by so many questions. I haven't got anything figured out, after all. Now that I'm closer to the city buildings, their beauty when seen from above is gone, and I register the sinister drabness that was masked in shadow in the view from the bridge. The sameness of the brick rows of apartments depresses me.

Nothing there but universal needs. Like everything else. Like everyone.

So why claim to be "different" from the mass? This has been one of the proud themes of my new-found religiosity. But doesn't everybody claim the same thing? And aren't the claims almost always a sham?

Chapter Ten

"I feel sorry for the gentiles," said a wasted-looking rabbi I'd come to know. The old man had just finished a stint in the hospital. "All they did there was watch television all day."

The rabbi was dying of cancer. His black wool suit hung limply on his small frame. His compact scholar's face, dominated by shrewd eyes and framed in an uneven white beard, was drawn as he told me how he pitied the gentiles and their television. I knew that he himself was in terrible pain every night.

After he died, some of his students undertook to transcribe the Hebrew notes he had written during that last illness. I saw some of those notes. They were comments on Talmudic law. His work was scholarly, but despite the abstruseness of the material the method was remarkably direct and orderly. The constant pain apparently had not scattered his thoughts. His notes posed problems for the medieval Talmud commentaries by positing cases that set their logic at odds with itself—forcing a conclusion that, if consistent with precedents from one point of view, was unacceptable from another. He raised more questions than he answered. You might have thought his unanswered questions would have weakened his faith in the system of Talmudic legislation, but they didn't. I know, because I heard him discuss his work with his son-in-law, whom I knew well, and I saw his eyes twinkle as he made his points. As he revealed the extent of his painstaking study, I could recognize in his voice the love of this vast legal and theological corpus that had driven him to the paradoxical extreme of—well, of teasing it half to death.

"Show me where I'm wrong," he challenged his son-in-law in Yiddish on one point – as I watched, one sunny Sabbath afternoon. His cancer was in a brief remission and he'd been released from the hospital, though most everything had been eaten away from his diseased hip. He'd just explained one of his arguments to the son-in-law, an earnest, stocky Jew with a reddish beard. Walking with difficulty, the rabbi used only a cane. (A wheelchair would have been forbidden on the Sabbath.) The son-in-law shook his head.

"It must be wrong," he answered. "But I don't see where."

The old man's eyes glittered. "Find it."

I was listening with only half my attention. My eyes were on a young woman dressed in tight jeans, walking away from me down our sidewalk through the calm midday glare. My body might be resting in its dark Sabbath suit, but my mind was somewhere else.

The rabbi didn't even notice the woman. He and his son-in-law kept arguing about his Hebrew notes. The old man leaned forward on his cane to renew his arguments. He seemed very happy, and I don't know what sort of perversity made me suddenly realize—watching his thin face, the skin stretched almost to the point of transparency over his cheekbones, and comparing it involuntarily with the youthful grace of the woman who had just passed—that he would soon be dead.

Sure enough, the old man's disease worsened after that and he went back to the hospital. The rabbi's son-in-law, Laibel Katz, spent alternate Sabbaths with his father-in-law, not wanting him to feel alone there. I knew all about it, because on the other Sabbaths, Laibel always invited me to his apartment for the two main Sabbath meals, Friday night and midday on Saturday. In fact, he insisted on it.

Laibel already had six children, the eldest of whom was thirteen years old. Despite what seemed to me the crowding in his apartment, he pressed his hospitality on me so eagerly it was hard to refuse.

"You've got to come again," he said to me after my first Sabbath meal at his apartment. "You hear? Got to."

I usually have no trouble turning down invitations. But Laibel enjoyed his hospitality so much that refusing it felt rude. "Nobody else knows how to eat," he lamented, and as I had with Reb Baruch, I gave in.

I went to Laibel often, even though I knew his interest in me was essentially impersonal, at least to start with, deriving simply from the fact that I was Jewish and single, had no relatives nearby, and was in his neighborhood. Laibel's hospitality was not a pose. He genuinely loved the opportunity to share some of the joy he took in life, and in Judaism, with someone else.

Like Shmuel Lehrman, Laibel was determined to lead me right. He had been astonished to discover that I had no Orthodox family members, not even miles away. Such a situation seemed to horrify him. "What do you do for the Sabbath?" he asked me. "The holidays?" He couldn't imagine a Sabbath or holiday meal without a family gathering. So it was with some embarrassment that I explained I almost always ate alone, reading, on those days.

Laibel's apartment was essentially like mine. The same black and white tiles on the kitchen floor. The same long narrow white-painted room in front, with its faded wooden *parquet* floor, which Laibel used as the dining room on the Sabbath. Like me, Laibel had no money for draperies. (But the place was spic-and-span; my own suffered greatly from my rabbi-roommate, Moshe, and the grime he seemed to leave behind him everywhere he went.) I suppose the biggest difference was the packing of Laibel's kids into bunk beds in every bedroom except for the one Laibel and his wife slept in. Well, there was another difference. In the front room, the most noticeable feature my own apartment lacked was a huge wooden bookcase, from which Laibel, in his, would pull down scholarly Hebrew books (beautifully bound, with deep black or gold print on the spines) to make his religious points for him. Considering his threadbare finances, the books must have been difficult for him to afford.

Of course, books didn't monopolize Laibel's attention. Or mine. The eldest of Laibel's girls—eleven years old—was a very pretty, willowy girl with serious eyes and fine, light brown hair. Her charm extended beyond her looks: she was curious, bright, and talkative without being tedious, little-girl fashion. Like most pretty girls she had already learned some of the tricks of the trade. She would persuade Laibel to let her stay up late by pleading (*not* whining, but with smiles and winning tosses of the head), while stroking his hand.

One Friday night, after young Sarah finally did go to sleep (in the living room, on a couch, in sight of the rest of us, since she had refused to go to her own bed), Laibel confided to me that he was hoping she would marry a rabbi, in another seven years or so when she'd be eighteen. Laibel had very clear ideas about it.

"One thing," he said soberly, "I definitely know. She'll never go to college."

"Really?" I said it more to make conversation than for any other reason. But Laibel took me up at once.

"Of course! I went to college, and I know what it's like there. That's not for my daughter. You understand, college—college the way it is today, anyway—isn't right for any Jewish woman."

Laibel knew I had studied six years for a masters degree at the University of Virginia. Did he intend a subtle criticism? Or was he appealing to a sympathy he assumed I felt? I didn't try to decide; my mind wasn't on the past. It was a very warm Friday night. We were both tired. Laibel worked two jobs in those days, in a bakery and in a small office doing graphic arts. I don't know when he slept. As for me, I used to read much too late into the night. Rather than tire myself further by speaking, I looked out the curtainless window of Laibel's dining room, down at the sidewalk full of people Laibel would refer to collectively as "*goyim*"—non-Jews. On the wide city street the lights of the passing cars were a prickling of white and red.

"Once you get outside the Jewish world," he said quietly, "everything you see is immorality. Well, of course, that's what they live for. What about you?" he asked, startling me for a moment with his sudden turn toward my private life. "You're planning to get married soon, I hope? It's the first commandment in the Torah, you know."

Most people in our urban neighborhood were Puerto Rican, apart from the Jewish population. Under the pressure of Laibel's unease with them, I suppose, the figures below seemed to me, as I looked, no longer bodies and faces, but brilliant dabs of color—red lipstick, black Latin eyes, white teeth exposed in laughter. Dehumanized as the result was, I still felt guilty for noticing even that much. Laibel's attitude made me feel as if I were betraying my ideals—our religious ideals—by looking at the people outside at all. But a lifelong habit of noticing things isn't shaken off easily. The smell from the street was not very good—tuna cans and newspapers in the gutter, that sort of thing. Still, under the enchantment of the street lights, the jewelry at the throats of the women sparkled as they walked by, and their hair shone.

I realized my silence might be taken as a comment in itself. "I'm trying to take things one step at a time," I said cautiously.

"How are you dealing with your family?"

"Well enough."

That wasn't quite true. A quarrel had broken out when my mother, in Washington, asked me to visit her for the Jewish New Year. That would mean praying in a Reform temple, which was forbidden to me because of Reform deviations from Orthodox ritual. My mother, for whom religion was a family affair, couldn't understand how Orthodox scruples could interfere with a family wanting to pray together.

"We're Jews. We pray. We blow the *shofar*. What more do you want?"

"There are rules," I'd told her.

But it was difficult to explain why the rules were so important, or why they should mean so much to *me* if they didn't to *her*. A pluralistic approach to matters of religious right and wrong has never much appealed to me, but it isn't at all obvious that ritual observance falls into the category of right and wrong. Except that if it doesn't, what's the point of it all? What is ritual without rules?

That Friday night at Laibel's the whole issue seemed very far away. No one in his apartment would have raised any of my mother's questions. The Law was taken for granted there. Besides, the Sabbath—with its traditional ban on electrical appliances, telephones, televisions, radios—seemed to have arrested time. My family problems belonged to another world, a past that seemed to have moved on into oblivion while Laibel's stood still. Looking out at the couples on the street below Laibel's window didn't bring the problems any closer: *they* would have laughed at my worries, if they'd bothered to have any reaction to me at all. But through my weariness a sort of vague resentment, an envious itch, nibbled at me. Those people weren't alone or misunderstood. They didn't live with religious conflict. They had their lovers, their wives. They had the happiness they wanted.

"If you have conflicts with family," Laibel said gently, "just handle them as best you can. The non-religious don't understand us. I've found they generally don't want to understand. When you decide to live the Jewish life they've decided not to live, you're an accusation to them. They go on the defensive and don't want to hear you. Believe me. I know."

As a matter of fact, Laibel had a sister who was largely nonobservant. The two were on fairly friendly terms, but argued often.

"Torah creates a different life, anyway," Laibel said. He stifled a yawn, then nodded. "A completely different sort of life, a new dimension to the world. That's what they can't understand. It's a life not really of this world at all. Living it makes you a new person, too. You'll see."

Tired as I was, I wanted to believe that. There *was* a very un-American charm about Laibel's apartment—its Yiddish phrases, the courtesy and generosity of the children, Laibel's unfailing hospitality. The other children were hard put to help Laibel and his wife with the oldest child, Danny, who was autistic. But they never complained about it, much less resented or insulted the boy for his oddities. (In my own elementary school days, gangs of my coevals used to taunt a neighborhood boy who suffered from Down's syndrome—and me, too, because I felt sorry for the boy and played with him sometimes.) No matinee idols adorned the walls of the children's rooms. In three years of visits, I had never heard a harsh word in the Katz home.

I looked at the girl we had begun by talking about. She had dozed off, curled up on an overstuffed couch against the wall. She had kicked off her shoes, revealing white cotton stockings; a precociously flattering, brightly colored dress was bunched around her legs and clung tightly to her sides.

What was I thinking about? I have sometimes had the perverse thought that innocence in women is appealing just because no man can ever quite believe in it. Earlier that night, young Sarah had asked me a series of charmingly disconnected questions about a picture book of endangered animal species. Then she'd dropped into my lap and guided my hand to the photo of the cheetah she had wanted me to see. Her touch was light and cool. The long-limbed cat had stared silently at me from the page, a look somewhat too knowing for my taste, yellow eyes brimming with primitive danger.

Laibel sighed again, joining me in looking at her now, asleep. The warm, damp summer air (Laibel couldn't afford air conditioning) held a too-intimate feeling. A lonely car horn wafted up from somewhere outside.

"She likes to read," he said. "She's bright. My wife is bright, too. But why should a girl be bright?" He looked at me with the same puzzled resignation he had once used to describe the trials of living with his autistic son—his tantrums, his unpredictable habits, the serious scratches he could inflict on himself the moment no one was looking, his way of throwing valuables out the window. Watching Danny mutter to himself and wander around aimlessly sometimes made Laibel feel like crying. And here, in his daughter's surprising intelligence, was another act of God that mystified him. He said: "What does she need brains for, to get married, have children and raise a family?"

He shook his head. The autistic child was Laibel's eldest. He was now *bar mitzvah* age. Had he been normal, Laibel would have held a celebration on the boy's thirteenth birthday. There would have been blessings, Jewish toasts.

I said nothing. I was looking at the girl with my own regrets. Soon she would be thirteen and forbidden to touch me. She'd blossom physically, turn prim, go out on dates arranged by her father and the local rabbis, keeping her distance, never touching or kissing a man, skirted to the ankles. And then...Why did it matter? Except that it seemed strange that, in the name of God and all his mystery, so much innocent flirtation should meet in the course of time with such a businesslike end.

A new thought struck Laibel. It was three weeks before the Jewish New Year, and a Hebrew saying describes that special period with the words, "I am my beloved's, and my beloved is mine."

Laibel reminded me of the saying, then asked, "You know what it means? What the real marriage is?"

I didn't.

"It's between God and the Jews. That's really what the words mean. A spiritual marriage. It means that we Jews, we're married to God. The others can't intrude on that relationship. If they did, it would be like adultery—like rape."

I looked at his eldest daughter where she lay on the couch, fast asleep now. I thought of her in another five years or so, turning up her nose, as her father already did, at the "street" that was the border of her world. Untouchable. Constrained with a man, as a Jew was constrained always.

"Imagine that," said Laibel Katz.

CHAPTER ELEVEN

It was time for a change. Though I was in the first deep flush of religious enthusiasm, I was also in the heat of—well, heat.

A married couple, the Rubins, who were my friends in Far Rockaway—friends of Shmuel Lehrman, whom I had got to know because they lived in the same building, and to whom I would rush on Friday afternoons just before the Sabbath, when Shmuel was late (as usual) and I got tired of waiting in the corridor by his locked door—said they had a solution for me.

"She's not completely observant yet," said Rachel Rubin—a stout, blunt-spoken type. "But she's tired of the dating scene. She really wants to get married. And, well, she wants—you know—a traditional sort of guy."

Traditional?

I wasn't at all sure I qualified. True, by that time I'd absorbed the conservative focus of the medieval Jewish codes, including their frowning on all premarital sex. I'd spent much of my free time during the last two years (between work and law school) studying the Talmud, praying regularly mornings and evenings, rearranging my life so as to avoid writing or business on Saturdays and Jewish holidays. That approach to life certainly seemed angled toward a conservative spin, but buttoning down my view of the world at large hadn't turned me into a Jewish Gary Cooper. To me, "traditional sort of guy" still meant the football players I'd watched enviously in high school—guys who always came to class in ties on game days. Bristling with unconscious physical health and vigor, they called the coach "sir," seemed bored already with girls, and would one day,

I assumed, acquire wives and children as easily as I might pick out oranges at the supermarket.

That was "traditional." I was just a Jew with his nose in the Talmud and his imagination in *Last Tango in Paris*.

On the other hand, I had already met the woman in question. She'd been at the Rubins' one afternoon when I'd visited along with Shmuel. I had been prepared to dislike her, because Shmuel had once dated her for a while, and he said she had broken his heart. (Not that that was an unusual complaint for Shmuel.) But the sight of Sarah dozing on my friends' living room couch, curled up against the old backrest like a child, her long brownish hair scattered in sweet disarray around her cheeks, was, well, disarming. And she was pretty, in an unassuming way. Rachel, my stout friend, assured me she was friendly; I was still painfully shy, and the businesslike interrogations to which young Orthodox women had subjected me on my own infrequent dates hadn't made the gauntlet easier to run. So all I said about the idea of dating Sarah was, "I see."

I saw Sarah again just a week later—this time under that stretched-thin tension that comes when you know you are being investigated as a possible future husband. Again, we were both at the Rubin house. It was a Jewish holiday of some kind. I don't remember which. My friends had asked me, as they always did, for some sort of scholarly comment on the holiday or its regular Torah reading, which I dutifully attempted to give. (In Orthodox households, it is proper to discuss religious subjects during holiday meals.) And Sarah sat there at the same table, more or less across from me and the dinner dishes, listening. She also listened when I talked about other things. In fact, she did a good deal of listening to me. Which was unusual. In fact, it was so unusual that it unnerved me, I'm afraid, and a rapidly rising pulse hammered in my ear during a needlessly lengthy comment on some political matter of the day, so that I have no idea at all what I said.

Since being in love and being unnerved are cognate experiences to me, I decided then and there to take the next step, for which all that was necessary were a few words to Rachel. Almost before I knew it everything was arranged. Sarah and I were going together, the next Sunday, to the Bronx Zoo.

All right—it wasn't exactly a night on the town. But for me, it was the first *real* date in a long time. To make matters more nerve-shredding, it was the first I actually looked forward to as much as I agonized over it.

What to do? To my own frantically assembled list of self-interrogation items, I eventually gave the following answers: long sleeves; oranges and pears; no, absolutely no preaching; back before suppertime, certainly!—and—well, only if *she* kisses *me*.

That seemed to take care of the major issues. But there was still plenty to fret about. Which long-sleeved shirt? Was white too formal? Would an older, more comfortable one be insolently casual? Even the oranges and pears posed problems. What if I brought unripe ones she couldn't eat? Wouldn't *I* look like a dope! On the other hand, overripe pears might be ruined during the trip. And what if I dropped the bag on the subway?

In desperation I called Shmuel Lehrman, who laughed, not at the questions I had planned to ask, but at the one I blurted out without forethought.

"I didn't break up with her," he answered at once. "*She* broke up with *me*. I think I was too religious for her. That was the main trouble. Funny thing is, I think she wants to be religious now."

She wanted to be religious. And *there*, oddly enough, was the crowning anxiety in all my fears. How did I simultaneously play the suave suitor *and* the earnest Orthodox Jew? I didn't even know how to manage the first, and now I had to try to be both at once.

Foolishly, I suppose, I actually tried to discuss the subject with Sarah herself, as we walked that Sunday between fenced-in wild birds and cavorting sea lions. Well, perhaps I didn't appear terribly foolish (though I felt it) since she really did most of the talking.

"I hope you're not feeling any pressure about seeing me—about how to act, I mean," she said, looking at a Bird of Paradise through one of the zoo's unobtrusive fences.

No pressure? What would marriage to her mean, after all, given my new commitments? The thought led me in unexpected directions. There was Sarah's hair, for instance. What was going to happen to it if she married me? Orthodox women are supposed to cover their hair after marriage. Sarah's ran down her back. I had visions of her lopping it off with shears, or matting it down under a wig, or binding it in some coarse rope or net. Any of these thoughts made me wince. But should I say so? Or would I be spoiling everything if I did?

"You're not, are you?" she asked. "Feeling pressure?"

I lied.

"I'm glad," she said. "I know how they can make you feel. I love the Rubins," she went on sunnily, "but sometimes they can really make me feel on *edge*."

I tried to imagine things from her point of view and made a quick, sympathetic guess. "Sure. Everything's so serious."

"Oh, yeah! And dating, especially. It isn't even really supposed to be called dating. It's '*shidduchim*.' I mean, here I am, just getting to know someone, and already I'm supposed to think about a marriage?"

"That's tough," I said. "People keep telling me marriage is a commandment. As if that helped. To Orthodox families a single man of thirty is a loose nail."

"Please! What about a single *woman*? She might as well be a tiger escaped from the zoo."

As a matter of fact, we were nearing the area of the zoo where the big cats were kept. Sarah was a lively walker. I followed her up a hill to get closer to the leopards and cheetahs. She was dressed unpretentiously in a light blue blouse and a denim skirt—a welcome change from the Orthodox Brooklyn girls whose shrill accents, expensive dresses and deadly-serious, carefully applied makeup always made me feel like an animal within leg-length of a baited steel trap. Put one paw into this blouse, their looks blared at you, and you're never getting out again. It was a setup only a very lonely or a very horny man could have fallen for. But of course,

93

that's exactly the sort of young man the Orthodox sexual mores are bound to churn out by the schoolful.

Sarah led me around the jungle cats. We saw two leopards, a male and a female, stretched out on their sides in the cool grass, their taut muscles a pair of smooth passages from neck to tail, playfully pawing at one another. She talked cheerfully. She told me about her parents ("When I was a baby they never even let me fall down—overprotective? I'll say"), Rachel Rubin ("A real friend. She's really seen me through a lot of trouble"), even some of her past problems with men ("The thing is, I'm really honest, and that just invites some people to walk all over you, you know?").

And then it was my turn to be honest. I told her that religious study had both galvanized and confused me. It had galvanized me by shoring up my sagging sense of historical identity. It had also given me some intellectual space in which to work out my fascination with questions of right and wrong.

But it had confused me, too. I was confused about the stern array of limitations, boundaries, warnings. By the notion of people skimming over their lives as though life itself were a stretch of treacherous rapids whose dangers were to be kept uppermost in mind and were to be avoided as much as possible.

"Yeah," she said. And smiled at me.

Did she realize, I wondered, that the most baffling of these anxieties was about sex? Orthodox Jewish law imposed a number of severe restrictions on my behavior with Sarah at that very moment. No touching of any kind. No seclusion. We must be in a public area at all times, and if we should ever go somewhere behind a door, that door should not be closed.

Yet I had no idea how this anxiety sat with Sarah herself. She had been dating for years as a normal, young American woman. Of course, that dating had involved some physical intimacy. (Rachel had told me how Sarah had been crushed, in the past, by men who began a date by kissing her and ended it by telling her they'd never see her again: "the kiss of death," Sarah had called it).

We live in our bodies, I wanted to say. Our words can only speak for a part of us. The whites and browns of ribs, breasts, bellies, the pressure of hands—this is language too. One is pinned to the world by it, or propelled to heights where the syllables disappear. And the oddest thing about the off-limits status of this sort of thing in religion, I thought, was how deeply the same patterns that shape that language, essentially sensuous, figure in religion's own emphasis on the non-verbal—the rhythm of ritual, the rising above time in its celebrations of resistless sequences: birth, love, death.

But Rachel had told me that Sarah was interested in Orthodoxy and wanted "a traditional guy." Was "a traditional guy" supposed to be rubbed so raw in the grip of tradition? *What was I supposed to do?*

Usually one date was all it took for a woman to reject me. Whatever was supposed to happen on one of those tense, buttoned-down encounters, it never seemed to happen. I would be told afterward by the *shadchan* that the episode was over. The marriage for which I had already half begun to prepare myself would never happen. A little more violence to the soul; a resolution to try again; a sneaking suspicion that it would never quite be the same.

But I dated Sarah almost two months without such a mishap. And on top of it, I was enthralled.

But what to do now? The strain of uncertainties was exhausting. Rachel Rubin only complicated my dilemma by informing me (after first swearing me to secrecy) that Sarah had confided to her that *she* found it difficult to keep from touching *me*. This just added a layer of confusion to my already raw nerves and religious uncertainty.

We reached a sort of crisis on a Sabbath night, when we met—once again—at the Rubins' house in Far Rockaway. Sarah and I lived pretty far apart, I in Manhattan, she in a distant New Jersey suburb. Neither of us had acquaintances near the other's house. So it was natural to meet at the Rubins'. Sarah would stay there over the Sabbath; I planned to sleep at the house of a family I knew around the corner from them, and we would all have Friday night dinner together at the Rubins'.

The Rubins had moved to a house of their own that year. They had paid for added size with shabby wainscoting and rundown grayish indoor-outdoor carpeting on a strip of which the two of us sat after dinner, wearing our best holiday clothes—me scratchy and uncomfortable in a wrinkling black worsted suit, Sarah as calm and natural as if she had been on her way to an outdoor concert. Part of the paradox of the situation was that I dislike clothing, especially fine clothing. The comedy extended to our shoes. I had on some new, polished black leather foot-traps I hated; I envied Sarah's sandals, but I hated them more than I envied them, because her exposed feet (with painted toenails) added to her allure, which, I suppose, is why Orthodox women rarely wear such things.

The Rubins had been invited to a *shalom zachar,* that is, a Friday night party held by the parents of a new-born boy who would be circumcised in the coming week. So the two left immediately after supper, inviting me to stay with Sarah. They reminded me pointedly, though, not to fasten the front door. Jewish law, you know?

I was in a quandary. Everything in Sarah's generous, un-pious manner encouraged me to move beyond conversation—if only I knew how. But once again I was restrained by religious principle. That is, until she threw me into a panic by saying, "I wish we could— oh, you know, not just talk."

I don't know if the pose that resulted from my trying to look calm conveyed helplessness or stiffness, but whichever it was, Sarah was determined to circumvent obstacles. We were both sitting on the floor, for some reason, our backs against two low-slung facing chairs very close to one another. My feet were therefore within her reach. Reaching over to me, she quickly untied my right shoelace.

She didn't take my shoe off. I suppose she was determined, no less than I was, to behave like a good newly-Orthodox Jew and not actually touch me—either because she knew she shouldn't or because she thought it would upset me, I don't know which.

But as far as she knew, only touching with actual parts of the body was forbidden: no one had told her it was forbidden to touch me with the tip of my shoelace. And no one had told *me* I was supposed to stop her if she did it.

So for a while we played a strange game. She went on talking to me, telling me what she must have supposed I wanted to hear—how she liked and respected me, and admired my religious ideals, and how she thought she herself wanted to live more traditionally after what she'd seen of life in a middle-class Arcadia. And all the while, my shoelace tip, between her fingers, played lightly around my ankle. Up, down.

It was unbearable. It had been a long time since I had been touched by a woman, and now the very indirectness of Sarah's touch made the longing it aroused all the more poignantly intense. Even worse, she turned out to be really talented in the use of the shoelace tip.

Can a woman ever really know all the things she can be to a man? Friend and temptress? Solace and torture?

It had to stop, of course.

Some time.

Impossible as the scene was, it had a giddy charm that grew every moment, and I feared that the slightest change would destroy it. So I did nothing. I was as enthralled with Sarah's cleverness as with her indirect touch. What generosity, I thought, what originality, and what innocence, all at once!

And then, in another moment, the sensations in my ankle told me she had gone beyond the use of the shoelace tip. Now it was her fingers on my ankle.

I had forgotten how something like that could feel. The world slipped through a crack and turned into heaven. I wanted to kiss her out of sheer gratitude.

But I didn't.

Maybe it was because of the Sabbath suit I was wearing, and all it reminded me of. Maybe it was because I knew the Rubins were coming home soon and I didn't want to disappoint them by having them find us caressing each other.

Or maybe it was...what? The courage of my convictions? Or my cowardice in the face of their frailty?

Anyway, with what I hoped was a winning smile, I said, "I think we'd better stop now."

She removed her hand.

I had to leave, and we both knew it. It was very late. Anyway, I thought vaguely, there will be other times. The giddiness of the experience had not worn off, and it made the time ahead stagger beautifully, if unpredictably, in my breathless gaze as I slowly stood up.

We said our goodbyes and I walked to the house around the corner where I was supposed to sleep, feeling on top of the world—and right into a tongue-lashing from the host, a middle-aged sobersides who could not believe I could have been out so late with a "non-religious girl," as he put it, without any impropriety having occurred.

I was certain there would be many more encounters with Sarah. Plenty of chances to finish what had been left hanging in that heady summer-night air.

I was wrong. Sarah invited me to her parents' house after that, which I took to be a sign that the relationship had ratcheted up in seriousness, but the signal proved a false one. Not that the visit went badly. As Sarah had told me in advance, her parents were protective of their only daughter to a fault, but in a good-humored way. I liked them. They seemed to like me. Sarah and I collected wild strawberries in a farmer's field near her house and she baked a pie with them. She was as beguiling as ever, and when she showed me the miniature of Michelangelo's David she kept on a ledge in her room ("my David," she called him, as if he had been her lover), I felt she was inviting me into a private world where nakedness was not off-limits.

But something in her was slipping away from me. I couldn't understand it, but I knew what was happening, and remembering my mad self-restraint of that Friday night at the Rubins', I cursed myself and my religion for the change in direction. So close, I thought—and I'd spoiled everything.

Ironically enough, my religion was rapidly becoming hers. She stopped working on the Sabbath. She ruled out non-*kosher* food from her diet. She started going regularly to lectures given by Orthodox rabbis—in fact, she enjoyed them rather more than I ever did. She even made up her mind to spend a few weeks at a school for newly-Orthodox women in Monsey, New York.

But however much we seemed to share, we seemed to share less and less of each other. The last time I left her on a railway platform near her parents' house, I looked from the window and saw her looking wistfully after my departing train, as if regretting the rupture I knew full well she was about to confirm once and for all.

And when she called me to break the news, I couldn't get angry; she seemed so concerned about me, and so grateful for my affection and sympathy—even my "example," she said—that the contrast between her natural kindness and my inhibited lust only sickened me with dejection about what, just a few weeks earlier, we had both agreed to accept as religious ideals.

CHAPTER TWELVE

Seven-fifteen in the morning. Prayers had just begun at Ohr Somayach ("joyful light"), the *yeshiva* for newly-religious Jews in Monsey, New York where I had enrolled myself earlier that fall. I was in the main room of a clapboard building that had once been a house, surrounded by other Orthodox Jews, swaying in prayer. Outside, I could hear two crows in a coarse duet. They were not far away but plainly aloft; from the directions of their calls, I figured they must be spiraling around each other, rising into the air over the fir trees that framed the wooden cube of the study hall.

Listening to them outside, with prayers going on around me, I had an unusual experience. I was standing behind a wooden desk, in a throng of swaying young men reciting Hebrew prayers. But at the same time I was also somewhere in the air, orbiting with those crows, a rough voice and its echo fifty feet above my head. I was standing on a floor, aspiring toward the sky. And I was also rising into a pale light that absorbed the noises the birds made and waited for me to catch up to them.

"Worship is transcendent wonder," says Carlyle. And here are some relevant words George Eliot wrote about prayer:

> The most powerful movement of feeling with a liturgy is the prayer which…is a yearning to escape from the limitations of our own weakness and an invocation of all Good to enter and abide with us; or else a self-oblivious lifting up of gladness, a *Gloria in excelsis* that such Good exists; both

the yearning and the exultation gathering their utmost force from the sense of communion in a form which has expressed them both, for long generations of struggling fellow-men.

Maybe you'll say that the sense of being in the air above my own head was so obviously an illusion that it's not worth mentioning. But is it really unthinkable for someone to be in two places at the same time? I mean, everybody can be, in fact must be, several incommensurate things at once: a history, a blob of protoplasm, a mind. Maybe prayer is just the strand that ties those things together, presenting us as we really are, the bearers of multiple needs, multiple realities strung along a bigger-than-we-are axis.

A month earlier an overloaded friend's car, with me inside, had pulled up a driveway that turned out to be an unpaved incline, a rising slope of sparkling gravel muted by surrounding rows of stern-looking fir trees. The November sun was already more down than up. The dust kicked up by the wheels, as we ascended a curve into a bank of even more forbidding oaks, turned the thinning light of early evening into a sickly pastel, like paint when too many colors run together.

Jeff Murray, the friend who had given me the ride, helped me carry my luggage. The man I would soon know as Rabbi Gold (with whom I had as yet spoken only over the phone) intercepted Jeff, and the two of them talked about New York, the highways, baseball, pleasant things. Students hurried by, dressed in black suits and hats. My new roommate, Izzy Markstein, lanky and red-headed, Orthodox a couple of years, took me to the ramshackle prefab cabin that would be my new home. He introduced me to the vagaries of the place. It had four small bedrooms—each one for two students—a single bathroom and a common room, which was damp, full of pine needles, with an old swaybacked card table in the middle of the sagging wood floor, and one molting old sofa against a wall. Everywhere there was a smell of rotting sawdust.

My own room, like the others, held two beds, and was so small that the only way I'd be able to do morning pushups would be to position myself between the beds, my feet under the desk between the heads and my head brushing the far wall.

Izzy stuttered a bit. "I hope you'll like it here," he said to me. "It isn't a H-H-Hilton exactly, and some people grouse about the food. But…"

Food is a serious subject to me, so I asked him about it.

"Oh, it's all right. Mrs. Moskowitz does it all herself. She checks every s-s-single bean, looking for insects. That's the kind of woman she is. You know, Jewish law doesn't allow you to eat insects." Suddenly he let loose with a clownish giggle that seemed out of place in a school filled with serious young religious students in business suits. Maybe he thought it was funny to be soberly discussing a prohibition against eating aphids and caterpillars. He wore the uniform too, including a rather wide-brimmed black hat, but uneasily: the hat was forever being pushed around so that he could scratch his head, the agile, expressive face was never still. I learned later that he had terrible sinus problems, which accounted for the humidifier that filled our desk, our one piece of private furniture. "But wait," he went on, "until they serve the 'red fish.' Then you'll really find out what you're made of."

Mainly, I wanted to find out some other things. I was an eager beaver, or wanted to appear one, so I wanted to know: when did the studying start?

"What about right now?" Izzy asked. "I'm in the middle of a difficult page of Talmud, and maybe it could be a sort of introduction for you."

A month later, we had seen so much, so fast, that the rasping of the crows overhead, a wordless affirmation of life, was a blessing to my overloaded brain. The birds reminded me that, however busy the tangle of words and laws, I was still somewhere between earth and— well, somewhere. I couldn't speed up the journey no matter what I did. And maybe—the thought occurred to me for what I believe was the first time in my life—I didn't want to speed it up, anyway.

Returning to my cabin that morning after prayers and breakfast, I found a stocky, densely bearded, square-featured young man seated on the sagging foot of my cot. He introduced himself to me as Shlomo Richter. He explained that he had slept in that cot until October and had come back for a look at his successor.

It seemed odd that he would ever be tempted to return to that spot. The room was dirty and in desperately poor repair, with splintering shelving and cracking walls. But Shlomo seemed mostly interested in *me*. He made a more or less approving inspection of my black suit (I'd just bought it). Then he found out I didn't own a hat, and the real grilling began. Didn't I know that Orthodox Jewish men typically wore hats over their *yarmulkes*? At least, the really and truly religious ones did. This made the subject an important one. Did I know how hat sizes were determined? Did I know how a brim was shaped? What "blocking" a hat meant? What makes of hat went with what sort of style? What sort of hat denoted a Hasid, and what denoted an Orthodox *yeshiva* student?

Within minutes he had pegged me as a hopeless amateur. But at least I was a willing student.

"Of course, now that you're in *yeshiva*, you'll want a good one," he said. "Otherwise it doesn't look good for the school. But take my advice and don't listen to the people who'll tell you there's no substitute for a Borsalino. A Stetson is just fine." He proved his point by removing his own and displaying it to me. His head, exposed without the hat, was sturdy, round, close-cropped. His suit was formidably correct, the tie tightly knotted. His face was all seriousness. He rotated the hat slowly, upside down, on his palm. My eyes were drawn to it; as I had once watched storm clouds pile up in a top-heavy Georgia sky, I stared at that upended hat as if it, too, might suddenly leave me trapped in the downpour of my ignorance.

Meanwhile Shlomo was giving me a concise lecture on the wearing of hats. "Stetson" and "Borsalino," and now other names, fell from his lips like books of the Bible.

"You see," he said, showing me his brushed-smooth, coal-black Stetson—"it has shape, good color, strong brim." Then he showed me how to turn the brim down in front. "Not up, like the Hasidim," he said.

Years later, on his wedding day, he would handle a large framed photograph of Rabbi Eliezer Schach, the Hasid-hating head of the Ponevezh *yeshiva* in Israel, with just such precise, confident movements of his hands. His school friends, who had presented him with the portrait, must have known that the fiery old Talmudic scholar would appeal to Shlomo. He had come to Monsey answering to the name of Seymour, hardly reading Hebrew. In just a few years he'd accumulated a scholar's collection of Talmudic volumes, a wardrobe full of black suits, a steady government job, an equally steady contempt for secular culture—besides a large-hipped, fertile wife who visibly doted on him. It was an Ohr Somayach success story.

At the time he inspected my cot he wasn't married yet, of course. He already held a tight grip on the other acquisitions, though. In fact, he seemed very nostalgic about the cot. He kept looking at it wistfully, with its narrow, rusty wire mesh and ancient mattress, as if it represented one thing he might not be able to keep with him throughout his life. That is, one thing he couldn't keep that he wanted to keep. For he'd obviously left a good deal of his former self behind when he'd landed at Ohr Somayach. He had cut his hair short, grown a beard, assumed a Hebrew name.

Now he looked all around my ramshackle room. "This is a good place," he said finally. And to me: "I hope you're worthy of it."

Rabbi Gold, after a short conversation with me in the forlorn neatness of his office, had pronounced me a suitable candidate for the Ohr Somayach education.

"You'll gain from us," he said, addressing me not as "Michael" but as "*Mee-kho-el*," the Hebrew form of my name.

I should mention that from the day I entered Ohr Somayach I almost never heard myself called anything else. *Mee-kho-el.* The full significance of this did not strike me for a long time, but I want to mention it now, because it bears on the shift in identity that was so much a part of my experience of those days. On arriving at Ohr Somayach I ceased to be Michael. I had not only changed my dress, my location, the nature of my reading, the language in which I would mainly study. I had even changed my name. Or rather, it had been changed for me. No one had asked me. It was just assumed that Jews, or at any rate Orthodox Jews like those at Ohr Somayach, used Hebrew names. And so this name, which I had never actually heard before becoming Orthodox, was suddenly thrust upon me—as *me.* A talisman of my identity had suddenly been turned inside out, belonging more to others than to myself.

(A further irony, as it turned out, is that this wasn't even my actual Hebrew name. Just about the time I left Ohr Somayach my mother unearthed a certificate written when I was eight days old, indicating that my Hebrew name was "*Melech Leib,*" after a great-grandfather of mine. So in a sense my Ohr Somayach name was a ghost identity, belonging to no one who lived before or after that time.)

Without waiting to figure out how Rabbi Gold knew I'd "gain," or even what that meant, I flew at the curriculum with almost maniacal energy. No one much noticed, because most of the other students worked like maniacs too. Nearly all of them, like me, were newcomers to Orthodoxy, which made us all eager to make up for lost time, and meant that I was never too much out of my depth among the others. On the Lower East Side, I had learned how to read the Talmud; while in law school, between morning prayers and the legal publishing office, I had squeezed in a daily study session.

Now I quickly discovered that, however much or little I looked the part, I was well adapted to the *yeshiva's* intellectual program. I loved moral philosophy, legal riddles, the grammar of analysis.

A Talmudic argument about the degree of legal liability in a complicated accident might veer suddenly into a question of Biblical hermeneutics. Was the Torah meant to be interpreted according to the reasons underlying the commandments? Or was each obligation understood as an end in itself? And what were the general rules of interpretation? A trip through the commentaries only complicated matters; the Talmud contained confusing or contradictory authority in different places within its great bulk, and all of it had to be straightened out.

I was also intrigued by the things I couldn't straighten out. Orthodox Judaism places great stress on the accuracy of the Bible. The arrangement of words within a verse may provide the basis of a law. Every detail is treated as meaningful. So what about details that cast shadows over the whole text? What was I to make of claims like the revelation at Sinai, for instance? Did Moses really converse with God, as he stood at that rocky site, about everything we studied in our Talmuds, written over a thousand years later? Could anyone prove he had?

On the other hand, as Izzy pointed out, could anyone prove he hadn't? Centuries of tradition endorsed the revelation; could we know more about an ancient event than the ancients themselves did? Not having a ready answer to that, I plunged ahead in my Talmud.

(I had not yet considered the possibility that the answers to such questions are not really factual but normative, that we decide on an account of revelation in order to secure a fruitful reading of the text. This isn't exactly a scholarly approach, I know. But I often find the Talmud's treatment of the text of the Torah, even when its readings are historically impossible, more interesting than the more "accurate" readings of Biblical scholars. The Talmudic commentators always knew what they were about, and their readings are alive with the shrewdness and the seriousness of men for whom the text is a living guide to real problems.)

All the study at the *yeshiva* meant a good deal of discipline. Its physical comforts were sparse. Izzy had been right about the food. There was never enough, and what there was left much to be desired. I was always hungry. But to squeeze in extra study time with Izzy, I used to eat supper in fifteen minutes, then dash back to the study hall. It was exciting in a way, the hectic attacks on our big volumes, and the demands of the curriculum made the sacrifices seem worthwhile. Still, I felt the strain on me physically.

"Izzy," I asked one afternoon, "how long does it go on like this?"

"As long as you want."

In fact, there weren't enough hours in the day to cover the material we might use for the next few lines of Talmud. I thought at first this was due to my weak Hebrew and weaker Aramaic, which forced Izzy to do a lot of translating for me. But as my reading improved, my problems actually multiplied. Questions were constantly presenting themselves to me and Izzy. Had they ever been addressed? Usually they had been, somewhere over the centuries of Talmud commentary, but this meant swimming through still more texts to arrive at something like a definitive view.

"Not b-bad," said Izzy, his head bobbing in the manic way he had, after one of our bouts with a problematic piece of Talmud. "I think we got something out of that commentary from the *Sea of Solomon*." It had taken us hours just to *find* that commentary, or rather to find one that addressed the question that had been troubling us.

Behind the clear blue eyes Izzy was a puzzle. He was a prizewinning bowler in Detroit, Michigan. I know nothing about the game, but I've always associated it with blue-collar types. Izzy must have cut a strange figure in that crowd with his intellectual tastes, not to mention his stammer, his sinus problems, his wild giggle. He did have the nervous energy of the sportsman, though. He once told me his biggest problem in *yeshiva* was an old habit of restlessness: "I was always in a hurry to be someplace else. I knew I could coast in college and get good grades, so I coasted and moved on." During his year of study in a Jerusalem *yeshiva* he went around in a long jacket, side curls, an aureole of red beard, his head shaved Hasidic-style.

He was a dazzling student at Ohr Somayach. But the restlessness remained. He would borrow a car sometimes and just drive away, engine roaring, to no place in particular. On the other hand, he once astonished me by announcing he was putting a stop to trips into neighboring Spring Valley, a dumpy town if there ever was one. "If I'm really on a spiritual path," he said, "I've got to establish some discipline. I shouldn't need to drive around Spring Valley. If I want novelty, I should find it in the Talmud."

He shook his head, with an expression on his face that was much older than he was. "When I drive into Spring Valley, I end up getting too interested in the things around there and spending too much time just looking," he said.

CHAPTER THIRTEEN

We all knew the buildings of the *yeshiva* couldn't last. Building inspectors from the town had already visited and had left, after little more than a cursory look around, in stunned silence. I think they must have noticed the mushroom that was growing from our bathroom floor. And the gaps in the sides of the cabins—once, quite by accident, a student literally put his foot through one of the walls. On frigid winter mornings the bathtub (the bottom of which was literally outside the cabin and two feet off the ground) was almost intolerable. Any water left in the tub froze to the porcelain. The cabins had no insulation. The heating system, which had been hastily installed in cabins obviously designed originally for summer use only, was atrocious. In the summer, mildew grew everywhere and mosquitoes sailed through cracks in the windows.

Soon the condemnation notices started to appear. We had known they would. Still, the administration reacted in Orthodox fashion—perfect complacency, and inaction, until the last possible moment.

Meanwhile, life in the *yeshiva* flowed on in a way that seemed timeless, following patterns laid down through centuries of tradition. It was remarkable how quickly we all adapted to them. You would have thought we had known them all our lives. But then, routines in general are easy to accept. It's the ideas behind them that are not always so easy to absorb.

The center of our lives was the study hall, or *bais medrash*. It was our school and our synagogue. In front was the Ark, where the scroll of the Torah was housed. This was a simple wooden affair, but to me, at least, there was something impressive in its stately barrenness. The rabbis sat in front, in their dark suits and black hats, facing the rest of us. They read from lecterns broad enough to hold the huge Talmudic volumes that were almost all you could find on the shelves. Every morning we squeezed out corners for ourselves around the tables that filled the room, pulled up plastic or folding chairs, drank coffee or tea from Styrofoam cups, and got to work.

Work was the study of the Talmud, and it consumed all our energies. It was a noisy affair; twenty pairs of gesticulating students argued over their texts, in a cramped room, like traders on the floor of the Stock Exchange. Study began immediately after 7:15 morning prayers and ended no earlier than 9:30 at night, when we recited evening prayers and went to bed. Breaks were for practical purposes only. On top of this, many students would remain after hours, studying until 11 pm or midnight. This was especially popular on Thursday night, the last night before the Sabbath.

"This is an old tradition, and a beautiful one. You want to greet the Sabbath Queen with a gift," said neat, phlegmatic Rabbi Gold. "What gift could possibly be better than Torah?"

The word "Torah," to Orthodox Jews, refers to the entire body of Jewish law. But in *yeshivas* it has a more specialized meaning. We were actually discouraged from considering practical applications of the Talmudic principles we learned, except in matters of ritual observance. Our studies were meant to be "pure"—that is, abstract and theoretical. We knew more about the communal problems of third-century Pumbeditha (an ancient Babylonia city) than about what was happening to Jews in Manhattan (a place generally to be ignored anyway, according to more experienced students, because it abounded in "impurity.") If someone tacked a poster to our one bulletin board urging, on religious grounds, some political initiative in Israel or Brooklyn, the rabbis would generally take it down.

"We need nothing here but Torah," Rabbi Gold would say.

If that course of study sounds dull to you, I can only say that you have probably never tried it. It has an intoxication all its own. The Talmud may be a hothouse flower, but it is a breathtaking one. Even in an overcrowded converted shack at the center of Ohr Somayach, cold in winter and stuffy in summer, students fell for it, and in most cases stayed fallen. I suppose it has always been like that.

Not that there were no problems for the rationally-minded student. I once asked a rabbi about a passage dealing with demons. Did we really believe in such things any more?

"Probably not," he said with a sigh, looking up momentarily from his Talmud. Regret was written all over his long, bearded face. And in an instant, I understood. It wasn't whether demons were real or not that concerned him. It was the fascinating use the Talmud made of them, which it would be a shame to remove from the rich tapestry of text and legend.

The rabbis realized that analysis of tort law didn't fill all our religious needs. There were many classes on Jewish practice and ritual, and many of these were larded with inspirational anecdotes. We were frequently encouraged in the "spiritual path" we were pursuing by the school's dean, Rabbi Kosovsky.

In addition, once a week we got a hortatory lecture from one of the rabbis. The traditional word for this is *mussar,* and it has its roots in a popular movement that swept through Eastern European *yeshivas* about a hundred and fifty years ago. Over the years the tone has changed somewhat, but the substance is largely the same: the world exists for the study of Torah, the study of Torah aims at breeding a lofty personal ethic, students should press on and never flag in their efforts, lest the Torah be disgraced, *et cetera, et cetera.*

I always had difficulty concentrating during these talks. For one thing, I don't like lectures. Call it a personal quirk: I have never enjoyed sitting in a crowd listening to someone speak from a podium. Besides, for some reason, maybe just a delight in violent contrasts, I kept finding myself thinking back, during those inspirational lectures, to sex education talks delivered to me and some classmates in a narrow, tiled basement room of an eighth grade gym class in Atlanta, Georgia many years ago. Twenty-five of us sat with our backs against a sweaty cinderblock wall in the basement of the school building—a place not all that remote from the crowded study hall at Ohr Somayach, come to think of it. The embarrassed, sweatshirted coach, a whistle around his neck, would be trying to sound both inspirational and natural—while talking about gonorrhea.

"Cut off your dick," someone yelled from the shadows—the coach having just cleared his throat and asked us what we thought we could do about "this, uh, V.D. thing."

The class roared, and the poor man chuckled nervously. "Now, seriously, guys. I mean, this, uh, thing…"

I guess I still half expect religious teaching to fare just as badly with young men. When I was growing up, piety was clearly on the defensive. Kids from religious Christian families joked about what went on in church. To this day, the Christian kids' jokes remain my main source of first-hand information about Christian ritual. Is it really true, I wonder these days, that Catholic boys sometimes gag on the Communion wafer because the nuns have told them it's human flesh?

But in *this* setting, religion was taken very seriously indeed. One day Izzy prevailed on me to hear a lecture by Rabbi Sirkin. In Talmud class, Rabbi Sirkin was taciturn, perceptive, relentless. But I'd heard he could really let fly with opinions when given the excuse of "Jewish philosophy," and it was a lecture on "Jewish philosophy" by Rabbi Sirkin that Izzy wanted me to attend.

I went.

What I'd heard about Rabbi Sirkin's quirky tirades turned out to be true. That afternoon he was full of bile about Christianity. I should mention at once that this sort of thing was not common at Ohr Somayach. Whatever my mother might have imagined about the school, very little of its time was directed at anything like formal religious indoctrination. Still less time was lavished on criticism of rival faiths. This may surprise the outsider, who might well suppose that the curriculum of a school intended for religious converts would consist of little else. But in this as in many matters, Ohr Somayach was a product of deeply-rooted Jewish traditions. Traditional Jewish education is not theological—it is Talmudic. And for the most part, so was Ohr Somayach.

But Rabbi Sirkin was an exception. When I came in to the tiny, cluttered classroom that afternoon, a little late as luck would have it, he was already on the scent of a demon, rocking back and forth on his base, his black hat bobbing, his dusty jacket bunching around his shoulders. I think I should describe Rabbi Sirkin, because the reader would be very much mistaken to imagine him as a red-faced, blowharding fanatic. He was a slender, swarthy man with large, very dark eyes, a neatly trimmed beard, sallow skin, a sour smile, remarkably delicate hands. (I remark on the delicacy because, as I would later learn, his inner restlessness drove him to subject them to the rigors of all sorts of rough work—building an expansion to his house, knocking down walls, cutting beams, hammering pipes and sheet metal.) He dressed in the usual Monsey Orthodox uniform (black suit, white shirt, black hat) but the carelessness with which he came to class with wood shavings or oil stains on his suit was in marked contrast to the fastidious grooming of his hair and beard. I never heard him raise his voice, and he may have been one of those people who are really incapable of shouting. But this too could be misleading, because it did not suggest a calm temper. On the afternoon in question, he was brooding over something that had brought him near the boiling point—though he showed this only by stroking his black mustache rather more rapidly than usual.

What had infuriated him was a well-publicized appeal, by a group of Christian clergymen, calling on members of churches to light candles in their sanctuaries in memory of the Nazi Holocaust. As I found my way to an empty chair, brushing against the young men next to me in the crowded room, Rabbi Sirkin was glaring off into space, searching for words to convey his contempt for the project.

"Ah, remembering the Holocaust," he said caustically. "What a nice thought from the Christians, don't you think? Remembering the Holocaust, now that they're finished with it, for the time being."

He glared at the students seated at the room's one table, or lined up against the veneered walls (some hadn't ventured to look for a chair, as I had, once the rabbi had begun his musings), as if daring someone to disagree.

"Why do you suppose the Jew they worship had to die on his cross? Because they all love Jews so much?" He stroked his mustache, somehow managing to make the gesture as eloquent as spitting on the floor. "You don't suppose the Holocaust really bothered them, do you? And now that their church attendance is dropping, they want to use Jewish blood, of all things, as a drawing card. And call it compassion? Is that all they can mean when *they* talk about 'remembering the Holocaust'?"

I raised a hand.

"What *should* they do?" I asked. I didn't mind the way everyone in the room seemed to draw in his breath at once, turning around to look at me.

From his seat at the head of the table Rabbi Sirkin gave me a long, icy stare.

"What do I care?" he demanded. Then his expression changed. He gazed intently around the room, out the window into the unkempt grounds of the school, full of massive oak and birch trees that on that Indian summer day tantalized the soul with a lazy profusion of swaying reds, yellows, browns, moving sometimes closer and sometimes farther away from the glass panes. Rabbin Sirkin, as I would soon know, loved those trees, and they seemed to lead him somewhere deeper into himself, but they could not soothe his irritation. He rubbed the right arm of his worn black suit jacket. Both ends of his mouth twitched now.

"Well, maybe if they just feel properly guilty," he murmured at last. "I wonder if that's too much to ask. For six million victims. Is it? Or is it just going to be—candles?"

There seemed no way to reply to that.

"Candles," he repeated. His face twisted around into a sardonic smile. "The Church likes burning things, no?"

I kept my mouth shut afterwards.

As I got to know him better, I avoided such subjects with him whenever possible. I found—and this is what made his tirades tolerable, when they couldn't be ignored—that what rose to the surface only vaguely reflected what was churning around in the depths below. You didn't know the real man from those fragments that came up on politically charged subjects. The real man was brooding away somewhere down there, cogitating a surprising variety of subjects—American law, aesthetics, semantics. Fortunately, on non-political topics he was less edgy, less pugnacious. I found that if I could guide him around his internal warning lights, he would talk about almost anything. As a child he'd been fond of *The Twilight Zone*. He still remembered entire episodes, and he was fascinated by the show's what-if themes. He had studied in a very large and very famous *yeshiva*. I'm not sure what they made of them there. He was a brilliant scholar, but not the standard article: an inner restlessness was always driving him. His lack of comfort even showed itself in practical details. For such a slight man, his physical daring could be amazing; he not only insisted on building an extension to his house himself, but on one occasion, when two students (press-ganged into helping him) accidentally dropped a heavy wooden beam they'd been negotiating down a long flight of stairs, he actually caught it in his arms, ignoring their shouted warning—though the impact could have broken bones.

He was at his most talkative while walking vigorously around Monsey—unless a third person appeared, for he hated "company." In class, he treated the Talmud as if it were a cryptic friend who had to be prodded for more information. He never wanted to leave a problem behind. He would unconsciously wrap an arm around himself, as if to squeeze an answer out of his body; he would rock violently in his wooden chair. Once during class he sat grimacing at the page in front of him for nearly ten minutes, apparently forgetting about the rest of us. He told me once, while walking down a sidewalk at night, that chasing down a difficult point in one of the major commentaries was the chief joy of his life.

He did have other pleasures. He used to take his wife and seven children on camping trips to remote lakes, enjoying the anonymity he found in such places. Was he running away from something? Sometimes—notwithstanding his caustic remarks about Christians—I felt that it was more than anonymity he found far out of Monsey.

"An old fellow actually waved at us when we drove by," he told me moodily, after a trip through some deserted, wooded spot in Michigan. "This old gentile. He saw us driving by, so he just waved at us." His voice dropped to a musing growl. "I realized something when I saw that. Something about being human has been ground down by 'civilization.' Why does something like that seem so strange to us? Just a friendly wave of the hand. But it meant something. People used to have a way, an *art* of living. Do you know what I mean? That simple enjoyment of human things."

He looked at me, then back somewhere, vaguely in the direction of the *yeshiva*. "I'm afraid, you know, we've lost touch with that."

Almost without realizing it, I was slipping into the rhythms of *yeshiva* life. Imperceptibly my idea of time began to change. I had been accustomed to thinking about time in terms of whatever I was working on—how far from the end, how far from the beginning. But now the cycles of Jewish study and observance began to take over. I stopped thinking as far ahead as the two years I had planned to be a student at Ohr Somayach. Now I floated in weekly suspensions between Sabbaths, each one describing an arc which, every Friday night, consummated in the predictable twenty-four-hour day of rest. And one Sabbath followed another in the slow orbit of the seasons and their holidays.

But life, of course, couldn't let me slide so easily into timelessness. Shocks could come at any moment.

One night I polished my black shoes, put on my Sabbath suit, and set out with the rest of the guys in my cabin to a building some way across town, where a former classmate was getting married.

I didn't know the fellow. But everyone seemed to be going. It was Shlomo Richter, himself a former student, who had told me of the upcoming wedding, which (he said) it was everyone's duty to attend.

"Especially yours," he told me. "Now that you've taken over my bed, you have responsibilities to fulfill." I'm not sure whether he was joking. Anyway, I went.

I remember I had to fix a stopped-up toilet in the cabin that evening before I left. I remember that because I was almost the only one there, and had to do it in my Sabbath suit, and the place was so small I was afraid the toilet would flood and I'd be up to my ankles in sewage. I remember, too, spotting another ghostly white mushroom growing from a dirty crack in our bathroom floor—I guess the floor there was more dirt than tile at that point. (Later, when I had pointed out the mushroom to the other residents, someone pulled it up. But no one thought to repair the floor.) Then the sun went down and some other young men, dressed as I was, gathered on the dirt path outside the cabin. We headed off.

Very few of us had cars, and the few available ones were unreliable. We walked instead. We had a long walk across Monsey to reach the building, even taking paths through a large wooded park to shorten the distance. But it was a summer night and the walk didn't seem unpleasant.

The others talked a good deal. One of them was an Israeli—tall, reed-thin, with long black side curls. I later found out that the side curls were fairly new. He'd arrived at Ohr Somayach in jeans and shoulder-length hair. Within six months he'd become a fire-breather. Hanging down his thighs were the ritual tassles, or *tzitzis*, of Orthodox Jews. He went nowhere without a black hat and a knee-length caftan that, considering his exceptional height, made me think of a clown on stilts wearing an oversized coat.

Yoel (his name) went on at some length about Darwinism. "A fiction of the scientists," he declared, in his Israeli accent.

"Is it true you're working as a tour guide in Washington?" asked someone, when he had finished.

"Yes," Yoel said happily.

"With *your* English?"

"I do not need so many words to say, 'This is center of world's corruption.'"

"Is that what you tell the tourists?"

"It does not matter what I say," said Yoel, loping along the sidewalk. "They don't listen."

"Somebody should make you a tour guide of a natural history museum," someone else put in.

It was too dark to see Yoel's face, but his voice told me he was still smiling. "I would say also that this is center of corruption. Business and government in America pollute the ground. Scientists in America pollute the soul. Theories, theories everywhere, not the Almighty."

"Do you think they really believe them?" the first interlocutor asked, after a pause. "The theories?"

"Yes," said Yoel. "They must. Because it is their religion. The scientists are priests of this religion, and frightened people need a priest."

We were in the park now that was our short cut across town. The path through it was paved for the most part, but overgrown with weeds and scraggly shrubbery in places. Trees leaned down at us from overhead. There were no lights, and at night the place looked much wilder than it really was. The deep blue of the sky was slowly leaking away to black. I could smell the excess warmth of goldenrod, the stuffy scent of dead grass. There were no stars.

"Dostoevsky said," I put in, "that a man has to believe in something inexpressibly great. Otherwise he will die of despair."

"Hmm," said Yoel. Moving through tree-shadows, he looked like a shadow himself, and as stern as a twisted trunk. It occurred to me that he wanted to ridicule the "scientists," not to sympathize with them.

"Is that only for men?" someone asked, "or does it mean women, too?"

"Not women," said Shlomo Richter. "At least not necessarily. Women don't think about things in that way."

"Rabbi Sternbuch says that women think with hearts, not heads," said Yoel. "That's what Rabbi Sternbuch says. Probably a wiser way."

Some others were murmuring in a chorus of agreement. We had almost reached the *yeshiva* building. We adjusted our hats.

"Make him proud of us," counseled Shlomo Richter. "And don't look at the women."

The doors in front of us were exactly like the doors of my high school—the same metal handles, the same dense paint, same high, suspicious windows crisscrossed with wire. Under the circumstances, the apparition stunned me with its lack of novelty. I remember actually wondering whether I would be able to grasp the door and pull it open. But somehow it opened anyway. I cannot remember whether the arm that opened it was mine. The strangest and most salient part of the memory is that it wouldn't have mattered; I was feeling as out of touch with my arms and legs as I was with my old school memories.

And then, inside the door, there was Sarah, standing not twenty feet away from me.

"Well," she said, and stopped.

My breath flailed inside the stone cave my body had become.

The others had walked off; I longed to have even Yoel back.

Sarah had on a silk pastel dress that hung nearly to the floor but still managed to show the smooth curves of her hips. Her figure had never been breathtaking; its beauty was in its candor, an artless wholesomeness that the added covering she gave it, now that she was fully Orthodox, only made more appealing to me.

"Hi," was all I could manage.

I had heard she was in Monsey. In fact, I knew the fellow she had just married. He had come to Ohr Somayach soon after I did. He was a good-natured, pock-marked, horse-faced fellow with short brown hair and prominent teeth, an accountant, I think.

Sarah seemed genuinely pleased. "I'm glad I saw you here," she said. "I mean, I guess I'm saying I've always wanted to thank you."

"Thank me?"

I don't know what I had expected, but I hadn't expected that. How is anyone grateful for failure, the male in me wanted to know. And yet—I suppose I did know what she meant. She was thanking me for bringing religion into her life, sharing with her what she supposed was the best thing I had.

"I mean..."

Of course, she didn't see me from *my* point of view: still wanting her, hating everything (including religion) that stood between us. And I couldn't very well insist on the truth against her much prettier version of it. What could I say? That I, a full-time religious student, a man who had helped introduce her to Orthodoxy, was standing there on my way to a wedding, half wishing I could rape her?

"And I'm glad," she went on, not bothering to finish her previous sentence, "that you're in *yeshiva*. I know you'll benefit from it."

I searched my mind for an answer to some of this, any of it, but the words I needed weren't there. Hadn't she herself been the one to teach me that?

Somehow, I got away.

Back at the cabin that night I spent a few of my life's most miserable hours on my cot (the cot Shlomo Richter still pined for). I felt sure I hadn't learned anything and never would. No words came to me, not from the Talmud, the Bible, or any book I knew.

I tried to frame some words of my own. But nothing I could think of did anything to lessen the pain.

Chapter Fourteen

A Jewish legend:

When the first rains of the Flood began to fall in earnest, while its first waters lapped at Noah's ungainly ark, his fellow-townsmen—realizing finally that trouble was at hand—began to crowd around the ship, clamoring to be let in.

The prophet drove them away. Who knows why? Maybe they had deserved it; maybe he was reminding the troublemakers of their rough treatment of him while he had built that ark, when (say the Sages) these same people had laughed loudly at the pious old fool with his hammer and timber.

Anyway, at that moment the Almighty slid back the gates of the underworld. And the anxious crowd around the Ark was granted a glimpse, not of the ship's dry interior, but of the terrible judgment that awaited them all below: thus, a final chance to repent.

And? According to the legend, the chance was rejected, and the world was drowned.

Now this may be—and usually is, in Orthodox Monsey—just an excuse for a bit of pulpit-pounding. *You see!* See the stubbornness of evil! Its refusal to change course, even at the last extremity! See where the unbelievers will lead us, if we let them!

But the more I think about it, the more I believe an opposite reading is possible. I mean, mightn't hell have its attractions? Couldn't a world sick to death of having its nose rubbed in its corruption actually *prefer* the isolating experience of supernatural punishment? Or, to put it another way—was the clamor of a crowded ship, shadowed by the wrathful superiority of its prophet, so obviously a fate more appealing to the multitudes?

Ohr Somayach in summer was a tiny group of bungalows bunched together in what must once have been a beautiful wilderness of oaks and towering firs. The summer resort the place had once been was abandoned in the 1950s (when the availability of air conditioning allowed affluent New York City dwellers to spend their summers at home, thus putting the resorts thirty miles away, like Monsey, out of business). The gardeners and landscapers had disappeared and the woods began to grow, uncontrolled, on all sides. The paint peeled, the walls warped. Weeds invaded everything. It was a ruin so worthless no one even bothered to demolish it. Eventually some rabbis who were determined to spread the faith bought the whole mess for a song, and that's how Ohr Somayach was born.

So, thirty years after the summer people had left for good, the place was inhabited again. By us. But now *we* were the intruders. And the wild things seemed to know it. Brambles tore the students' black jackets on our way to the study hall; burrs worked their way into hats. At night, swarms of mosquitoes rose from muddy pools, penetrated our rusted window screens and plagued us in our cots. Wild deer would spring out of waist-high grass and stare at us, glassy-eyed in the *yeshiva's* outdoor arc lights, before fading back into obscurity. It may sound quaint, but it could be unnerving.

And it also lent force to my growing suspicion that the school, and the religion it represented, might be too isolated for the students' own good. Or anyway, for the good of people like Moshe the priest, whose story I am about to tell—a man for whom a very small heart of darkness would have been more than enough.

When I met him he had already been at Ohr Somayach for a day or two; it was the demanding schedule of the *yeshiva* that kept me from meeting him at once. It was Friday afternoon before I knew that the newcomer and I had been "assigned" to the same host for a Sabbath meal in town that night; Friday night before I knew anything about my stout, taciturn, dark-featured companion except that his name was Moshe and that he came from South America.

He didn't talk much during our long walk. I remember only one comment of his. Spotting a two-month-old Easter wreath on one of the houses we passed, he turned to me suddenly and asked: "How many Christians are in Monsey?"

I told him I didn't know. The school was located in a hamlet so heavily Orthodox that non-Jews generally seemed to disappear into the crowds of black hats and beards, outsiders among outsiders.

A slow smile deepened the mystery of Moshe's face. He wore a black woolen suit despite the heat, and a thin black beard was curled around his cheeks: a Svengali.

"Ah, but there are *some*," he said. He pointed an index finger at the Easter wreath. "And they're celebrating the death of a Jew, don't you see."

Our host that night was one of those well-meaning Monsey Jews who supposed it the soul of kindness to pump a guest for every detail of his life history. In twenty minutes I learned: that Moshe was born and grew up in Peru; that he had no brothers or sisters; that he had once lived in Rome; that he was married and had no children (not *yet*, he was encouraged to add); that he was schooled in classical languages; and that his wife, of Moroccan ancestry, was at home in Chicago.

But when asked why his wife wasn't with him, Moshe (who had seemed poised, even a little arrogant, up to then) astonished me with the childish way he avoided the question: he pretended to go deaf—literally reaching for his glass of water as if the room were silent. That was when, unexpectedly, I began to feel a little sorry for him.

But he kept his trouble inside, until we had left the house and headed back toward the cabins that served as our dormitories.

By then it was about midnight. A solid black glaze, unbroken at the edges by any trace of color or far-off city gleam, had clamped down over the summer sky. We had a long walk back to Ohr Somayach. As we walked down the edge of the one long, narrow road that led through the oaks and firs toward the distant *yeshiva*, a sour mist, an aftertaste of a rainstorm the day before, rose from the cracked asphalt, making it difficult to see. The trouble got worse when occasional passing cars blinded us with their headlights. But Moshe, ignoring all this, walked on at an exhausting pace despite his stout frame. And now he was no longer taciturn: he kept talking, in steady if thickly-accented English, about the Christians.

They were deadly, he said. They could not be trusted. They were liars, they celebrated the death of Jews. And their priests were worse. His talk, punctuated by stentorian gestures, rose and fell.

"You don't believe me?" he demanded suddenly.

"Well…"

"You simply don't know the facts. Did you know I studied at the Papal Library once? I know what I am talking about. They are the biggest liars, the Christians. The Jesuits most of all. I read dozens of their books."

I had never met anyone who had studied at the Papal Library. I had certainly never expected to find one among the students at an Orthodox Jewish *yeshiva*.

"I wanted to know," he said, aggressively rather than defensively. "I went back to all the early works, in Greek and Latin. I read their whole history. That's how I know. Christians are liars."

"Not *all* of them?"

He stared gloomily ahead as we kept moving. His right arm kept making gestures, as if addressing an invisible crowd.

"The only thing we have like it is the Lubavitcher Rebbe," he said. He was referring to the leader of a Hasidic sect notorious for the missionary enthusiasm with which it tried to popularize Orthodox rituals among other Jews.

"They worship that man," he went on. "He is not a human being to them, and he knows it. It's the way Peruvian villagers treat their priest. If he says, drop dead, they will do it. I tell you," he repeated, "it is like a Christian cult, this Lubavitch. That man, the Rebbe, he is like the Pope."

He pushed on for another gloomy minute, apparently forgetting about me, as I struggled to keep up with him. Long, limp grass hung in rank and entangling patches over the sidewalk, making the way even more treacherous, and to this day when I remember the story of that night it is with the sour bite of that grass's smell in my nostrils.

After a while he sighed.

"Listen," he said. "I am not going to sleep tonight. I could not tell our host, because I saw from the pattern of his mind he wouldn't understand."

"And I will?"

"Ah, I know more than you realize. There are two gifts..." Here he used two Greek words I did not understand. "You see. These are two gifts I happen to have."

His smile again cast its strange shadow through the gloom. I was glaring incredulously at him, but whether he was doing it deliberately or not, he was managing to intrigue me.

"Yes," he said, "I'm not proud of these gifts. They come from a power of impurity. And they can be dangerous, too. When you can listen to people's thoughts, when you can see some of their future taking shape..."

"Just a minute," I protested.

"I told you I wasn't proud of them. But listen!" His voice was oddly professorial—a quality that deepened, rather than relaxed, now that his subject was personal. He even raised his chin for emphasis. I wondered where he had picked up the habit of such high-handed speech.

"There was a time when I cared more what people thought of me than anything else," he was saying. "But I'm not like that any more. Believe me, I'm paying for it. Oh, yes." His voice dropped. "I miss my wife. And do you know where she is?"

His eyes, through the night's faint mist, were torches raised to the faggots. "She is brainwashed by these Lubavitch people in Chicago. They don't even let her answer my phone calls."

He took in my look and then quickly shook his head.

"I won't do anything terrible," he said. "I've given up their methods forever, don't worry. When I was in a village of simple people in Peru, they thought *I* was God. I would walk everywhere with a suit of clothes made to look like gold. Like the sun. Yes. I would tell those people what they were thinking. I made them fear me."

I could only stare.

"I was right about you," he said, to my still greater astonishment. "You are offended, but you understand."

"Not a bit," I said.

His finger split the air angrily. "Don't deny it. I am a Peruvian! My family didn't live as Jews. We were Peruvians like other Peruvians. Haven't you heard what Latin Americans do when they have talents, but are not born into the right families? What *profession* they take? Even the Jews, sometimes?"

And then the odd smile again darkened his face—he saw that I understood. Even under these circumstances he was taking a little pleasure in shocking me, I suppose.

From there the story came out rapidly. Moshe had officially converted to Catholicism while still in his teens. At the time his only motives had been practical: social obstacles and humiliations awaited a Jew in professional Peruvian circles. Many of his relatives had done the same thing long before he had.

But with Moshe, the conversion had turned out differently. His religious reading changed him. In fact, a few months after the conversion, he entered the priesthood in Lima. He ignored the feelings of his parents, who disapproved strenuously, and the startled hostility of other Jews. He understood their pain and their opposition. He hadn't become a priest to hurt any of them. He simply didn't care, or rather, he *couldn't* care. Something more important had happened to him. He had fallen in love with God.

He finished his training and was ordained. He took the name Diego. At his request, he was assigned to a remote Andean village. He told his bishop: "I want to save the humblest sufferers there are."

Well, that was his mistake, he told me that night. As his extravagant impulses always would be. The people in his mountain village had no taste for the spiritual drama their new priest had hoped to orchestrate in the depths of their desolation. They were poor. Their main concerns were the price of beans and the health of the local *burros*. If they thought of their unhappiness at all (which seemed to happen only rarely), their thinking took forms that were useless to Moshe—ideas connected with the shadowy bands of guerrillas to whose ranks, now and then, a young villager slipped away, and who were feared and hated by most of the peasants as much as the minions of the local aristocrats.

At first he sank into despair. Then a saving alternative seemed to present itself. Moshe's "gifts" had been with him since he could remember. Now, trapped in his Andean village, he began to use mind control. In utter frustration he began to work on susceptibilities more accessible than the villagers' hearts. He would awe his congregants if he couldn't save them. Moshe told me how he made himself an elaborate costume out of cloth of gold. It sparkled when he walked—"like the sun," as he had already told me. It fascinated his flock. When, in church, he panted in the grip of a vision of God, a hundred candles would catch the trembling gold mirror of his cassock, so that he shone with supernatural splendor. From his pulpit he would stare above the congregants' heads and thunder, *God has chosen this place to be clothed in light, can you see?* They couldn't, of course. But they believed their priest.

And they believed even more when, in his confessional, Moshe began to reveal to them things they had not told him.

"How did you know I felt that, Father?" one of the villagers would ask, astonished.

"Never mind!" he would say. "Confess!" Moshe's sternness would instantly draw the supplicant's submission, a cracked, thin voice that would say: "Father, I can hide nothing from you."

Once at his mercy they could be rebuked whenever he chose. He told them they were lazy, lustful, proud. They told lies. Worse, they had tried to hide all this—to keep secrets from God. But not from him. Fearing his power, they confessed everything now.

And then they really were suffering, they were begging him for absolution. But even that wasn't enough. He gave his absolution. And then they forgot all about their sins—and him—until their next confession. A routine like any other.

And Moshe's own agony grew. No matter how passionately he tried to believe himself in his new role, he saw through his own game: how he tricked the villagers into turning on *him* the devotions he had once wanted only for God. He had sought out humility. But now, could he bear to be insignificant?

Worst of all was the villagers' attitude toward the church. To Diego/Moshe it was an arena for the most lacerating desires: God and Devil literally at war for the soul. Sometimes, halfway through Mass, Moshe would feel as though his exaltation lifted him bodily from the floor, the power of God overmastering the weight of mere flesh. But there were other times, bitter times, when even as the holy words left his lips the power of darkness took possession of him. Then he would be nearly overwhelmed with a desire to seize Christ, if he could, to attack him bodily, to curse. And in that way, he told me, to put an end, not only to the church and the stupid villagers, but to himself—and the humiliation of his tormented unworthiness.

For who was he, anyway? An apostate Jew in a gold cassock, making dumbshows for illiterate peasants! Why *not* break the illusion? He would long to hurl the chalice across the church...

And then he would glance back at the worshipers in their cracking wooden pews. And there they would be as always: stolid, half
dozing, fanning themselves, waiting patiently for him to finish. He
could have tolerated their rebellion or hate or contempt, even their
indifference, better than this—their listless, unthinking obedience.

He began to chastise them. At first he managed to restrain himself so that he doled out only minor penances: to abstain from the
marriage bed a few nights, to fast for a day. But when he saw how
meekly they accepted his punishments, his contempt flared into
hatred and he wanted to hurt them in earnest. What would it take
to prick their spirits? To make them struggle with the knowledge of
the soul's appetites, as *he* had done?

Alone at night, he begged his Savior to intercede. He was going
crazy and knew it.

And for once, his prayers were answered. The guerrillas—the
same guerrillas who had always been the terror of the village—
went on the attack, surrounding Moshe and his townspeople. The
villagers were cut off. For weeks his people could not get down their
mountain to buy food. They were close to starvation. They killed
the village dogs and ate them. "Not so bad as you might think," was
how Moshe described it. But real terror had descended on them all.

And in that terror Moshe at last discovered that before God
everyone is equally human. Small, frightened, hungry—that's all a
person really is, he told me. At bottom a man is always crying like a
child. Hoping, like a child, for a little help from above.

When the guerrillas were finally beaten back Moshe left the village
and went to Rome, pleading a scholarly objective. A new life was
already growing in him. In Rome (the Papal Library), he devoured
all the books he could find on the history, the origins of Christianity.
He found no answers to the doubts that were consuming him.

And then he looked up a rabbi with whom he had once cor-
responded during his early religious education. Fresh from his

disappointments in the study of Christian theology, Moshe soon discovered, with the rabbi's help, what he had already begun to suspect in the Andes: that his mind had never really accepted Christian dogma. It was the struggle of his own soul that had made its Satan, and its Redeemer, vivid to him.

Now, for the first time, he changed the direction of his religious study. He began to learn Hebrew and to pore over the ancient Jewish texts, the mystical books as well as the legal codes. He found that Jewish law was constructed with the same painstaking care as the best scholastic theology. But its consistency and moderation fascinated him. In the Jewish view, he learned, no priest was needed to bridge the gulf between God and man. The Law was a human one granted from above—not a divine instrument skewering unworthy man.

That was when he gave up the use of his psychic power, he told me. He quit the Church, resumed the name Moshe, grew a beard. He began to wear a *yarmulke*. For the first time, he felt completely Jewish. A new world lay before him. The steady gaze of the naked eye toward heaven, without the aid of any special lens, seemed as much as he would ever need.

He married and moved to Chicago. His wife was a Moroccan Jew who loved to cook. Her specialty was pumpkins. She cooked pumpkin pies, pumpkin stews, and some Moroccan dishes that involved a sort of pumpkin curry. She even began to look like a pumpkin, Moshe told me—short and rounded, and orange-skinned. That pleased him; such simplicity was exactly what he thought he needed.

But then his wife discovered the Hasidim of Lubavitch, who were numerous in Chicago. These people placed a mystical emphasis on everything in Judaism. His wife's ancestors, in Morocco, had believed without hesitation in spells and in mystical formulas, good and bad. That didn't bother Moshe. Her tradition agreed with his own experience that such things held a power to be feared.

But the Hasidim in Chicago offered a different view. There really was something like a sorcerer's way to God. True, it wasn't available to ordinary mortals. But one could reach it by grasping the coattails of a special leader: the Rebbe.

A trip to Brooklyn was arranged, ostensibly to visit relatives. While there, Moshe's wife paid her visit to the great man's shrine in the heart of rundown Crown Heights. Moshe never found out what they had said to each other. But she returned to Chicago a full convert.

Already there were those who claimed the old Rebbe was the promised Messiah—the leader who was to bring the Jews out of exile and back to the Promised Land. Even the ones who questioned this believed that he had access to visions of God they themselves would always be denied. The study of the holy texts wasn't enough, they believed. The books' secrets were not accessible to ordinary people. How, then, could one benefit from contemporary prophecy? The Lubavitchers had the answer: join the ranks of the Hasidim, read the Rebbe's sermons, travel to Brooklyn for his blessings. (If travel was impossible, there was the telephone, and a full-time secretary; even a fax machine.)

The faithful in Chicago enjoyed a special advantage. The local Lubavitch rabbi was himself reputed to be a remarkable man. Though young, he was capable of communicating the Rebbe's will to the rest of his flock. He attracted an entourage. Not content with hearing his publicly spoken words, several of the Hasidim took to accompanying the rabbi whenever he walked from the synagogue to his modest Chicago apartment. On top of everything else, he was a strikingly handsome man. Look deeply into his eyes, one young Hasidic woman whispered to Moshe's wife—"and you'll see a glimpse of the next world."

It was the Peruvian village all over again. But this time it was the local rabbi, in his *yarmulke* and black coat, who had taken the place of Diego decked out in gold. And this time the victims were not mountain peasants but Chicago Jews—one of whom was the former Diego's wife.

Moshe couldn't stand it. It seemed a perverse joke of fate, too perfect to be endured. And whom could he turn to? Who would understand him, even if he dared to reveal to some rabbi-counselor his own Christian past? In a desperate showdown he told his wife that the Lubavitch rabbi was a fraud. How did he know? she asked. She didn't know about his background and he was ashamed to tell her. Never mind, he said.

She didn't listen to him. She simply left his house and took refuge with other Hasidim, who were familiar, they said, with uncomprehending attacks by Jews not yet fully enlightened. As Moshe's demands became more strident, she had insisted on a divorce. After that Moshe's memories blurred. He was too miserable to be sure of anything, he said. He was not even certain whether he and his wife were actually divorced under Jewish law. He did not want to believe that they were. Technically, that was what he had come eastward to find out. He was scheduled to meet with rabbis in Monsey, Brooklyn, Far Rockaway. My school had simply offered him a place to stay.

"I have to ask you a favor," he said. "After the Sabbath. Please, call my wife for me. I must talk to her. Can you do that? If they hear my voice they won't even call her to the phone."

The cabin I shared with Izzy and six other young men had the advantage of a telephone on its front porch. Since, on the Sabbath, Orthodox Jews do not use them, it wasn't unusual for several people to come to us Saturday nights and line up on the dilapidated planks outside the front door. They'd wait their turn at the pay phone, which hung across from a fantastically degraded vending machine that had once dispensed Cokes. (It was too massive to remove without smashing the planks of the porch, so it had stayed there.)

That night only Moshe used the phone. I had kept my promise; I had got his wife on the phone for him, but it obviously didn't do him any good. Pleading with her by long distance telephone, Moshe was a different man from the professor who had lectured me about the Christians and boasted of his powers of mind control. As it became obvious that his wife was giving him only cool, short answers, he lost his self-control, shouting at her from our porch, his voice echoing in the tangle of woods nearby.

"Don't you know who I am? How can you talk to me like this? Please! Listen to me! Please!"

He broke down, begging her to leave Chicago. (A parody of his voice echoed back from the woods.)

"Please, please…"

I sat inside, across from Izzy. We both gave up the pretense of not hearing what was happening on the porch.

"He's pretty upset," Izzy said.

"He has a problem with his wife."

We waited uncomfortably for several more minutes.

"I hope he doesn't go on too long," I muttered. His voice had dropped to an unintelligible moan. "He's using my mother's long distance card."

It was a heartless thing to say. But I was beginning to wonder why I had let him disturb me as much as he had. Moshe had entranced me—and all night the trance had frightened me with the shadows it cast. He had talked about a lot of things: about American foreign policy in Latin America; about evolutionary theory, in which (unlike many Orthodox Jews) he strongly believed. But mostly he had talked about his wife, whom he loved almost insanely, and about his certainty that the mind control techniques mastered by the Lubavitchers had caused her to break with him.

On my cot in Ohr Somayach's Cabin Four, I kept thinking: if the pursuit of God means life in the boldest possible colors, then I should be like this man, shouldn't I? Anyway, I shouldn't be *here*, in a little camp in rural New York, enjoying scholarly analysis of remote legal problems. When we talked about "the spirit," weren't we talking about Moshe?—and his tormented Masses, his villagers, his mental "gifts," the wife who was punishing him unwittingly for all of those things?

Or were we? Wasn't there something crazy about all this martyrdom? Of course I could feel sorry for Moshe. But to take his story seriously? Mindreading! Of course, he'd done a pretty good job on *me*—I admitted that. But for that sort of clairvoyance you don't need telepathic powers. You don't need much of anything.

When Moshe finally hung up the telephone, he came inside the cabin and collapsed into a chair, sobbing.

"You don't know what it's like," he said over and over. "You can't know. You can't."

Izzy tried to comfort him. "Whatever it is, it isn't forever, right?" He didn't answer.

After a while Moshe became as taciturn as when I'd first met him. He shed no more tears. He just sat silently on our beaten-down vinyl couch, staring ahead so impassively that eventually all we could do was to go to bed, one by one, leaving him to find his own way out—which he apparently did. He left Monsey the next morning, which was Sunday, not before promising me to pay the long distance bill he'd run up once he reached Chicago. (He never did.)

I never saw him again. But I thought about him a great deal during the next few weeks. Just as I thought of the legend of Noah and his doomed fellow-citizens, while I sat cramped in one corner of the noisy study hall, arguing, like all the others, about a basket tilted on the Sabbath, or about who suffers the loss of an injured ox that had been entrusted to a watchman. And while the rank woods waved and twisted outside around our own crowded little ark, unnoticed by any of us. While I listened to weekly lectern-pounding sermons about the "spiritual path" we had all taken.

Nothing much consoled me—not then, and not while I sat at Friday night meals, between courses of *gefilte* fish and baked chicken, looking at the white tablecloth, the black hat on the host's head, the sparkling crystal, the wooden bookshelves, and the carefully bound, gold-titled Hebrew books—all of which had suddenly seemed so arbitrary and powerless next to the wild spirit, cloaked in a gold cassock, who had escaped a Peruvian mountain hell to fall helplessly before one Chicago Hasid and a pumpkin-woman from Morocco.

PART 3: FAMILY AND STRANGERS

You have often complained to me that people didn't
"understand" you! Goethe and Newton didn't complain of
that...You are perfectly well understood. And if you don't
understand yourself, it is not the fault of others.
> — Anton Chekhov (in a letter to his brother Nikolai)

Always it was Abram, the man from Uru, or more correctly
from Harran, of whom the forked tongue spoke—calling
him the great-grandfather of Joseph. Both of them, young
and old, were quite aware that, unless by moonlight, Abram
was not the man, that unquiet subject of Amraphel of Shinar;
likewise that no man's great-grandfather lived twenty generations before him! Yet this was a trifling inexactitude...
> — Thomas Mann, *Joseph and His Brothers*

CHAPTER FIFTEEN

"**I**t's your mother," said a fellow student, handing Cabin Four's phone to me in the thick, crickety darkness. After a brief conversation, I handed the phone back to him, not knowing how to answer his question, "Well, what was that about?"

My brother Jeff was engaged.

If my brother and the rest of the family had been a survival of the Yiddish theater, this would have been the moment when Mama would have fallen in a faint, her hands clasped over her breast, while the curtain descended and the orchestra throbbed an echo to her last words: *"Oy, mein kind, mein kind!"*

But the real Mama wasn't fainting. And her role, the one of unutterable shock at Boy-Meets-*Christian*-Girl, or rather Boy-*Marries*-Christian-Girl, seemed to have been offered, in anachronistic drag, to me.

Was I meant for it?

At the last family wedding, in which brother Rob had married his Christian sweetheart in an evangelical ceremony (and the "pastor" had tried to convert me, and a circle of Rob's friends had babbled in "tongues," holding hands while Rob furrowed his forehead in prayer), I had actually been best man. That was before my interest in Orthodoxy, of course.

"I love these *opportunities*," the pastor had said to me in such an oleaginous voice I'd hoped, for a second, that he was joking.

"Opportunities?" I'd asked, once it was clear he wasn't.

"Oh, yes." He stood there beaming at my brothers and me. He was a very young man, with a permanent smile plastered onto his face. The treacly effect was crowned by watery eyes that seemed ready, at any moment, to burst into tears of pious gratitude. He wore some sort of white smock with cut-out felt letters spelling "PEACE" glued to it for the occasion.

During the worship service, in a room that might have been a hospital auditorium, several people made me briefly wonder if we weren't in fact in a mental hospital: they began babbling gibberish in loud, clear voices. It was only a slight relief to know that this was really not mass insanity—this was a religious practice called "speaking in tongues," or glossolalia, one that in some Protestant churches was even considered a sign of divine favor. It was no relief at all when my turn came to play a part in the ceremony: it was my job to propose a toast to bride and groom.

But of course, back then I'd been just another Jewish agnostic. And Rob was my brother.

Now it was different.

The plot thickened after I had handed back the battered phone, left the Israeli next in line gaping curiously at both of us, and sat down on my cot to try to write Jeff what my current principles deemed the proper letter.

What *was* "proper"?

Memories assailed me as I tried to write: Jeff and I sharing a room for one delightful year at the University of Virginia; Jeff washing our dishes in the bathroom sink (we had no kitchen in that tiny basement apartment and cooked on a card table); Jeff moving his mattress out of our bedroom, with infinite tact, when Janet spent nights with me. The two of us had shared jokes about brother Rob and his Christian friends, even scampered around Mom's kitchen with fingers raised like horns over our heads, pretending to be devils, on late nights after the friends had finally finished their sermons and gone home.

I could remember sitting near him on the polished wooden pews of Temple Rodef Shalom, oppressed by the stained-glass gloom, both of us fidgeting as the rabbi droned on about the need for Jewish self-preservation and the dangers of intermarriage. The elegant phrases hadn't meant much to us then, and they still sounded awfully murky as I tried to formulate them in my letter.

What was I trying to say? It was all very well to invoke the specter of Jewish extinction. (My mother's first comment on Jeff's engagement, later recanted, was that he was "handing Hitler a victory.") But after all, that threat turned on the ancient law that deemed the children of non-Jewish mothers gentiles, regardless of the religion of their fathers. What was that sort of religious technicality supposed to mean to someone like Jeff?

I could try oratory, but that was dampened by another memory, this one of the last time a Christian had tried to convert *me*. At the time I was a Radio Shack salesman, and the Christian was a customer. He was a confident ass, whose tall frame, like a steeple or a watchtower, sharpened abruptly as it rose to a face that was long and narrow, dominated by burning dark eyes and an aggressive nose. Nothing really memorable lived there, but he was impossible to ignore, and I remember very clearly his faith in the power of his own resonant phrases. When I told him I was Jewish he tilted his head back and literally shouted at the ceiling, "Jesus Christ is Lord!" When that didn't seem to have the desired effect (we were alone in the store; a flat dull night pressed against the picture window at the front, and his voice boomeranged off the walls and made a strange counterpoint with the drone of a stereo in a sales case), he programmed the demonstration-model computer in the front of the store to print the same phrase infinitely—"JESUS IS LORD JESUS IS LORD JESUS IS LORD..."—to add weight to the claim, I guess.

"God," he said, turning to me, "is laying his finger on your heart."

Of course I couldn't bring myself to intone any such phrases at Jeff. It wouldn't matter that the phrases would be Jewish, not Christian. I hated the very taste of them. And even if I could get over my revulsion and deliver a cautionary sermon, how was I going to respond to the obvious objection that I had gladly done for brother Rob what I was refusing to do for another brother?

It's a melancholy business searching my life for purposeful symmetries. The Radio Shack proselytizer's love of phrases pursued me to Ohr Somayach, where I often heard one or another student repeating aloud a handful of Hebrew words in the loud, oddly sorrowful chant that has been a tradition of Jewish schools for hundreds of years—and where I was once advised by another student to repeat a hundred times daily the words, "If one leaves the Torah, fire consumes him!" (By the light of any sufficiently fussy theology, the most fundamental claim can become a matter of mental hygiene.) But there's no logic to the assortment of marriages I have attended and not attended. I was best man at Rob's; didn't go to my father's second (but invited him and his second, non-Jewish wife to mine); once went to a Christian stranger's, years ago, in a distant church, because Janet asked me to; but didn't go to Jeff's because his bride was an agnostic non-Jew.

On the fine spring day of that wedding, several months later, Ohr Somayach's flimsy cabins, with their odor of sawdust and pine needles, had never seemed stuffier. As I nodded at fellow-students hurrying past me on their way in and out of the study hall, I reflected that according to everyone there I had done the "right" thing by staying where I was. Rabbi Gold, too, had said so. I had even traveled to Brooklyn to obtain the opinion of the head of a distinguished academy.

He had agreed with Rabbi Gold. All the rabbis said I must not demonstrate approval of such a marriage by attending it.

And to prevent any misunderstanding I'd better say this now: I more or less agreed with them.[3] A person has a right to set his own priorities. I had made Judaism one of mine. Jewish culture, Jewish existence, whatever you want to call it—it does stand for

---

3 At the time. Today I don't consider it my right to impose my religious priorities on anyone else; but this is not the traditional Jewish attitude, certainly not the Orthodox one.

something, and you can't commit yourself to defending it and, at the same time, ignore its dangerous weakening though assimilation. And, of course, Jeff was contributing to Jewish assimilation by intermarrying, whether he chose to look at it that way or not. He was free to make that choice, denying the public, religious significance of his private love. I was not. The choices that had defined my life made it impossible for me to deny what Jeff's marriage meant for Judaism. That had to be part of my point of view.

All the same, I hated the words I was forced to use to justify myself. I hated the stiff gesture of non-attendance. I hated the feel of the rigid letter of the law, designed to safeguard a consistent definition of Jewish peoplehood, digging such an arbitrary impression into my family's well-being. And I felt like a primitive, swinging a club of theology at the delicate flower of love.

"What's the point?" I myself had asked my mother way back when, on the day she'd first broached the idea of brother Rob's marriage, and wondered aloud if there was any way to prevent it. "What's the point of saying or doing anything? Nothing we can say will make any difference."

That was certainly true. While a graduate student, I myself had fallen deep into the charms of a Catholic woman with Italian parents. Religion was the last thing on my mind when, after a long infatuation tormented by shyness, I suddenly found her in my arms. I have seldom tasted anything like the poignant indirectness of her kisses. And I've never been able to think of any rationale that would have driven me away from her at the time—even though she ended up dropping me herself, after just three weeks.

"Who am I to tell other people who they can and can't marry?" I had asked my mother, and the words haunted me now.

I had asked Shmuel Lehrman the same thing when we worked together for the Manhattan publisher. At the time he was in the mood for a religious dispute. Texts and principles never did the trick for Shmuel; he needed a *casus belli*, and by wondering aloud whether Judaism had a monopoly on virtue I had given him one.

We were walking to Penn Station to catch trains home, and Shmuel was grousing about the number of corners I turned on the way. (He had a strange conviction that a city diagonal is most quickly traversed by walking a long straight path in one direction, then turning at right angles to make another long, straight walk along the other axis.) Between complaints about the turns we were taking under my lead he insisted, against my skepticism, that "assimilation" was as bad as "what the Nazis did."

"You mean, my brothers are Nazis for intermarrying?"

"For heaven's sake," he growled, "stop talking like a liberal. Look, the point is that the Jews can disappear just as surely through intermarriage as through concentration camps. Isn't that clear? Only liberals pretend not to see that."

"Meaning what?"

"Either the existence of the Jews matters or it doesn't."

"Isn't there some sort of question about how *much* it matters?" I pursued. "Or how much it's supposed to matter to a given individual in love with another given individual?"

"There's a right and a wrong," he said. "This is what life is all about. Knowing what I know, I can see that intermarriage is wrong. So, if it's wrong, I have to do whatever I can to stop it. And so do you. I really ought to kill some of these Christian missionaries. It doesn't matter if they're 'sincere.' They're arguing against the *truth*. That's *wrong*. I should put a bullet right through their heads."

"I see."

"No, you don't. You're still thinking like a liberal. A marketplace of ideas, with coupons handed out for good behavior. Then the next year they burn down the synagogues, and you don't even know what's happening. Oh, but Americans are different, is that it? Well, yes, they are! Why should they burn down the synagogues? They don't need to, when all they have to do is make friends with us and let nature do the rest. Why destroy us with guns or gas when we're doing such a good job of destroying ourselves? With the help of missionaries. I ought to put a bullet through their heads."

"Why don't you, then?"

"I wouldn't get away with it," he said simply, "and it would look bad. People would say, 'Jews are fanatics.'"

"You mean, the ideal is to *be* fanatical, but not to show it?"

He grunted his impatience. "While you waste time talking about it, Jews are disappearing all over the place. (I'm going crazy with all these turns!) Because some gentiles are 'nice people,' let the Jews disappear, is that it? How many Jews will be left in the next generation? It's a silent Holocaust!"

Now that the "silent Holocaust" had actually reached me, reality seemed more complicated than Shmuel's logic. Jeff accepted my position with more understanding than I had expected, but my father wrote me a rather harsh letter. (After all, he too is married to a non-Jew.) He accused me of placing my personal beliefs before my family. Which was true, of course, in a way. But then—not true. I mean, here was my old question thrown back in reverse: If *I* didn't have a monopoly on truth, did other people? If you assumed that Judaism might, after all, be true—and by now I was committed to believing it was—wasn't my father reasoning in circles? Asking me to condone in my brother what was, in fact, harmful to him? Asking me to "love my brother" by committing a form of spiritual fratricide?

"The main thing," Rabbi Gold counseled—in the relative privacy of his office, with its papery wood-veneer walls and its one soft brown vinyl chair, in which I fidgeted—"is to maintain contact with your brother. Remember that if he thinks you're a fanatic, *Mikhoel*" (I was always *Mikhoel* to him) "he'll never come any closer."

This was another familiar theme, the flipside of Shmuel's "I wouldn't get away with it": what people "think"—in this case, what other Jews think, the hope that non-religious Jews will be "brought closer" to Torah if the religious people make a good impression on them. An understandable policy. But is policy enough to govern one's family relationships? And how was I supposed to bring Jeff "closer" after I had spit in his eye by refusing to attend his wedding? Did any of us really know what a "good impression" meant to the people we were trying to impress? To say nothing of drawing them "closer"? Are we really so certain we have something that needn't move at all—something they, not we, need to approach?

I have seen Jeff's wedding on videotape. It would have enraged Shmuel Lehrman. A Reform rabbi and a Chicago minister teamed up to legalize the Lesher-Bess couple. Watching it, I was struck less by the religious irregularities than by the small number of guests, compared to the number who later attended my own wedding. The hall was huge, its vertical scale—polished walls, chandeliers, high ceilings—emphasizing what seemed to me the emptiness of the great rooms.

Yet on its own terms the wedding was perfectly successful. It's just that Jeff couldn't compete with the scale of Orthodox communal involvement. That is, with Ohr Somayach and Monsey and the hundreds of Orthodox Jews who made it their business to come to my wedding, dancing, juggling, offering advice or just slapping me on the back, not because they were all great friends of mine (they weren't) but because—well, because it was a Jewish wedding, and they were Jews.

On the day I sent Jeff my awful letter, I was too weary to imagine anything of the sort. Early in the morning, after dropping the envelope into a mailbox, I went into the study hall. I sat down at my designated square of tabletop in the crowded room. I opened my folio volume to the bookmarked page and reentered an ancient dispute about the meaning of a particular sort of vow. As the subtleties of argument enfolded me, I forgot about the bruising human world, with all its loud voices, its competing claims and layered quarrels. I backed out of the endless circling of real-life ethical dilemmas and lost myself in the Talmud.

CHAPTER SIXTEEN

L ooking back on things, I suppose it should have occurred to me long ago that Rob—the eldest Lesher child after me—would become the truest believer of the bunch.

Rob was always the most conservative of us—the one who most dearly loved order, discipline, ritual. At an age when the floor of my room was littered with shirts and notebook paper, his was so neat that he could tell if someone had so much as looked through one of his dresser drawers during the few minutes he had been downstairs watching *Perry Mason*. Everything, each sock and coin and button, was cleaned and stored with military exactitude.

These days, my mother refers to me and Rob as "the fundamentalists." To her we're two peas in a pod—both believers in old-fashioned absolutes. But this pairing contains an irony. True, Rob and his family celebrate Passover, Sukkos and the Sabbath—just as I do. True, Rob observes the traditional dietary laws. He spends time regularly on Bible study and Hebrew prayers. Even the insularity of his religious world mirrors my Orthodox community.

But our similarity ends there, even from my mother's point of view. Rob, having become an evangelical Christian while in college, has drifted into the subspecies of evangelical Christianity that calls itself "messianic Judaism." His Hebrew prayers are offered in the name of *Yeshua,* or Jesus; his theology is based on the New Testament, not the Hebrew Bible; and his highest religious goal is to awaken other Jews to "the true Messiah." So, although his answering machine message begins with a *shofar* blast and a loud "Shalom!" Rob is an outcast (or worse) to most Jews, while to the same people my Orthodoxy, even where unpopular, places me firmly on "our" side of the lineup.

For me, the irony is enriched by the fact that Rob and I reached our religious destinations by remarkably similar routes. In Blacksburg, Virginia, where Rob was a college student, he met the first really pious people he'd ever known—Christians—just as I met the first religious people *I'd* known after I moved to New York. Rob was impressed by the depth and simplicity of the Christians' conviction. Also, I suspect, by their ability to quote Scripture in support of everything they thought or did. (Rob retains, as I suppose I do, the very Jewish faith in the power of texts.)

While I was meeting the first pious people *I* had ever known, and learning the ropes of their religion-centered social arrangements, Rob was making friends with people whose lives revolved entirely around Jesus Christ. Here, however, there were some differences between my brother and me. Rob fell in love with his religious acquaintances; I was only impressed by mine. In fact, I wonder sometimes if the different endpoints in our religious odysseys might have more to do with our approach to religious friendships than with the differences between Christianity and Judaism. Or is that just ducking the most important questions? Would the solution to one riddle unscramble the other?

In my family, Rob has always been said to resemble my mother's father. Philip Eisenberg—Grandpa Phil, as we called him—died from burns he received when his house went up in flames. More precisely, he died from injuries suffered after he reentered the burning house he had left minutes before, while the fire was spreading, insisting that he had to remove the fuses from the fuse box—for "safety reasons." I mention this because the similarity between him and Rob has to do mostly with stubbornness and fastidiousness. I don't see much physical resemblance between the two, but then I only remember Grandpa Phil in his declining years, when two heart attacks and a stroke had left him rather gaunt, his aggressive nose almost skeletal, his long legs frail. In those days he didn't look like the headstrong young man he had once been. Emphysema racked his chest every morning. (Despite that, he never did quit smoking Camels, in which he took a slow, ritualistic pleasure quite unlike my father's nervous chain-smoking.)

As a child, I remember hearing Grandpa Phil's tormented coughing from the bathroom at six o'clock on mornings when he was visiting. I swear he sounded like a man pulling in his last wheezing breaths. After half an hour of that, I'd pull my sheets up over my head in the morning cool and think, God, we're going to have a corpse on the floor.

He didn't die, though. Not then. Grandpa Phil clung stubbornly to life, even died of stubbornness in the end—the neighbors tried in vain to stop him from braving the flames of that burning house. Grandpa Phil was stubborn about a lot of things. He even went on believing in the gospel that hard work pays, no matter how often his own hard work ended in failure. I don't know how many different jobs he struggled at. As a child I was told Grandpa Phil used to deliver large blocks of ice in the days before refrigeration, and for years I visualized frozen cubes the size of boulders, veined with blue, gripped in fierce-looking iron tongs, propelled up a dim flight of stairs by the incongruous figure of my bald and wheezing grandfather. It's an image that deserves to stick, however inaccurate the details. Grandpa Phil failed at many things, but it is impossible to visualize him giving up.

Certainly stubbornness is the trait that connects him with Rob in my own mind, since the baptismal water in which an evangelical minister doused Rob defied the family's notion of common sense no less than Philip Eisenberg's re-entry into the flames that killed him. The irony in the similarity is that, for years, it was part of Rob's Eisenbergian stubbornness to insist that Grandpa Phil hadn't just died in a fire but had been consigned to an eternal one—Hell, that is—since he had died without acknowledging Jesus Christ as his personal savior. That's how Rob viewed all of us, for a time.

Rob says now that his religious quest began in early 1978, while he was a college student at Virginia Polytechnic Institute. "I was introduced to a living, real God that I had never known before," he says. The name of this "living, real God" was Jesus Christ, as I know from our conversation aboard a Trailways bus, whose shuddering shell as the old engine churned up the highway north of Charlottesville seemed as cold and shaken as I felt, hearing my brother use phrases like "reborn in Christ" and "liberated from Satan" and "true salvation."

That wasn't all he had to say. He attacked everything in which the two of us had been raised. Real religion, he told me then, couldn't be found in the Reform temple to which our family belonged. "A lifestyle and cultural thing," he called the sort of Judaism practiced there, by which phrase he—like my Orthodox coreligionists—meant to dismiss it as unimportant.

The people who introduced him to this religion, Rob says, did not "push anything down my throat," nor were they "stereotypical Bible-thumping kind of evangelists." He may be rationalizing somewhat after the fact; all the ones I ever met quoted constantly from the Bible and were monotonously, even oppressively, given to proselytism. But even if I shared my mother's view of Rob's conversion—which boils down to a conviction that he was seduced by the enemy—I would have to grant Rob enough independence of mind to be troubled by the "enemy's" attitude toward Rob's family and people. Clearly their callousness did trouble him. Most of his Christian friends knew nothing whatever of Jewish history. ("The traditional Christian view is that all history collapsed; nothing happened before Jesus," Rob says now.) They knew even less about Christian history vis-à-vis the Jews. They could not understand why most Jews wince at the sight of a missionary. They did not know, and could not seem to grasp, how the age-old charge of deicide— still embraced by evangelical Christians—looks from the receiving end. A "real Christian" during World War II, Rob has told me, was one who "stood up against the Nazis and stood up against persecution." Of course there were such Christians, and none of Rob's new friends was any sort of Nazi. But most of them did believe that Jews were damned, which meant that Rob's family, grandparents and all, were already doomed to eternal torments, whether or not they had been disposed of in European crematoria.

Yet Rob found his way to live with this, at least for a time. The rock inside the sugary powder puff the evangelicals served up to Jewish converts—that is, that unconverted Jews deserve whatever they get—did not drive him away from his new faith. His stubbornness bore him along then, the large domed forehead (very much like Grandpa Phil's, come to think of it, if you take away the hairline) grimly furrowed, the deepset brown eyes gleaming, the unmistakably Jewish beak of his nose pointed dead ahead from an auditorium seat, while an evangelical speaker one Friday night explained how all the messianic references in the Hebrew Bible actually refer to Jesus of Nazareth.

Rob has told me that on that night he was literally the only Jew in the audience. And it was another ten years before he himself was ready to affirm that his own Jewish heritage mattered to God. But one day, he did.

"Are non-believers in Jesus really damned?" I have asked him since.

"You can live a Godly life without believing in *Yeshua*," came Rob's ready reply—and then he hesitated, rubbed his nose and went on, head lowered self-deprecatingly but with an unapologetic forefinger adding emphasis: "but I don't believe you can be saved and go to heaven unless you believe in *Yeshua*."

What fascinates me is the earnestness involved in Rob's mixing of opposed creeds and cultures, and his own position at the unlucky center—a place somewhere between old-fashioned Jewish guilt and a sort of prophetic arrogance, a Christian uncomfortable with Christianity, a Jew still more uncomfortable with his discomfort.

I suppose I see myself in him, to some extent, though in a sort of funhouse mirror. For instance, as I juggle with his description of the need for belief in "*Yeshua*" to secure salvation, I find my memory repeating a variant of an Orthodox mantra: "You can be Jewish without being Orthodox, but you can't live a really Jewish life, satisfying to God, without Orthodoxy."

Am I, too, mixing oil and water when I combine Orthodoxy with modern American education? When my coreligionists invoke popular political slogans of the New Right to explain traditions more than a thousand years old, are *they* fudging the relationship of the old books to the new world?

Around 1986—about a year after I moved to the Lower East Side and officially embraced Orthodoxy—Rob attended services at a "messianic synagogue" in northern Virginia called Beth Messiah. He liked the place, but found the services rather "too Jewish" for his taste at the time. Meanwhile, circumstances propelled him onward. He suffered a financial collapse after unexpectedly losing a job in a bank. He and his wife Shelley (whose maiden name is Martinez and who believes she had Jewish ancestors in Spain), with their two children, were forced to sell their house and move.

There were other problems. "We were fed up with some of the abuses we saw in the charismatic type of churches" to which they had belonged, says Rob. "They had great music... but there was infidelity... they weren't walking out a character walk."

Like me, Rob and his wife were intrigued by Jewish ritual rhythms. In December 1992 they did not get a Christmas tree, for the first time during their marriage. Like most Jews at some time in their lives, Rob was experiencing his differentness.

"We didn't feel comfortable in the church world any more," he says. "We started to feel different—outsiders."

Rob and Shelley responded by joining the growing "messianic" movement. Many of these "messianic Jews," as they call themselves, were first converted to Christianity during the evangelical youth movement of the late 60's. But, to my surprise, and at first to Rob's, there were also a great many non-Jews in the "messianic" movement—an actual majority of the congregants, in fact. To these people, Christians by birth and choice, Jewish ritual was just exotic enough to be fascinating and just familiar enough to be comforting. Which, I must admit, mirrors rather well the attractions of the rites for any number of young American returnees to Orthodoxy, who were raised in a culture largely void of religious ritual.

The authoritarian side of Rob's religious life is also similar to the world I got to know at Ohr Somayach. Rob says that if he has a question about a point of religious practice, he consults an established rabbi, or an "elder," reads Scripture for guidance, and prays for enlightenment. Substitute "Talmud" for "Scripture" and you have a pretty good formula for the religious decision-making life of a *yeshiva* student. Like the "messianic" Jew, he is trained to consult a rabbi, to study his texts, and at difficult moments to pray that God will enlighten him.

There are other similarities between my community and Rob's on the politically fashionable issue of the "traditional family." Returnees to Orthodoxy talk a good deal (as Rob does) about the atomization of the modern family, and tend to place the blame (as Rob does) on the abandonment of old-fashioned religion.

As it happens, Rob's views are easy to document, because he and his wife, for some time, circulated a newsletter to fellow Jewish Christians. He's never offered to send me a copy, but I've got hold of quite a few through my mother. ("Can you believe this?" she scrawled on a note placed atop one.) In one issue, Rob offers a summary of his own family values, in a passage that is a distorted replica of the Orthodox propaganda I heard pretty regularly in *yeshiva*:

> Both of us [Rob and his wife] had grown up in either broken and/or dysfunctional homes...We also had not been raised with proper G-dly, loving discipline.... [Later], when we were in [a community] church we were convicted of our own selfishness after having seen the fruit borne [sic] in those families. The children were respectful and obedient, not only to their parents, but to other adults in the church.... There are many passages throughout the book

of Proverbs that make it clear that an obedient child is a delight and a blessing to his parents.... We learned that if we apply proper and loving discipline, we will reap the fruit of the harvest with the reward of a delightful and happy family in the L-rd (no matter what the size).

Here are all the themes of "family values" reaction, with a vengeance. First there's the association of "broken homes" with modernity. Then there's the self-flagellation for the "selfishness" of remaining childless even temporarily. (Why is it so hard for reactionaries, Christian or Jewish, to stomach the idea of enjoying their own lives?) There's the remembered pain of family "dysfunction" and—curiously—its reshaping and internalization as an ideal of "Godly discipline." (The adjective "loving," twice applied to "discipline," suggests the poignant delusion that the violence and fear that damaged our own childhoods will save our children's, if only our hearts are pure.) There's the half-hidden fear of children's supposedly limitless appetites, and its deflection through the emphasis on "obedience" and "discipline." There's the revealing resort to Biblical authority to "prove" the rewards of raising children—suggesting that the pleasure is willed, not felt.

Most ominous of all, there's the smell of self-sacrifice, the idea that we raise children not because we want them but because an implacable God will have it so—an idea brought into rather horrible focus by the following paragraph from the same newsletter, in which Rob announces that after three children of his own he wants to adopt another one:

G-d has brought *all of us* into His family by adopting us as sons.... We must be brought into the throne of grace through the shed blood of *Yeshua* of whom the Father said, "This is my Son, in whom I am well-pleased." As G-d...has adopted us as His children by the blood of His own Son so can we respond to that model here on earth by adopting a child through the laying down of our lives and laying down our selfishness and bringing one who is less fortunate and lost into the family of G-d.

Here, adoption actually takes on all the gory theological burdens of deicide and atonement. God allowed the murder of his natural son to make room for the unnatural human race; now, we must imitate him (with our *blood*, the *laying down of our lives*), adopting children we don't really want (we are guilty of *selfishness*) in order to expiate our ancient crime.

I'd like to say my own religious environment gives me no clue to these ideas, but that wouldn't be quite true. Stern rabbis, lecturing from Sabbath pulpits, sometimes point to the typically small American family as a symptom of self-indulgence. In Orthodox circles, too, I have actually heard some rabbis connect birth control with the Holocaust, a sort of guilt-mongering not so different from Rob's variety.

There are equally depressing similarities between Rob's religious community and mine on the subject of "discipline." Rob has always been quiet: the one wildness of his childhood was playing the drums, and he has since atoned for his fondness for rock music by playing in strictly "Christian" bands. So I can't picture his "Godly discipline" as particularly harsh. Likewise, I don't know any Orthodox Jews who openly promote flogging or beating their children—though I have heard that among some Hasidim the level of violence is considerably higher than in the communities I've lived in. But using children as fair game in a sort of moral target practice does seem to appeal to the broad right wing in Judaism, including most of the newly-Orthodox. An Orthodox friend of mine—raised, like me, in liberal middle-class circles—once told me flatly, "I don't talk to my children about their feelings. I'm the parent, they're the children. They have to do what I say, and that's it. Otherwise, how do they learn values?"

All the grim theologizing about children touches me in an especially sensitive place when I hear it from my brother. I suppose that's because what Rob is really doing is rattling the skeletons in our family closet. Rob won't quite say so, but his preaching seems to reflect childhood scars his new religion is meant to remove. His love of order and predictability was badly wounded by our parents' divorce. Then there was the incipient religiosity—evident even when he was ten and the two of us invented a fantasy "religion" in which he was high priest—which found pretty barren soil in my father's aggressive skepticism and my mother's equation of religion with family functions. (My father's typical comment whenever anyone mentioned religion at the dinner table was, "Well, if God is all-powerful, did he want the Holocaust to happen?" And my mother might murmur, looking down at the table, "A Jewish boy ought to have a *bar mitzvah*.")

Is religion just a bandage for such scars? If so, how effective a bandage? And why did the two of us choose different brands?

I'd like to ask Rob about this—who would better understand the question? If I don't, it's largely because I know how Rob would answer: he'd preach at me, protecting his creed, not exploring it. Maybe Rob's creed wouldn't serve his purposes if he *could* question it. But then I'm left wondering if his creed is a blessing or a curse—and turning the same question, a little desperately, back at my own.

I'm much more at home with people who don't claim moral certainty—yet there's something in fundamentalist Jews and Christians that touches me in a place the others seldom reach. Maybe that's because theological certainty so often shares the same heart with the deepest personal confusions. Maybe the frustration I feel at trying to understand my brother reflects deeper frustrations—with the impermanence and insecurity of all human arrangements—that lie alongside my religious quest, and Rob's.

If that's so, then our stories can never be fully untangled. So maybe it's fitting that they should contain so many pregnant similarities and incongruities. Juxtaposing him with me is like reading a palimpsest: the obscurities are part of the text.

CHAPTER SEVENTEEN

From time to time, during that fall and winter at Ohr Somayach, I telephoned Shmuel Lehrman from my ramshackle cabin lying halfway down the gravelled, rutted "driveway" from the study hall. Standing at night on the ruined porch of Cabin Four, I'd talk over with him what I'd been doing. And learning. Why? What was I looking for? A certain stability, I think—a perspective from which the transition to *yeshiva* life looked like a smooth movement along a continuum.

Not that Shmuel was the best person to give me such a perspective. Nor was anyone else I met at the *yeshiva*. If I was looking for a comforting sense of self, I didn't find it.

What I found instead was The Creature.

Nothing proved Izzy's native generosity as quickly as the way he introduced me to his "older friend" when I came back from the study hall at my regular ten o'clock one night, and found The Creature slouched against Izzy's cot.

He was significantly older than I—at least forty-five, quite possibly older. The Creature was tall and thin—almost gaunt. Every scrap of his hair was hidden by a childish knit cap that a cartoon character might have worn, and his face had the sort of angular roughness that can swallow up decades. But there was certainly nothing cartoonish about his face. He was pale, and though the face was square-jawed and looked strongly built, the overall effect was one of exhaustion. His every gesture seemed grudged out of an infinite store of world-weariness.

"Hello," he said to me, and his voice turned out to be the most self-consciously listless thing about him. "Your roommate exaggerates in calling me his 'friend.' He has invited me to stay in your cabin out of a kindness for which I am grateful. I plan to be here a short time. So I won't be in your way long."

Evidently feeling he'd said enough, he fell silent again, not even looking in my direction as I assured him I didn't mind at all. He was reading a battered book he'd brought with him. Political philosophy, I think. There were a lot of other books in a half-open canvas backpack that lay on the floor near him. The hands in which he held the book were a puzzle: the fingers were long and pale, as if unused to sunlight, but the nails were thick and coarse.

He was obviously accustomed to simple living. There was (to me) even a hint of romance in the way he had drifted into town with nothing but a stack of books and an offer to do some editing for a local rabbi who was writing about anti-Semitism. The books he carried were real books, too—political theory, Jewish scholarship. I was then very interested in the editors of opinion magazines, and he seemed to know a good deal more about them than I did.

"No one has spent more time pissing into the wind than William Buckley," he said grimly that first night, when Buckley's name came up (I do not remember how).

We were by now solidly in the grip of winter. The soil outside was frozen in irregular lumps, and cold winds clawed through our cabin walls. The cabin, having been built originally as part of a summer bungalow colony, had no insulation at all. Notwithstanding the electric heater Rabbi Gold had kindly allowed me to use in my room, the main room of the cabin had to be warmed constantly to keep the rest of the inhabitants from freezing in their beds. This seemed sensible enough to me, but it soon irritated The Creature, who was used to the cold and who slept on a vinyl couch in the main room.

"You people are infected with the American love of overheated rooms," he told me on his third day there, after he'd spent two nights on the couch. He had slept in his clothes—had been doing it ever since he arrived—which were wrinkled and gave off a soft, sour odor, though he himself was irreproachably clean.

"Don't forget that this is the only room with any heating system at all," I reminded him. "And you happen to be sleeping in it."

"With this 'heating system' of yours," he said, "it's a wonder they don't close this building down."

The heater really was very funny. The cabins, designed for summer, had no provision for heating. Ours was on stilts, a few feet off the ground. To add a "heating system," someone had actually knocked out a piece of the floor, fitted a metal grate into the opening, and installed a sort of gas grill underneath. When you turned on the heat, naked flames leaped up at the grate from the dark cavity under the floor. Izzy had warned me, grinning, against drying my shoes on the grate on my first day at Ohr Somayach. "You may be tempted when it rains and your shoes get wet. But d-don't do it. We've melted a few shoe-soles that way," he'd said. *Yeshiva* legend had it that students had once grilled a hamburger on that grate. The flames certainly would have made that possible, but if the students really grilled a hamburger there they must have eaten it together with a wad of pine needles and a few generous flakes of rust, because the grate could never be thoroughly cleansed of either.

"They *are* closing this building down," I said to The Creature. "We've been given a condemnation notice. They must have seen the mushroom growing on the floor of the bathroom. We'll have a new place by springtime."

He didn't smile. "Well, I'll be long gone by then. I suppose I can accept prevailing conditions for the time being."

His gloom began to make me uneasy. Like Dostoevsky's Svidrigailov, he always managed to give off the feeling of decay.

"Will you come back?"

"No," he said shortly. "Of course, I said that last time I left, and here I am. But I think this time will be different."

"Why?"

"Oh, I suppose there are limits even to this administration's patience. True, I'm working now, but that's not quite enough to justify extending hospitality to an irreligious type like me. You ought to know how it is. I might 'influence' the youngsters." He sighed. "They can't abide that sort of thing here, you know. I suppose they're talking about the danger I pose over at the 'office' right now. A rabbinic conclave, and I'll be getting the Gold rush."

That seemed a rather harsh picture of Rabbi Gold, the school's administrator, and I said so.

"Well, as I said, this administration has shown patience. So far. I don't mean to complain."

"*Are* you irreligious?"

I suppose it was a rude question, but he didn't appear to mind. "Let's just say, I'm not attached to this place."

At the time I found the place irresistible. "Why not?"

"Do you really want to know?"

"I think so."

He looked at me wearily for a moment before answering. Then he looked away. "The truth is, I've never been attached anywhere. Since you asked."

Though he didn't show any particular interest in me, I was drawn to his saturnine presence. Why didn't he like Ohr Somayach? Might he know something I didn't?

"I'm curious to know whether our thinking runs in the same universe," I told him, cautiously as before, when I gave him a couple of my short stories to read. The next day, I gathered from his guarded comments that I had a way to go on the road to intellectual sophistication before he could really communicate with me. But I was touched that he had read the stories at all.

"I thought you might not have the time," I said.

"Because of my work? That doesn't take much time."

"Why do you do it?" I was still trying to figure out what he *used* to do. He'd clearly been accustomed to doing something.

"I don't like to stagnate entirely. And it's valuable work, I suppose. The rabbi I'm working for is doing some important writing on anti-Semitism."

I may have looked skeptical, because his gray eyes suddenly lit up with irony. "Your roommate, like you, seems to find it incredible that I should care so much about anti-Semitism and so little about Judaism. Frankly, I think you learn very little about either from sitting here, in a school like this. You make up a world out of your books and then make life imitate myth."

I couldn't tell whether he expected a response.

"He likes to act cynical, but he really isn't," Izzy had said about him. "You should hear some of things he's told me. The advice he's given. And it seems like he really knows what he's talking about." Izzy had burst out in one of his startling giggles. "Of course, he's always trying to talk me into leaving this place, but even that's sort of an act. If you watch him carefully when he eats, you'll see he says the blessings."

I said I found that hard to believe.

"You don't know him," Izzy said. "He isn't easy to know. But deep down he's really nice."

"Not that anyone here would dream of letting me teach," The Creature was saying, as if to himself. He blinked—his only movement. "And they're probably right. What if any of my pupils turned out as I did?"

A few nights later he was sitting up late in the main room. Izzy was in Brooklyn for a date and wouldn't be back; he planned to return to Monsey late and spend the night at the house of a friend of his, so he wouldn't disturb the rest of us in Cabin Four. Across the room from me, The Creature sat so still, even for him, that for a moment it occurred to me he might actually have died. I expected, at least, a fly to buzz around his head—like Svidrigailov's.

After a long time, from its pale height, the face spoke. "May I ask you a question?"

"Sure."

He didn't look at me. "What are you doing here?"

"Trying to learn something about Judaism." What did he think I was doing there?

He nodded very slightly. "And why does one want to learn such things?" he asked, with a dry shift to the third person.

I told him—as well as I could, I suppose. I told him that a single life was too short to sustain a great notion like "identity." Which, I supposed, was why we all spent so much time probing into our unconscious pasts or grumbling about the "cultural influences" on our conscious present. So I was trying to become part of a traditional encounter with the things that mattered most. And thus clarify my approach to those things in my own life.

"Is that what Judaism is to you?" he asked, his gray eyes fixed on me.

"I don't claim it's perfect," I said, wondering where he was leading me. "But whatever you call it, our religion isn't an illusion. It can still be studied and applied."

"When I spoke to you before about life imitating myth, I had some particular myths in mind."

"Such as?"

"The myth of the big, bad *goy*, for one." Now, suddenly, he moved a little. "Do you know what I mean?"

I shook my head.

"All right, I'll tell you. Do you know what the average non-Jew thinks about us?"

I was silent.

"He thinks we're obsessed with suspicion. That we blame everyone for the antisemitism of a few."

"And is he right?"

"Of course he's right!" Now The Creature was angrier than I'd ever imagined he could be. "And don't tell me another Holocaust story, please. I know them all. That doesn't change anything about *us*."

His anger evaporated quickly. Now he just looked tired. "We're only too happy to have the Holocaust to point to," he said, his voice weary. "It keeps all the right walls in place."

"But they're up there for a reason," I protested after a moment. "Isn't that the whole point of your own work on anti-Semitism? Is it your job to knock the walls down?"

"Oh, my *job*," he said scornfully.

"Well?"

But now he was The Creature again, listless and taciturn.

In fact, he was silent for so long I thought he had finished with me. But then, without warning, he went on softly: "No one will ever knock those walls down. How many of these students would stay in the *yeshiva* if they didn't think they were better than everybody else, huddled in here on our side of the wall? Oh, I know you don't think it's that way, but I know better."

And then he *was* finished.

A week later he told me he was on his way out.

"Where are you going?"

He grimaced. "Your roommate asked the same thing."

"What did you tell him?"

"Nothing. In fact, that's why I'm on my way out. I want to leave before he comes back."

Slowly, he paced from end to end of the room. Then he noticed my puzzled look.

"Are you trying to be sympathetic or naive?" he asked.

He sat down on his usual battered couch in the main room, the place he'd been sleeping. He looked paler than before. There was no one else in the cabin. "Damn it all," he muttered, and passed a hand over his face. "I feel like a penny waiting for change."

I didn't understand the expression. He looked at me, too weary to be pained at my stupidity.

"I mean, I feel like the lowest thing there is."

He rubbed his cap over his coarse mass of hair. I was astonished at the amount of hair he kept bound up in that cap—unkempt, iron-gray.

Then he spoke, still looking away from me. "It isn't enough that the guy gives me hospitality here—he's even offered to lend me money, which I won't accept, of course. Now he wants to know where I'm going. How to reach me. He thinks he's going to call or write me, I suppose."

He sat still for a few moments. "That's really your roommate's trouble," he said softly. It occurred to me that he had never once referred to him by name. Nor had he ever addressed *me* by name, come to think of it. "He's a real Jew, your roommate. So busily helpful. So naively concerned."

I had heard a little of the conversation, the night before, between Izzy and The Creature. From inside the room, as I'd sat up studying (it was very late, and the place was otherwise quiet), I had heard Izzy say in the common room: "I don't get it. I care about what happens to you, that's all. Isn't it enough that I care about you as a friend?" I hadn't heard The Creature's answer.

"Well," he said now, getting up very slowly, unfolding long legs, awfully resolute for someone so given to listlessness. "It's time to go. The rabbi's work for me has hit a pause, so there's no reason to stay in Monsey. I might come back, of course. But I hope I won't have to."

"You really don't want to tell m—to tell Izzy where you're going?"

"It wouldn't matter," he said. "If I need to call, there are always gas stations." He was putting a few books into his duffel bag. What was he reading now? William Buckley? Jewish philosophy? "You won't have to tell Izzy anything. He'll understand. Well, maybe he won't. But he'll get over it. He's very young. He'll find better things to do than trying to make a phone call to somebody who doesn't have a phone."

After his bag was full he sat down again on the couch and stared ahead of him. I was already late for a class; since he didn't seem to be going at once, I excused myself. He didn't even look up. I kept thinking about the expression he had used: a penny waiting for change. Then I thought about the fact that I hadn't actually asked him where he was going, though I had started to. I hadn't thanked him for reading my stories, for sharing his thoughts with me. I hadn't asked if there was something, anything he might want me to do for him. And I started feeling pretty low myself.

After class I hurried back to the cabin, hoping to find him. But I was too late. He had gone. The manuscripts I had given him to read were carefully stacked on the desk next to my bed. Next to Izzy's bed were a few coins—probably change Izzy had lent him for phone calls. There was no note.

CHAPTER EIGHTEEN

My father and his second wife paid me a visit that summer. They probably intended it as a peacemaking gesture, since my father and I had exchanged some hard words over my nonattendance at Jeff's wedding.

But it wasn't peace that stirred in me when I left the crowded study hall and found the two of them standing on Ohr Somayach's long gravel-and-earth driveway, squinting in the sun of a July afternoon.

My father was dressed comfortably in cotton slacks, red-and-white striped knit shirt and golfer's hat. He'd been gaining some weight, but his bulk was pleasantly arranged inside the shirt. As a youth he'd sported a pompadour. That was long gone now, but his wiry hair and swarthy complexion were still young-looking. I wouldn't say my father always looked as though he'd just stepped out of a magazine; it would be more accurate to say that he always looked as though he *wanted* to look that way, with his eager brown eyes, his engaging, full-lipped smile. What I looked like to him and to Nancy, in my tie and *yarmulke*, the navy blue suit plastered under the summer heat, I can only imagine.

"How've you been, son?"

Nancy, always awkward in unfamiliar social settings, silently eyed my fellow students, sweating under their black Stetsons and Borsalinos, hurrying in and out of the study hall, as my father and I shook hands. Her reddish hair, cut short, framed a face that seemed too white and timid for such an unforgiving summer sun. Accustomed to my religious scruple about touching women, she didn't attempt to pretend friendship by shaking my hand.

The ramshackle room I led them to in Ohr Somayach's Cabin Four clearly bothered both of them. I had done my best to clean it up beforehand, but in their presence I found myself seeing it as they obviously did: dusty, hot and dirty.

I flushed with embarrassment—then a touch of anger. Wasn't it *his* place, not mine, to feel a little shame?

I was fifteen when, just after my family moved to Washington during the notorious "Watergate" summer of 1973, calamity arrived. It arrived in its most awful costume: the door-to-door salesman's dress that announces doom in the accents of cliché.

Throughout the cross-country drive, my father had kept disappearing from the restaurants and gas stations we stopped at to make long, mysterious phone calls. Once settled in Washington, as a reporter for *Newsweek,* my father had disappeared again—this time into the crisis that was then engulfing the Nixon White House. For some time, I saw too little of him to revive my uneasiness at his odd behavior during the trip.

My first real memory of him during that summer—and the one that sets in motion all the others—is of the slow, hot Washington afternoon my mother answered the phone, turned pale, dropped one hand to the formica counter, swung around to face me (I was eating a popsicle) and gasped, "Your father's had a heart attack."

A doctor would later call the episode "garden-variety." But it wasn't that to any of *us.* From his hospital bed, Dad confessed to my mother that he'd been involved with another woman—Nancy, to be exact—ever since his first trip to Washington, when he'd gone ahead of the rest of us by a couple of months to find the new family house. She was the reason for all those mysterious phone calls. This infidelity was not his first, he said, but it ran the deepest. And that made the situation intolerable. He was in love, and under life-threatening stress as a result. He'd have to leave the marriage or die. In fact, the pressure of the double life he'd been living since the cross-country trip had actually brought on the "cardiac event"—to borrow the title of the book he would later write about the whole thing.

On such pivots, Dreiser wrote in *The Titan*, swings the world. The confession did for the marriage. When my father left the hospital it was to move in with Nancy. Oddly, the heart attack was also just the thing to accelerate Dad's career: the *New York Times Magazine* immediately printed the long article he wrote on his "cardiac event." Soon came my father's first published book (cowritten with his cardiologist), describing in excruciating private detail the "identity crisis" he'd suffered along with that heart attack—and then, on the same downward slope the aesthetic of my father's moral life seems to trace in my own mind's eye during those days, a television series that ran on ABC. The show starred a black actor who had recently played a hard-nosed Navy instructor in a popular film, and featured a jocular rendition of the way my father had carried his extramarital intrigue into his hospital room while he recuperated. ("No wonder he's having heart trouble," mutters the show's "doctor," as he looks at wife and mistress, unknown to each other, standing side by side in a hospital elevator.)

"Thank the Lord for small favors," my mother said when the show failed after less than a full season.

"Well," said my father, looking around at the gang of shacks that Ohr Somayach was, above the dust in the harsh light of afternoon. "You sure didn't pick an elegant place."

He was half joking—rolling his eyes in mock dismay like Bert Lahr, a boyhood hero of his. The shacks were made of prefabricated boards painted a yellowish color, peeling and splintering in places. The windows were open because of the heat; rusted screens poorly covered the open spaces.

"I'm not here for the comforts," I told him.

"Well, I should hope not. What is that large house over there?" He pointed at the only real building in sight, squatting on top of a low hill. It had once been a house of sorts.

"That's the study hall."

"Is it hot in there?"

"We've got air conditioning."

"But not in the cabins." He looked back at mine with a frown.

"I can manage without it."

"I suppose you can," he said. "I remember you spent a summer at the University of Virginia without any air conditioning."

I told him that he was welcome to stay for lunch. "The eating cabin is a little cooler."

"No, thanks," said Nancy, probably guessing (accurately) at the quality of the food.

It was remarkable how my father and I could slide so dully along the spokes of polite convention. Even with Nancy there. Sad, that stiffness of the poses no past intimacy ever seems to erode.

"So this is higher education, Jewish style," my father said breezily. "I don't know if I ever told you, but your Grandpa Murray insisted on my going to Hebrew school in the afternoons for a while when I was growing up. But I wore him down. I hated it. Finally, he told me I could play ball in the afternoons instead. I remember that day well. It may have been the happiest day of my childhood."

"I guess I'm a little old to play ball," I said, wondering a bit at his choice of anecdotes.

He kicked at the blue-gray gravel in the driveway, as other students hurried past and threw curious glances at him. Looking around again, taking everything in, he seemed elaborately disappointed. Well, of course. He'd seen my cabin, with the paper-thin walls, the pine needles, and had probably concluded I had lost my mind.

"You're thirty-one," he commented.

My father at that age had four children and a speechwriting job for Senator Birch Bayh of Indiana. What did I have, besides a few mildewing religious books?

"Well, I won't be here forever," I said. And felt, again, a rising irritation as I heard myself apologizing for a decision I was proud of.

We were all walking down the driveway, under frowning fir trees, toward the street at the end of the rutted descent. Just to get a little space, I guess. Somehow Ohr Somayach's presence threw an oppressive consciousness over us all.

"I've been all right," my father said, answering a question I should have asked, but hadn't. "No recurrence of that business that had us all worried."

One day, earlier that year, my father had suddenly found himself unable to form sentences. Standing in his Westchester living room, he had tried to say, "Let's go," and had said, "Up the stairs." By the time he was rushed to a hospital, the doctors' probes and stethoscopes had detected nothing unusual inside him, in that red cavern where vital things happen. Of course, we all knew that given my father's history of heart disease, he could be susceptible to blood clots—and that one such clot, lodging somewhere in the labyrinth of tiny blood vessels feeding the brain, could cause a stroke, possibly crippling his mind.

"I've taken some blood thinner," he said, "but that's all. It's not bad."

Again, he and Nancy surveyed Ohr Somayach, this time from the foot of its unpaved driveway.

"You've always liked being a student," he said. "Well, you know, so did I. I loved my college days."

Those days had been a far cry from the academic asceticism of Ohr Somayach. My father had traveled all the way from Brooklyn to Missouri to go to college, because Missouri U. offered a journalism program, rare at the time. But what had really caught the venturing student's attention, once he got there, was a festive crowd of young, blond men outside a large brick building, all wearing stylish suits emblazoned with a three-letter Greek insignia. They were loudly cheering new inductees, one of whom every so often would run up the stairs to the porch of the Georgian red brick building.

"And then they'd all cheer, and jump up and down," my father would say. "Here was this great old Southern-style house, with real columns, and a porch the size of a city park. And all that cheering. I didn't hesitate. I ran up to the guy who seemed to be in charge, stuck out my hand, and said, 'I'm Steve Lesher, and I want to join *your* fraternity!'"

A Jew from Brooklyn, my father still had a lot to learn about the social realities of Middle American fraternities.

But one night that fall, a pretty Southern girl on campus cornered him under a magnolia tree (well, the decorative magnolia is my own imagination's addition), and hesitantly asked him, "Just what do Jews *believe*?"

"Suddenly," Dad had told me years later, "I realized I had hit a gold mine. So what if I couldn't join a WASP fraternity? After all those years as some kid with a pompadour, I was something *exotic*!"

It was a magnificent opportunity. But what *did* Jews believe?

"There was a Hillel House on campus, a place for Jewish services and education, I guess. The poor rabbi there was just about the loneliest man on earth. Well, when I showed up one day and asked him, 'What do Jews believe?' I was his godsend. I think he must have fallen in love with me at first sight. The next thing I knew, he was doing everything with me. Studies, holiday events. Best of all, because I had a good voice, he let me sing the Sabbath services every Friday night."

That was the killer. My father's new dating tactic was to invite a non-Jewish girl to the Friday night service. There young Steve would stand at the lectern before a small, admiring crowd (made up mostly of older townspeople who lived nearby), adorned with white skullcap and black pompadour, a white *tallis* wrapped around the shoulders of his best suit, the protagonist in an arcane drama—swaying, chanting, his tenor voice (a good one) running up and down over the traditional melodies, leading the others in the ceremonial Hebrew prayers and *kaddish*. From the back, the girl would watch—helplessly, of course, stranded in a foreign ritual and unable to do anything but admire the young Jew who was so much in command of it. The rich warm night, filtering in with magnificent, honeysuckle-scented laziness, must have deepened the magical effect.

"Those Friday nights," he told me, "would knock their socks off." He mugged for me, forgetting everything else in the sheer pleasure of storytelling. "And sometimes other articles of clothing, too."

I've never asked my father whether the "poor rabbi" knew that his protégé was using the Friday night prayers to knock articles of clothing off pretty, non-Jewish girls. Maybe he did. In any case, little more of Judaism seemed to have filtered down to my father in the years between then and my own Ohr Somayach days.

"Did you ever study the Talmud, Dad?" I asked him, standing in the gravel driveway. I think I had a vague idea of getting him into a book with me, knocking *his* socks off.

"No. I know it's a clever text, but remember, I don't believe in God."

One day, while I still worked for that Manhattan legal publisher, Dad had called me with a question about the Talmud. "Someone here at work just died," he'd explained (he was working for IBM's Communications Division by that time), "and I'm going to try to say something at his funeral. I thought maybe the Talmud could furnish some sort of relevant quotation. I wanted to ask you, since you might know: does the Talmud say anything about the virtue of doing one's job? I mean, doing it well?"

"You want to quote from the Talmud at this man's funeral?" I asked him.

"Well, I'm looking for a book of wisdom, and you know something about the Talmud. I thought maybe I'd use a quotation. You know, something about the virtue of doing one's job sincerely and well. That's something that would characterize this man."

At my antiseptic desk in the legal publisher's office, under a fluorescent light, everything around me a prim denial of the real-life trash heaps of the mind, I bit my lip. "To be honest," I said, "I'm not sure I'd want to dissect the text for a snippet of a topical reference. Not on those terms."

"Oh, come on." I could picture him at the other end, pursing his lips, rolling his eyes. "Is praising a man at his funeral such a bad use for the book?"

"But you don't even believe in God. How can you quote the Talmud as an authority?"

"Why do you imagine God as the source of all authority?" my father asked. "A good book is a good book, don't you think? Why does this have to turn into a theological dispute?"

"But it's hypocritical. It's..." I stopped, wilting before a wall of words. Taking religion out of the Talmud is like smashing a bottle to drink the wine, but if you're only looking for a few drops in the first place, what's the big deal? A quotation in a eulogy isn't exactly the revaluation of all values.

"And remember," my father went on, "I'm a Jew, too. Most of the Jews in the world aren't Orthodox. But we're Jews. We have as much right to Jewish tradition as the Orthodox do."

"Dad, what you know about rights isn't the issue just now. Or wrongs, either."

"I have a right to happiness," he had said to me, on the unforgettable night when I was fifteen and he had moved out to live with Nancy and had arrived in his new car to take me out somewhere, to "explain" things to me. We were sitting at a dark table in what I gathered, from the waiters' attire, was a fashionable restaurant. He was thirty-eight. He'd just shaved off his coal-black trimmed beard, explaining that it made him look "too old." Fresh out of the hospital after his heart attack, the newly smooth facial skin was one response to his new-found sense of mortality. Divorce, I suppose, had been another.

In his hand, as he talked, was the thin, sparkling glass that held his second Gibson of the night. He was becoming a regular drinker, something he'd never been before. Maybe the stress of his situation really had edged him close to a loss of self-control. Nevertheless, he managed for the most part that night to present his most persuasive manner, half winning self-revelation, half lecture.

"I'm perishable," he said. "Look at it that way. When you've had a heart attack, as I have, you begin to realize time won't run on for you forever. I've got a heart disease. And the fact is, heart disease is treatable but not curable. It will likely kill me. The figures say I'll probably have another heart attack in about two years, and die. I have a right to enjoy some of life before I do."

Tears came. His, not mine. I realized all at once that I wasn't really being addressed at all. I was a stage property in my father's midlife crisis.

"Of course, you think I'm wrong," Dad said. His Jewishly handsome face looked puffy in the inadequate light. "How couldn't you? You've been raised with Jewish morality. Well, so was I. My grandparents would never have divorced. They would have stayed together forever, even if it meant making each other miserable. That's how things were done."

He avoided looking at me, but I sensed that, too, was a pose—a way of minimizing my power, padding his senses to my pain. "Yes, divorce *can* be fair," he went on, "to escape from misery. Maybe one day you'll understand that."

It was after midnight when I got back. I still don't know how to describe how I felt, except that I hadn't cried. I knew that something central was being ripped out of my life, but somehow the story of its loss wasn't mine: I had no say in the drama that was tearing up my world, and no words to give anyone else.

Which I discovered even more vividly as my mother interrogated me for details of the conversation. She had her bedroom light turned off, partly because she would be getting up for work at the grocery store at five the next morning and partly, I suppose, so I wouldn't see her face clearly.

She was lying on her back in the big, white-quilted bed she has slept in, alone, for decades now. She kept a rolled-up pillow under her knees, legs slightly apart, her feet exposed, two white stabs in the night. It might have been a lover's pose, but maybe for that very reason my fifteen-year-old senses, as I heard her breathing from her pillow, waiting for my account, found her intimidating—as if she were waiting for expected disappointments. As I talked, her mouth drew into a hard pinch and she offered an occasional tart aside. Was he drunk? she asked. Well, was he drinking? Yes, yes, she'd thought he would. And he drove home, too? The creep. (My mother, raised by the puritanical Grandpa Phil, can't understand drinking and never really lets loose with profanity.) Wasn't that just like him? When I got to the part about "Jewish morality" she laughed out loud.

"Oh, I'll tell you about the Jewish morality in *his* upbringing. He wants a soapbox now, of course. But things were different in Brooklyn, with Murray, that father of his. When Steve turned sixteen, Murray wanted him to be a man. So..."

My mother still speaks with the accents of Montgomery, Alabama, where she grew up. Girls there, I suspect, did not reveal the sexual practices of sixteen-year-old boys they knew. But divorce changes things.

"So what did Murray do? He bought Steve a call girl. As a birthday present. At sixteen! That's the kind of background *he* had."

I thought of that as I watched my father and Nancy picking a path through the gravel on their way back to their car, to the normal world they'd briefly left behind. All in all, I knew more about my father than I wanted to. And yet there was a great deal about him that was still a mystery to me. He had developed a certain natural dignity of movement that still eluded me—maybe it was the solid middle, or the graying hair. I was still an awkward harlequin, with a comic oversized nose and too-tall profile, no matter how hard I fought to make it look like something more refined. In some ways my father looked younger than he'd looked during that awful conversation sixteen years earlier.

And me? I hadn't found a single word to communicate the new dimension of life I thought I had discovered. And none of my words could match the most recent story he had told me about himself: about the time his car had flipped over on the highway somewhere in Westchester, the small steel-and-aluminum body rolling around and around near an embankment, and awed onlookers, seeing him emerge unharmed, had asked him whether he'd seen his life flash before his eyes.

"I didn't have the heart to tell them the truth," he'd said to me. "You know what it was? When that car started going over, all I could think was..." —here he mugged, like Bert Lahr again, gripping an imaginary wheel, the eyes going comically wide—"all I thought was: 'Holy shit! *Holy shit!*'"

And there I was, once again doing the student bit that was all I seemed to do reasonably well—this time with *yarmulke*, ascetic arrogance and no air conditioning. And still trying, I suppose, to win my father's interest in something I had done. From his point of view—and my mother's too, probably—I hadn't advanced an inch.

CHAPTER NINETEEN

O ver Labor Day weekend that same year, I visited my mother. She still lived in the house my father had bought in the summer of 1973 and moved out of shortly afterward. In those days it had had a few more occupants, of course—including a miniature poodle and a cat, who between the two of them, over the years, reduced the backs of the upholstered family-room chairs to sawdust. Now that the rooms were largely empty, my mother had devoted her native energy to refurnishing and redecorating, so that the house looked better now—a floor lamp here, a refinished black armoire there—than it had while the Lesher family was splintering inside it.

After the divorce, Mom had worked at exhausting jobs, despite middle age and a bad back: first as a waitress, then as a meat wrapper in a supermarket. That was a matter of necessity, not choice. She had five children and had to provide for them. But she was good at her work. Over the years she'd stuck with the supermarket, defied the sneers of the men who'd been there before her, and gradually risen to delicatessen manager—from which position, as she sometimes put it, she wasn't likely to rise again. She wasn't particularly happy in her job. The work was hard. Privately, she also complained about the morals of the women who worked for her now that she was a manager. "That Susie," she'd say. "I swear that girl would run off with anything in pants."

But she was determined not to whine, not even about her broken marriage, though she had been careful to "remake" her bedroom—changing the wallpaper, adding a shag rug, eliminating my father's books—as if to render the place unrecognizable in the unlikely event Dad ever tried to scale the brick wall in the back and punch his way in through the storm windows.

"I'm not much interested in the past," she told me, looking quietly around the kitchen as I ate my *kosher* food off a paper plate. The past, in my mother's eyes, was an abstraction, something that belonged solely to the mind. Only what could be touched, smelled, washed or cooked seemed to mean much to her, at least on a practical level. Up to her elbows in food every day, slicing turkey breasts and pastrami, cleaning and re-cleaning the counters of her section of the store, I think her natural dislike of the abstract had deepened. But even when I was a child she had been suspicious of what she called "just words." Family, children, health were the important things. "Just words" were the tools of unreliable people, people who talked from "soapboxes," as my mother scathingly put it, people who ignored their wives and children, didn't care about earning a living, but kept on speechifying about "art" or "principles" while important things went undone.

People like Dad, that is. Or me.

So when she said, "I like to think ahead. Oh, I don't suppose there's a lot ahead for *me*. But I have my children, and soon there will be grandchildren to look forward to," I had to remind myself that in the end, to my mother at least, a grandchild was a grandchild. So it didn't matter what I was trying to learn at Ohr Somayach, what I had sacrificed for it, what sort of religion I wanted to give the children I would eventually have. The children themselves would matter—that is, if I ever stopped reading and talking and got around to having any. Everything else was "just words."

Except that it wasn't really so simple. Certain words still had power for my mother. It just seemed that I could never quite find them, or find out how to use them. I could never forget how, during my fling with the Italian Catholic woman, Mom had unexpectedly lit into me about non-Jewish grandchildren who hadn't even been born yet: "I will *not* have any, do you hear?"

She had been genuinely angry, and I was stunned. Bear in mind that I was only twenty-two; the young woman and I were only intimate for a few weeks; we had never discussed marriage; and having children, at that time, was about the last thing on my mind.

"That's not fair," I had protested. "None of us is going to get married specifically to father your grandchildren."

"I raised you Jewish, didn't I?" she demanded. "How can you even consider raising families of Christians?"

A believer in free choice, I had naturally defended Rob too, when his turn came—not because I liked his evangelical religion, but because my mother's narrowness struck me as bigoted.

"Suppose Shelley's family protested against *her* marrying *him*? Wouldn't you be offended?" I'd asked her.

"That's not the point." She'd been saying that to me, in one way or another, all my life. I never did seem to get the point. My mother considers herself practical—and it was adjudged long ago in my family that I am *not* practical, or as my mother puts it, that I don't have enough sense to come in out of the rain. (According to family legend I once really did forget to come in out of the rain. The truth is that I didn't forget. I'd been so fascinated by the twisting gray sheets of rain a storm had driven across the road in front of our house that I had stayed outside in it, rather than missing any of the excitement by fetching an umbrella.) To Mom, I'd always been "a dreamer"—an idealist who talked volumes about forests and walked head-on into trees.

I was used to that much. What I wasn't used to was the emphasis my mother, all of a sudden, placed on what seemed to me the most tenuous of abstractions. Did it really matter so much whether Rob's kids went to church?

"I've devoted my life to building a family. Is that family going to be cut short after one generation?"

"But I don't see…"

"If you don't see it, you don't want to see it. What kind of life could I have with grandchildren who grow up with Christmas trees, and who think all Jews are going to hell?"

That question came back to me over the weekend, but in an ironically twisted form, as I wondered—I couldn't help it—if something
like it couldn't also be asked of *me*.

True, my children won't number my mother among the damned.
But can they truly share my mother's family life, fulfill her trans-
generational aspirations the way she wants them to? Her slacks, her
uncovered hair, her seafood restaurant outings on Saturdays would
render her as foreign among Monsey's Orthodox as the Dalai Lama,
padding around in saffron robes over the Bermuda grass, would
appear in my mother's own suburb.

Or as I did, for that matter. My Sabbath walk around a couple
of suburban blocks, a casual custom from my point of view, drew
stares from neighbors, most of whom had moved in too recently to
remember me, but a few of whom had known me when my Saturday
costume was the same as theirs: tee shirt, jeans, an armful of grass
seed or pine mulch. The Talmudic tractate I'd brought along on
the trip to Washington was stashed away in my old room (where
I'd once confided my self-doubts to my diary), so they didn't have
gold-printed Hebrew titles to stare at, but with my suit, my beard,
my ritual tassels, I might as well have carried the strange names
under my arm.

And I suddenly remembered how the word "Jew" had been
hurled at me one day over the tinny crash of a snowball that broke
a window inches from my head, as I walked through my mother's
front door—this same front door—one frigid afternoon when I was
eighteen.

Suspicious as I always am of Jewish paranoia, I nevertheless
found myself wondering how I'd appeared to my neighbors before
I was self-consciously Jewish. Was I really just like them, even then?
How much like them did I appear in the days when I worked on
Saturday, but was a liberal atheist who loudly insisted on freedom
of religion? Maybe I was kidding myself in those days. Did the sight
of this grownup apparition, trudging around Mclean with beard

and skullcap, amount to a discovery or a confirmation for my old neighbors? Might they be nodding knowingly as I passed by? Had I always been foreign here, without knowing it?

Oh, of course I'd been mostly like everybody else. Which was exactly why the shrill laughter and the shouted words "Jew! Jewboy!" had disturbed me so much that winter day when I saw the broken glass on the floor, heard the receding footsteps and knew once and for all that windows weren't the only fragile things in our lives.

"The police say they can't do anything," my mother complained a week later. By this time the vandals had taken to driving a car through our front yard during the night. Dad was living in his Washington condominium with his second wife by then, so he couldn't sit up on the porch to threaten them with a shotgun even if he'd been willing to. (In fact, Dad had never been the shotgun type.) So my mother had called the police.

"They said there's nothing they can do. They said we might put up some obstacles around the yard to discourage them from driving through again. But we should be careful not to make them too dangerous, or they could sue us." She gave an incredulous little laugh.

After that, we just got used to hearing them drive through our front yard in the darkness. The screech of the tires as they tore around in a tight circle through the grass and over the concrete walkway was a kind of taunt, and it hurt doubly to hear it silently, staying inside, fearing to confront whoever was in the car—fearing, I suppose, what they might call us if we did. For it was words I thought of when I admitted my shameful cowardice, words I could do nothing to repress.

After a while it didn't matter any more: the disturbances stopped. I never saw any faces. I only saw the receding outline of the car as it roared its way out into the street and around the corner. To this day I don't know who they were, or who were the passengers and who was driving. For all I know, they may still be living around my mother. Even now, years later, I may see them when I visit her in Mclean, may even speak to them without knowing it. This knowledge colors my view of every face I see in the old neighborhood.

But I could never really feel at home or at ease there, even if everyone I saw there was a friend beyond doubt. Too much has happened to me, and to my world, for me to force myself back into this one.

"Write more often, darling," my mother said, kissing me on my way out of the house and back to Monsey. "I never seem to know what you're doing."

"Yes, you do," I said. We were standing on the artificial blue slate of the foyer, which my mother had always hated and I had liked, because when I lay face down on it, it looked to my seventeen-year-old eyes like the frozen blue surface of an ocean, arrested in its movement but endlessly vast.

"You know everything I'm doing," I emphasized weakly.

"Not as much as I'd like to."

Of course, she had watched what I was doing as, step by step, I had moved farther away from her. Every visit to Mclean must have brought with it an unpleasant surprise. First there was the skullcap. Next had come the *tzitzis* hanging from corners of the ritual undergarment—"your tassels," she called them, as if (to my impatient ears) she meant to call them my invention, my fetish. "It's Jewish law," I'd told her, as I was to tell her again and again—when I refused to eat the chicken she cooked, when I began buying my own food and ate it off paper plates. Finally there had been a real argument when, one Saturday evening before dark, Mr. O'Malley from next door had wanted to return a rake to our garage and I had hesitated to turn on the electric door opener. It was still the Sabbath. I could not use electricity. But how to explain that to Mr. O'Malley, holding our rake and resting his old body's weight on it? As it turned out, it was my mother who needed the explanation.

"You're acting crazy," she had hissed as soon as Mr. O'Malley had gone. "Do you want him to think you're a lunatic?"

"I'm *not* a lunatic. I'm keeping the Sabbath."

"How am I supposed to explain *that* to him?"

"You don't have to. I'll explain it."

"He's *my* friend. How do you think it would look to him if you behave this way and I don't tell him *anything*?"

"Well, we'll explain it together."

"I will *not*," she snapped. "I won't be made to look like a fanatic."

"Is Judaism so hard to explain?"

"*Your* Judaism!"

Remember those old men whose wild beards and mumbled Yiddish annoyed you when you were growing up, Mom? Remember how ashamed they made you feel in front of your American friends? Well, guess what? You gave birth to one of them.

"I'll try to communicate better," I said. "But I wonder if explanations are really very helpful."

"I'd like to know what you're *feeling*," she said.

"Haven't you?"

"Not really. Especially since you were in high school and all the changes started happening to us. I've always wanted to know how you felt all that time."

As sons have probably wondered for centuries, I asked myself how many of those old feelings she'd really wanted to know. Like after Dad was gone and the house was full of her grief, when my dearest seventeen-year-old dream had been to get my hands inside the dress of a girl named Karen Phillips who lived up the street. What do you say about that? Would my "honesty" ease the memories of those days, when she'd pinched pennies to pay the mortgage on a broken home?

"Okay," I said, hoping I really meant it. Meaning, that is, that I hoped my trip backward in time hadn't thrown up too many barriers between her world and mine. But I didn't even dare to put that hope into words.

She said, "Maybe you'll give me a Jewish grandchild after all."

As we walked to the car she added, "I just never thought it would come with such a price tag."

PART 4: TURNING BACK

And where shall this wealth of accumulated great impressions, which Jewish history constitutes for every Jewish family, this wealth of passions, virtues, decisions, renunciations, fights, and victories of all kinds—where shall it flow, if not eventually into great spiritual men and works?

— Friedrich Nietzsche

I dislike the everlasting European bustle around "progress," which in the end adds up to nothing...I am bored with Europe's "progress" and its "emancipated humanity," with the masquerade of little people who play God and keep sinking into the mire.

— Nathan Birnbaum (1927)

Is not the Distant, the Dead, while I love it, and long for it, and mourn for it, Here, in the genuine sense, as truly as the floor I stand on?

— Thomas Carlyle

CHAPTER TWENTY

I am heading back to Ohr Somayach from my mother's house in Mclean, Virginia. It's the fall of 1988. The trip involves, first, a train ride to New York; next, a subway to the "Monsey Trails" bus stop; finally, the bus trip into New Jersey and then northward, into the rolling hills of Rockland County, New York, back to the Orthodox enclave of Monsey where I live and study. I am a thirty-year-old man with no income, a student at the *yeshiva*, marriage a distant prospect.

Across from me on the Amtrak is a pretty young woman, one leg in soft blue denim tucked underneath her, talking with artless charm to her neighbor about her first year in college.

"My mother doesn't understand," she tells the neighbor. "She's never seen the way I live at college, and now she thinks I must be wasting all my time. Not to mention *her* money."

We are somewhere outside Baltimore. The young woman has blue eyes, long limp brown hair, an amused expression. She can't stop talking. She's probably on her way back to college, maybe Barnard or Brandeis or Radcliffe. School means freedom to her, whatever school it is.

"I mean, now I *never* get up before nine o'clock. And I'm up later at night too, like a grownup, not a kid. But to my mom? I came home at midnight once, the first week after finals?" (She has the youthful trick of speaking her declarative sentences as if they were questions.) "I thought she would *die*. 'I was so worried!' I had to explain to her, you know, I just don't live the same way any more?"

The neighbor keeps nodding amiably, and I too am somewhat lulled by the charm of this brightly meandering female voice. Amtrak train rides can be tolerated if you allow yourself sufficient distraction. Unfortunately, the only thing distracting me, besides the woman across the aisle, is the memory of a comment my mother made, when she mentioned some contemporary rock music group during my visit, and I went blank: "Well, you'll find out all about them when you have kids." But it's my mother who will be the one to find out, I'm afraid. Childhood in Orthodox Monsey is not the typical American affair.

I pull my Talmudic tractate out of my bag and try to study it. The text is familiar; dozens of my notes are scribbled in the margins of the wide, white pages. Nevertheless it is slow going. I'm feeling out of things from lack of practice, and I'm noticing (maybe for the same reason) the awkward incongruity of the ancient content bumping against the modern setting of this slicked-down train car. The Talmud speaks of transportation by donkey and ox-cart. And here I am, zipping along via Amtrak. The Talmud assumes the rigid public segregation of the sexes—and as I read I keep hearing, as if in ironic commentary, the voice of the young woman directly across the aisle from me.

Yet it's as though I heard her through a filter thickened by endless repetition, for in a way her comments seem as worn to me as the Talmudic text, though I can't push them, or her, out of my mind. Wearing dresses, she says, is a sexist practice. Chinese doctors are more "realistic" than American ones. And so on. Another text, familiar but not familiar any more, an echo of my past, if not my ancestral one, another invitation to reexamination.

Still, whatever I'm feeling, I'm not feeling superior. Age is supposed to coat one's experience in nothing-new-under-the-sun familiarity, right? But I've never been able to feel jaded. If religious conversion is supposed to make the convert cocky enough to ignore voices from his own former world, that hasn't worked with me. Even the idea of summarizing my own life jolts me. Can a life like mine ever be reduced to the flatland of Talmudic analysis? Or a young woman's exhilarated platitudes?

I disembark into the low-ceilinged confusion of New York's Penn Station. From here it is a matter of getting to 47th Street and Fifth Avenue, at the center of Manhattan's diamond district (a concentration of Hasidic-run jewelry stores). Usually I take a subway that I have to board one long block and a half east of the train station, which means that I walk directly across town from the station entrance until I reach the right staircase downward.

Passing along the dirty street to the subway station stirs uneasy associations. I've discovered that it belongs to a wild-looking Israeli who, in the night hours, has a way of swooping out of nowhere to confront religious Jews carrying their bags to the subway. Like many beggars the Israeli is a specialist: he prefers Jews wearing *yarmulkes*. And he has a pretty good repertoire of tales of misfortune.

"Do you know the way to Lincoln Square?" he snapped at me in Hebrew one night, materializing suddenly at my elbow, hungry-looking but clearly no ectoplasm, despite his having appeared out of thin air.

"Why do you want to go to Lincoln Square?" I asked.

He was lost, he explained in rapid Hebrew (I struggled to keep up), and hoped that at Lincoln Square he could get directions to somewhere he could sleep for the night.

"Ah."

I could see his appeal was guided by my *yarmulke* and aimed at my sense of religious honor. "Lincoln Square" referred to a large Orthodox synagogue in Manhattan, which, however, was some distance away and almost certainly locked tight at that hour. The voice of reason urged caution. The stranger's beard and his greasy, curly black hair were untrimmed and uncombed, and his loose corduroy jacket was torn in places, but for all that he didn't look like the real thing—that is, he didn't look *lost*. On the contrary, he seemed completely at home, moving around the dark streets with a native's confidence.

"Have you any money?" he asked, still in Hebrew. "Maybe you can help me. You see, my money is in Bank Leumi, and won't be available until Monday—so you see…"

I hesitated a moment, and then gave him what I had. He eyed the five dollars in his hand with the air of a critic.

"I don't think I should go to Lincoln Square tonight." He switched suddenly to English as he pocketed the money. "The streets are dangerous for a Jew. Maybe you have enough for a room to stay in?"

When I looked blank, he swooped away as quickly as he had come. In the distance a car horn sounded mournfully, but no lights pierced the gloom, so I didn't see the stranger's figure as he retreated.

Most money is given to beggars out of cowardice, says Nietzsche. Was I a coward? Needless to say, before my conversion I wouldn't have dreamed of giving such a creature five dollars. So why had I handed it over now? Had I done it only to prove (to him? To myself? To the invisible eye of Orthodox social opinion, watching at all hours?) that I really had changed—that my new lifestyle was more than a style? Or was I just an ordinary dumbbell, taken in as all dumbbells are taken in?

At one level, I guess, the religious life amounts to a new set of devices by which we can be manipulated. And against which we must therefore learn to toughen ourselves. At the risk—it sometimes seems—of losing touch with exactly the fire and tenderness that was behind the appeal of that life in the first place.

We want to be saints, and end up as calculating nebbishes. We want to transcend the limitations of ego, and we find ourselves struggling for some way to unscramble our own motives. People who think of Orthodoxy as a simplifying creed have never lived in our skins.

Later comes the familiar bus ride from Manhattan to Monsey. Now there are no coeds. No female chatter about what things are like at home. On this bus the men and women are separated by a long green chintz curtain stretched down the middle of the aisle, hung from a sort of rod the Orthodox-owned bus company has installed down the bus' length. Men are on one side, women on the other. The black-suited Hasidim who ride with me now have worked all day; it's a weekday, they are tired, most of them are nodding off. A large family means, whatever else it means, that one is nearly always busy. (Where do these people go for reflection, or self-examination? I don't know. Their synagogues are certainly not contemplative places.)

The Vizhnitz Hasid in the seat ahead of mine is asleep. His head has lolled off to one side. I recognize him as a member of the "Vizhnitz" sect by his dress, for Hasidim are extremely precise in these matters: the cut of a knee-length coat, the type of black hat, the haircut. A travelers'-size Talmudic volume is in his lap, but for him this ride is an opportunity for forty winks—little more than that, probably, given the ferocity of the Israeli driver, who is taking every curve in the highway as if it were a personal enemy. The Hasid is a young man, pale, rather tall, with prominent cheekbones and full Jewish lips. The high black collar of his suit rides tightly around his neck. He has recently had his hair cut, Hasidic-style, meaning that except for the long, coarse earlocks, and some downy and almost colorless hairs along the back of his neck, he is shaved nearly bald. The back of his head looks so smooth and pink that he reminds me of a child asleep, and I am tempted to reach out and stroke him; but knowing that his reaction would not be at all childlike I restrain myself and look out the window.

It is forty miles or so to Monsey, most of it through one of the busiest slabs of workaday New Jersey. As usual, traffic is heavy. The driver alternately pumps accelerator and brake. Impatient, he swings the long vehicle from lane to lane, inching up to the bumper ahead of him and then suddenly roaring to one side or the other, yanking us back and forth. The horizon, urban and industrial at this range from the city, is as irregular as our movements. As the bus lurches, the Hasidim sleep on, shaved heads in velvet *yarmulkes* bouncing a bit.

North again. Industrial names: Newark, Paterson, Passaic. The interstate cuts deep into changing terrain. Then the country begins to open out. The green signs along the Garden State Parkway give way to the big blue one that announces the New York state border. We have finally escaped the city, slipping through unclenching urban fingers into the green hills that presage the Kakiat Mountains, still many miles away to the north, their vague outlines now graying under the gathering evening.

Thus begins the New York State Thruway, the same road that runs to Woodstock, maybe an hour's drive beyond Monsey. In the summer of 1969, so many cars crowded the highway on the way to the concert that rural New York had the worst traffic jam in its history. "New York State Thruway is *closed,* man!" announced an excited spokesman as the "happening" began.

Long bus rides make me feel (briefly) superior to time. I can picture the pastoral setting of the Woodstock concert from the rolling hills visible from the window. I can imagine the arrested tension of all those cars backed up along the Thruway. But that's about all. Culturally I am far away—I can't grasp the remembered events. The images keep slipping, like the film in those old elementary school projectors from years back. In the long centuries of Jewish history, the twenty-year step from then to now isn't even discernible. My Orthodox coreligionists in Monsey won't have to expect to be asked, as Arlo Guthrie was once asked by some reporters, "What happened to the dream?"

Most religious Jews see themselves as hard-headed. Their own attitude toward the eventful interval of the Sixties is as smug as the reporters' mock bathos was silly. Incidentally, Guthrie himself was unsentimental in his answer: "I remember a lot of crazy things were going on, people were killing and dying, and a lot of us were pretty scared, but I don't remember a dream."

In Monsey, the Woodstock festival (when it is mentioned at all) is fantasized in grotesque terms, a referent for the orgiastic nightmare of modern permissiveness. The black-hats are not interested in hearing about what it was really like. A prominent Monsey rabbi argues against exposure to any "gentile" music—he includes Brahms and Beethoven—because, as he puts it, listening to "their" music is equivalent to "inviting them into our houses." And with them, presumably, come bikinis, drugs, promiscuity, adultery and, inevitably, religious assimilation. First Brahms, then the neighborhood pimp—finally the baptismal font, I suppose.

What I find most interesting in all this is the implied contrast between the Orthodox community's myth-making and its own self-image. The Orthodox community is quite certain it has the goods on everybody. The Hasid ahead of me on the bus, if he were awake, would tell me promptly enough what to do with my own youth's Aquarian fantasies: "Foolishness," he would snort, and go back to his Talmud. These days, confronted by an outsider, I might end up saying more or less the same thing.

But can anyone else see us the way we see ourselves? Even assimilated Jews are notorious romantics about Jews and Judaism. "Jews throw half their money away on philanthropies and fancies like Zionism," says Shaw's eponymous millionairess. Theodor Herzl was probably the nineteenth century's wildest nationalist dreamer. And even his ardor looks puny beside the two-thousand-year wait of religious Jewry for its Messiah. As for extra-rational experience—the long-frocked Jews who sell diamonds and real estate in New York City no more need Carlos Castaneda's psychedelic hero, Don Juan, to teach them the ropes of other-worldly life than the original Don Juan would have needed Joyce's *Ulysses* for pointers on seduction. Hasidim believe in angels, demons and magic. Their rebbes are forever rising right up out of the slums and visiting heaven, arguing with the Angel of Death. The current Klausenburger Rebbe made only a slight sensation among his flock when he disclosed a few of his previous identities. He claimed at least one lifetime in the Sinai wilderness, during which he observed the ancient debate between Moses and Korach over the leadership of the Children of Israel.

And it isn't only the rabbis telling these stories. I know a man who insists that when he met the late Lubavitcher Rebbe some years ago, the old man (then nearly eighty), to demonstrate the power of the Torah coursing through his veins, leaped out of his chair and over the large wooden desk in his private study.

What does all this mean? A friend and rabbi who specializes in twelve-step counseling says simply: "The community is in denial." Orthodoxy has built itself an isolationist culture as a mollusk makes a shell, not only for protection but for self-definition. The traditionally religious Jew has learned to identify himself so much through opposition to his surroundings that to take down the imaginary barriers in his relation to the world at large threatens his own notion of identity. He prefers a separate peace, in which even his standards of reality are those approved by his own community. No wonder the Orthodox self-image, and the Orthodox view of the outside, are both filtered through dark lenses. To see either the outside or oneself clearly would call into question the community's mythic distinction between the two. And those of us who are refugees from that "outside" world find it difficult enough to identify with the new one without having to shove our own wounds, and theirs, in the faces of the natives.

But can we really afford to be so credulous about ourselves? About others? Thinking of the Hasid ahead of me, the Klausenburger Rebbe's reincarnations, the way an old woman once protested to the driver about being left at her usual bus stop in Manhattan—"because it's Goot Friday, and it's not safe"—the fantastic view of America from inside the Monsey bus, I ask myself, as I have so often: What will I tell my children, as *they* grow up in such surroundings? And whatever I tell them, how much will reflect what I know? And how much what I want them to know? Or what I don't want them to know?

The entry into Monsey is prosaic enough. The bus turns off the Thruway. Billboards give way to shopping centers, shopping centers to neat suburban neighborhoods. A duck crossing. Neighborhood watches, watching. Frame houses, driveways, shutterless windows (the norm in New York, it seems) staring into space. Not the teeming ghetto my parents imagine. Not the earthly paradise we Orthodox sometimes pretend. Still, in the basements of some of the frame houses, study halls are crowded early every morning and late every night with men studying Talmud, the Bible, the old laws. And why not? Who am I, who is anybody, to say that *this* is not "normal"?

CHAPTER TWENTY-ONE

In his book *On Being a Jew,* James Kugel has the spokesman for traditional Judaism tell his American-Jewish interlocutor:

> You see yourself through American eyes, in that peculiarly American fashion of imagining that each person is no more than himself, made out of thin air...But what I see is, instead, somebody who was born, who came out from his parents and they from theirs, and so on, extending both into the past and into the future—so that a true understanding of who you are, and even of what you will accomplish, must begin with those facts.

Kugel is an American, and moreover a poet—that is, someone with a professional stake in grasping life from the "thin air" of imagination. Thus, there is something self-critical in his critique of the American taste for self-definition *sans* ancestry. I feel that I, too, am rebuking my own preferences when people ask me why I have chosen the life of Orthodoxy and I give my usual answer, which is: Orthodox life has chosen *me.*

Because that isn't what I'd like to say. I'd prefer to claim that "tradition" is a sort of menu spread out before me—an offering, not a command.

But I don't say that.

Why not?

Do I sometimes feel that the crimping of my life's boundaries makes more precious the experience of what's left inside, focuses life's muscles and nerves along certain limbs precisely because other parts have been pruned away? Under the weight of tradition my notion of time, for instance, has become less a straight line and more a sort of ribbon wrapped around the human continuum. Talmud study, with its ageless questions and layers of commentary, is one way of evading the limitations of the linear thrust of history. So is the revolving cycle of festivals. When a Jewish holiday approaches and I drop, naked, into a ritual bath, the water that closes over my head sweeps away the years and I reenter time's womb, so to speak, to emerge as a new birth a thousand years old.

But is that sort of thing reason enough to give up the rest? Better than most people, I know the cost involved. I sometimes feel that my life is peopled with ghosts. And when I say "ghosts," I'm not thinking of the dead. I mean my own absent family members. People who should be part of my life at crucial moments ... but can't be, because my religious transformation has imposed too high a barrier.

I remember vividly the sense of isolation during the first Jewish New Year I celebrated Orthodox-fashion. It was in Monsey (where I would later study at Ohr Somayach). The service was stirring, though by my standards monstrously long. Six hours crawled past between start and finish. I didn't understand all the Hebrew by any means, which added to the impression of slowness. But I wasn't bored. I will always remember certain moments, and in particular I remember one sound: the voice of the rabbi who led most of the service—floating, twisting, crying through the penitential text, out of a swaying body turned away from me, over dozens of other bodies packed together in prayer.

"On the New Year it is written, and on the fast of the Day of Atonement it is sealed!" the rabbi chanted in Hebrew, in the crowded auditorium we had borrowed from a local Jewish school. "Who will live and who will die ... how many by drowning, how many by storm..." His voice rose an octave—"Who will rest and who will wander"—then swelled into a roar: "But repentance, charity and prayer can reverse the evil decree!"

But the excitement chilled for me as I remembered that no one in my family was with me to hear it. On previous New Years, as far back as I could remember until I'd gone off to college—and even later when I was in my mother's house—we'd gone to the synagogue as a family. But here I was, finally celebrating the holiday as a traditional Jew should…and meanwhile my observance was too solitary to be traditional, for other Orthodox Jews celebrated in close family groups, even if temporarily divided by gender while in synagogue.

And I knew my own observance would remain solitary. My mother and siblings would never travel all the way to Monsey to participate in an old-fashioned service whose language and structure would make it almost as alien to them as an Easter Mass. Nor could I go to them. For one thing, religious law didn't allow me to travel on the holiday—the shrinking horizons imposed by refraining from cars and telephones, which is intended to throw a tight embrace around one's intimate circle, had for me the ironic effect of closing family *out*. For another thing, the law prescribed that the ceremonial *shofar* must not be blown in a congregation where men and women are seated together—as they were in my mother's temple. So from then on, I realized, my family members would only be with me on the New Year through the enforced sense of their absence. A door had closed on my personal past just as I had picked up the thread of an ancestral one.

Ghosts.

I felt the same way the first time I conducted a Passover Seder in my own apartment. My wife and son were there, of course, but I was oppressively conscious of the absence of siblings and parents as I donned the ceremonial white *kittel* and poured the first cup of wine.

I realized I couldn't be with my mother, who was presiding at a family supper table far away in Washington, the wooden tabletop spread with special white, just as she had done year after year when I was growing up. I could picture it clearly. She'd be serving stuffed fish, chicken, *matzoh* ball soup, and helping my brothers and sister with the reading of the *haggadah*, which describes the ancient Jews' deliverance from Egyptian bondage. My childhood memories were punctuated with the rich sensations of those late nights, once a year: the four cups of wine (the only time alcohol was ever served at our table), one drunk for each Biblical promise of redemption; the symbolic foods arranged on a special plate; the crumbly brown-and-white, unleavened *matzohs*; the velvet midnight sky under which I could stand for a few minutes after the meal, an exhilarated child up long past his bedtime, tasting the excitement of his own sort of freedom.

The repetitiveness of the background of all those memories, against which my mind's eye could see myself age as if in time-lapse photography, was part of their wizardry. Even the tablecloth—a glossy but rather ordinary embroidered linen, that seemed a little less magical each Passover—evoked the concentric power of the interlocking years. Against such a background, details that did *not* repeat themselves stood out with a special sheen. I'll always remember one Seder night when a lunar eclipse commenced toward the end of the ceremony. Hours after I would normally be asleep I stood in the dark outside my family's house and watched the moon turn a deep copper inch by inch, like a magic penny.

And now, instead of all that, ghosts sat at my Seder table. Ghosts who should have been among the people closest to me and my life. But weren't.

I felt this so strongly, year after year, that finally I wrote about it. What I wrote appeared as a column in *The Jewish Week* in the spring of 1996. I set out to describe my feelings about being separated from my mother on holidays, and expressed my hope that, whatever our differing religious commitments, we shared more than what divided us:

> In fact, we both share a poignant nook in the drafty castle of Jewish history.... Yes, we are suffering the stress of transition but transition is about continuity as well as change. In fact, it was my mother who taught me many of Judaism's crucial lessons: that there is no good life apart from good living; that no one can be complacent as long as someone, anyone

is hungry; that each generation's chase after "modernity" obscures the virtues that ought to bind them all.

I meant the column as a gesture of conciliation. But I hadn't reckoned with the bitterness of the religious divisions among Jews today. Orthodox Jews told me I was wrong to feel regrets: after all, I was in the right; it was my family, not me, that had gone astray. Non-Orthodox Jews were no kinder. One wrote *The Jewish Week* that it was a "sin" I didn't travel to Washington to celebrate Passover with my mother, brothers and sister, regardless of religious differences. Another man informed me that I belonged to "that great mass of *Baalei-Teshuvah* who learn all the petty details but miss the big picture," and snorted that I should "come down off [my] high horse." Several letter-writers complained that I left my mother "alone" on the holiday.

I suppose I was naïve to be surprised. For one thing, I had thought it would be obvious that my mother continues to preside over family Seders as in the past, still attended by most of the family, grandchildren included; I'm the odd man out at her table, not vice versa. But assumptions are part of the story; one reader wrote to ask me why I didn't simply invite my mother to attend *my* Seder, apparently never dreaming that my mother would scarcely want to leave her own Seder to attend one conducted in a fashion she considers archaic and tedious. For her I too am a ghost, and so is my religion, with its shadowy implications of bonneted grandmothers and bearded, Yiddish-speaking rabbis.

Maybe I really have to choose to treat some part of me as less than fully alive: if the religious part is not to fade out of life, then maybe I've got to oppose and devalue my own natural tastes for freedom and for community. Some part of the soul has to give way to another part. But what's left afterwards?

Maybe my unease with ghosts is perverse. Hadn't I deliberately sought out a Hasidic synagogue in Brooklyn's Borough Park (Rabbi

Rosen's) for one of my first experiences of an Orthodox Sabbath? And the place, a low-ceilinged, green-tiled room full of Yiddish-speaking youngsters with cherubic faces and side curls hanging below their jawbones, men in long coats, old-fashioned hats and unwashed beards, the odor of *gefillte* fish—wasn't it crammed with an unassimilated past? If I took it seriously, didn't that mean I viewed the scene as a tunnel through the modern world, linking me to my own ghostly history, preferring that? If not, why hadn't I just shrugged and left?

Very early that Saturday morning I awoke, in my guest bedroom in a small but comfortable Brooklyn apartment, to a vague rumble I at first took to be a distant subway. But it continued, never fading or growing, for ten or fifteen seconds. When my thoughts took clearer shape I realized what it must have been: an earth tremor, rarer in New York than, say, in Los Angeles, but not unheard of. As a modern American I had no difficulty classifying the experience. But even as the realization hardened in my mind, a small Hasidic boy in striped cotton pajamas, barefoot, with earlocks bouncing, tumbled into my room and announced, "Did you feel that? It's the *Livyosson!*" He meant the mythical sea monster, called "Leviathan" in English, whose size and power are described in the Book of Job. His father, as I gathered from our ensuing conversation, had taught him that unexplained movements of the earth resulted from the turning of the monster's tail at the bottom of some ocean.

That afternoon, the same father fussed over the vagaries of his modern (but malfunctioning) air conditioner. When the same people use electric air conditioning and blame earthquakes on sea monsters, most observers see only comedy. Why didn't I react like Kafka, who spent the Sabbath with a Hasidic community and remarked afterward, "After all, we could just as well have been with African savages"? I clearly remember how the muttering sounds of their prayers filled the air like the grainy background of an archaic photograph.

And what good is the archaic? Even if my ancestors fascinate me, they can't take the place of the living relatives and friends their dead world has shouldered aside. Too much has happened since they died. By what right do I invoke the name of their Torah in the first place? Considering the cultural differences between me and them, my religious reading almost makes me feel like a voyeur. Just to begin with, how does a religious person, today, read "the five books of Moses" with something like decency? I'm painfully conscious that I intrude into the prophet's world with neither the cautious respect of a scholar nor the complete sympathy of a fellow-believer. From a perspective thousands of years younger than Moses', I grab at him out of my own need, looking for something that gives *me* religious satisfaction. He, for instance, probably understood the Promised Land literally, the land in which God would be made manifest; for me, the vision can never be as simple or as intense. The horizon Moses contemplated just before his death has sprouted cities, armies, culture clash, and—religiously speaking—three thousand years of failure. Later Jewish sages had to sidestep the disappointing reality of the Promised Land by pushing its literal meaning far into the future. What can it mean for me now? History or vision, or what?

I think of a day near the beginning of my religious odyssey. A chilly, gray day in early fall, a wind whining through the Brooklyn streets.

The Brooklyn of my memory is a city of squat apartment buildings crowded together on slabs of asphalt and sidewalk concrete. Stores whose front windows close at night behind steel eyelids. A city in dense gray quadrangles strung together with power lines as with chicken wire. It's a week after Rosh ha-Shanah, the Jewish New Year. This has been the first New Year I spent as an Orthodox Jew. I've come here with Rabbi Rosen a few days before Yom Kippur, the Day of Atonement, to perform a ritual I've never heard of before.

Sometime during the Middle Ages a custom arose among Jews to perform a sort of sin-offering before the holy fast day, the dominant themes of which are purification and atonement. Shortly before the fast, a chicken, as it was prepared for slaughter, would be swung over the head of each penitent. A formula would be recited: This is your exchange, this is your substitute, this is your atonement. This bird is going to be killed, and you will live a happy and peaceful life.

Rabbi Rosen has told me that Orthodox Jews still observe the practice. So here I am.

A crowd of black-coated men and boys has pressed into one large Brooklyn street around an enormous truck. The huge trailer of this truck is crammed with chickens in cages. There must be thousands of them. In the chill wind young, bored-looking Hasidic men stand alongside the truck, pulling crates roughly from the trailer, removing the chickens from crates, one by one, handing the white birds to customers among the throng, who pay the young men with paper bills (which the Hasidim stuff clumsily into their pockets), then grasp each chicken by its legs and swing it upside down over their own heads. Then each man swings the chicken over the heads of his children, who stand huddled next to him in the crowd, while he recites a related formula.

This is your exchange, this is your substitute, this is your atonement. This chicken is going to be killed, and you will live a happy and peaceful life.

In the wind, white feathers fly from the crates in all directions, like clotted snowflakes. The crowd, black backs against gray, swirls around the truck, almost concealing it from my sight. Hasidic men throng it, eagerly shoving back and forth, buying their chickens, swinging them. Little girls with braided hair and bright cotton dresses, small darting boys in old-fashioned sailor suits with wide lapels and earlocks keep close to their fathers and stare up at the live chicken swinging over their heads. These are probably the only living chickens they have ever seen.

The smell of the birds, hundreds on hundreds of them, is thrown suddenly in our direction by the wind.

"I don't know about this," I mutter to Rabbi Rosen.

He turns his watery blue eyes in my direction. "What's wrong? You're scared of it?"

My pride is piqued. All right, I'll do it. The chickens are making a squalid racket, which mingles with the street-carnival sounds of all the Hasidim buying birds, reciting the ritual formula.

We near the truck, Rabbi Rosen propelling us through the crowd as if we were darting through bushes. I can see the truck clearly now. The dull, rusting side of the huge trailer is painted with the name of a Jewish meat company. Now I understand where all these chickens came from. They belong to the meat company, and are bound for a *kosher* abattoir somewhere in Brooklyn. Ordinarily they would go directly to their deaths. (Incisions made rapidly with a razor-sharp knife across the throat, according to the prescribed ritual manner, with a blade inspected by a rabbi.) Today, for our religious convenience, they are making one brief stop along the way. To be swung upside-down in the air before they are sacrificed to the slaughterer's knife. I have never before visualized just how many chickens are slaughtered in one region as small as Brooklyn, on any given day. The accumulation is staggering.

The thought of so much chicken-slaughter seems incongruous here, in this most inorganic of places. Sacrifice, however, does not. Acres of trees and grass, and all that went with them, must have been thrown to the blades and shovels to build the urban surface we're walking on now. And what about the crowd around me? For its religion, lives upon lives have been thrown away over the centuries. Now these Hasidim are prepared to sacrifice modern civilization, too, to keep the old flame burning.

Another truck is cruising by, a loudspeaker mounted on top. "Jews! Remember the poor before Yom Kippur. All Jews must remember to feed the poor." My sympathies are engaged in an unexpected direction as I look at the chickens in their cages. My particularizing vision takes in a nondescript white bird near the open back of the trailer. This bird, like the others, is destined to be a meal, not to receive one.

Another memory.

When I was very young, my parents took me to some sort of combination farm and zoo, where I was intrigued by a chicken in a cage. It waddled back and forth on fouled rags behind its prickling of wire, and I interpreted its indifferent clucking as an expression of pathos. When my mother wasn't looking I tried to touch it through the wire mesh. Jerky as a windup toy, the chicken hooked my finger savagely with its yellow beak, and my pity turned to fear and anger. I jumped back, nursing the bruised finger, and for a guilty second I enjoyed imagining the bird seized from the cage, having its neck wrung. I'm sure I was yelling my savagery out loud in what had begun as a cry of pain.

But then, a remembered parental reproof came to the surface: *How would you like it if I did that to you?* And I stopped yelling, as in a sickening lurch everything turned upside down. For at that moment I knew—that is, my young conscience told me—that I *was* that bird, that we had changed places. I was going to be punished, my evil wish had been its attack on my finger, and now I was doomed. Wasn't that what the bird and I both deserved, if we were now equally bad?

This is your exchange.

Now Rabbi Rosen is handing me a chicken he has bargained for. The same one I had noticed? Probably not, but I can't say.

"You're not scared?" he asks, smiling, still speaking in the nasal, high-pitched Hasidic way that makes him sound as if *he* could be the small child trying to play with a chicken.

"No."

I take it, thinking of that caged bird years ago, remembering my guilt. The harried-looking young Hasid at the truck hands me a wrinkled piece of paper with the Hebrew written on it. Quickly I start to swing the chicken above my head, and I recite the formula.

This is my substitute.... This is my exchange.... This is my atonement....

Is this how Jews expiate their guilt after all? Can killing possibly atone for anything? Or is atonement a kind of admission of savagery, acknowledging the animal inside? In my grip, my chicken opens its beak. I see a parody of tongue, a parched sliver of flesh.

My own tongue moves in response. This is my substitute. This is my exchange. My sacrifice... The bird seems to weigh a century in my hand.

My exchange.

For all you dead generations, I'm thinking, whose rituals didn't save you from fiercer predators. For you I enact your ritual of death. My substitute, my sacrifice. For your senseless sufferings, this senseless ceremony.

Swinging the bird, I repeat the formula a third and final time.

Now I hand the chicken back to one of the Hasidic youths and watch it being stuffed into its nameless cage.

And as I leave the scene quickly, through the overpowering chicken-smell, a surprising feeling rises to the surface: *relief.* It's as if I'd lost my virginity. Borrowing the savage anonymity of ritual, I came a step closer to the shaping forces of my past. It isn't a pretty feeling. But maybe atonement isn't meant to be pretty?

CHAPTER TWENTY-TWO

I want to devote a few words here to Rabbi Laszlo Berkowitz, the first clergyman of whom I have any clear memory.

Rabbi Berkowitz presided over the first Sabbath services I ever attended, when I was a young boy in Northern Virginia. He was (and is) a Reform rabbi, but when I was young I had no idea there was more than one kind of Jewish denomination. So I knew him simply as "the rabbi," and my family moved away from Washington before I was old enough to have sharpened my use of the word.

I knew Rabbi Berkowitz again when I was in high school, after my family returned to the Washington area in time for Watergate and my parents' divorce; I remember the startling apparition of his tanned face and short, stocky body in a striped knit shirt outside our door one Sunday afternoon, clutching, of all things, a tennis racquet. He had shown up to meet my father for a friendly game.

I laughed behind my hand at Rabbi Berkowitz's sermons during the atheist heyday of my college years, whenever my mother pressured me into visiting his synagogue during my visits home. Yet, years later, when I began to think seriously about Judaism, Rabbi Berkowitz and I had a talk about my idea of studying for the rabbinate, of all things. Then I became Orthodox and didn't see him for a long time.

For me, his round, boyish face and Hungarian accent defined the word "rabbi" at an age when I was just old enough to learn that words could be detached from people—that they were not just friendly and familiar names for particular grownups. Yet the relationship of the word "rabbi" to Laszlo Berkowitz has undergone a particularly violent transformation in my own mind. In fact, there was a time when, due to my own religious transformations, I refused to believe that Rabbi Berkowitz was actually a rabbi at all.

I really know embarrassingly little about Rabbi Berkowitz's life. He was born and grew up in the Carpathian Mountains, in Hungary, along with about half a million other Jews, eighty percent of whom would perish in the final year of the Second World War. He often mentioned that he grew up only a short distance from Sighet, the town in which Elie Wiesel was born. (He was also very close in age to Wiesel.) He was a farm boy and he must have looked it: compact, tanned, the face broad-boned. He has retained those features in adulthood; only the eyes and lips suggest refinement, which his modesty prevents from taking the form of hauteur.

Like many Holocaust survivors, he rarely talks about his wartime experiences, and so the years between 1940 and 1945 are an almost impenetrable veil over his early life. Still, I've heard him tell enough stories about his boyhood (he was in his teens when the war broke out) to know that he was good-naturedly ignorant of most matters not immediately useful to him. He says that he was not very serious about religion either. In one story I remember, he sat with other boys in the back of the crowded synagogue toward the end of holiday prayers. At that point in the service the men of priestly descent (*kohanim*, as they are called in Hebrew) would stand in front of the congregation chanting a special blessing, their hands outstretched in a position used only for that purpose. It was customary not to look at the men's hands when they did this. But Laszlo and his bored friends had decided among themselves to challenge custom and see just how it was that the priests held their fingers during the special blessing.

"Everybody had told us," said Rabbi Berkowitz to a tenth-grade Sunday school class in which I was a student, rubbing his slightly pudgy palms together in the pleasure of storytelling, "that if you looked at their hands during the blessing, you'd go blind! So all the men in the synagogue closed their eyes—some even turned around backwards. But we boys, one at a time, we stole a peek at those priests' hands."

And?

"They held out their fingers like this"—he divided the fingers of one hand like Spock in *Star Trek*, then smiled boyishly. "And none of us went blind."

Rabbi Berkowitz was just as curious about Germans as he had been in the matter of forbidden fingers. Hearing that German soldiers were to be seen "in the city" (Budapest? Warsaw?) he says he got on a city-bound bus in order to get a look at a few. This would have been in the spring of 1944, just when the first large-scale deportations of Hungarian Jews to the concentration camps were taking place. He knew nothing about the deportations, though. Like nearly all Jews in the mountain country, he was blissfully ignorant of the network of death factories that had been assembled on the other side of the Polish border. German soldiers were merely exotic creatures to him.

So when a German officer boarded his bus and asked if there were any Jews aboard, he naïvely volunteered. Then he went with the officer for a short drive that led to a roundup that led to a ghetto, that led to a cattle car that led, ultimately, to Auschwitz.

After that, what I know, or think I know, are stories that come mostly from a time at the end of the war, and most of the substance is really from my father, who may have heard more of Rabbi Berkowitz's stories than I have.

Anyway, the story goes something like this. As I've said, Laszlo was a farm boy. So were his friends, who seem to have been a tough and resourceful bunch. Having heard around the end of 1944 (on Auschwitz's secret shortwave radio) that the Germans were desperate for workers to man factories for war *materiel*, a few of them, Laszlo included, approached a guard and lied about their prewar mechanical experience. They told him they used to build automobiles. Maybe they'd be useful somewhere, they suggested vaguely.

The guard took the bait. He brought the boys to an officer. I'm not sure what the boys hoped to gain from the ruse. Their mechanical ignorance would have doomed them if they had actually reached their destinations in Germany. But getting shipped out would buy them precious time—even a few days might save their lives from the murder machinery, which was running at full tilt in the last months of the war. Maybe they hoped dimly that the war would end before they reached Berlin. In any case, the German officer quizzed them by showing them a part of a carburetor and asking one of the boys to identify it. The boy brazened his way through by claiming he could only name it in Hungarian, which he knew the officer did not speak. Asked to be specific, he said solemnly, "It's a radish."

The officer, expressionless, turned to another boy and showed him another engine part.

"And you, what's this called?"

"A celery."

The boys named another part "potato" and somehow or other managed to convince the officer they knew what they were talking about. Laszlo Berkowitz was one of several put on trains and sent somewhere inside Germany to repair Nazi tanks.

The train ride was a nightmare. It was bitter cold. There was no food or sanitation. Trapped in windowless train cars, the prisoners could hear the Allied bombs pounding Germany. Maybe the Allies would save them all. Or maybe they'd just kill them. Or the Germans would. Somewhere during the journey the future Rabbi Berkowitz's train was stopped by invading American soldiers. They captured the German crew and ripped open the doors. Young Laszlo was one of the prisoners who stumbled out.

That experience changed his life. His rare remarks about it suggest that his survival of Hitler's war made his religious identity suddenly loom in his mind as something both precarious and precious—two things it had never been to him when he was a child in a Hasidic village. That was why he became a rabbi, and why (I suppose) it was fitting that Rabbi Berkowitz introduced me to a religious culture that, throughout my early life, I thought of as virtually defined by its hazards. As late as the seventh grade (in Atlanta, Georgia) I was the subject of a running class joke: someone would toss a penny in my direction, apparently expecting me to reach down and grab for it. I didn't. But that never damped down the joke. As soon as the penny landed somewhere in my vicinity, everybody would laugh uproariously. And I would remember that I was a Jew.

I suppose it was natural that Rabbi Berkowitz, who belonged to the Reform movement, disapproved of my new-found Orthodoxy. But his attitude bothered me. Because I'd known him for so many years his disapproval seemed to pull away a piece of my self-definition.

True, by the time Rabbi Berkowitz had a chance to react to my new beliefs, my *yeshiva* classmates had led me to expect the worst from any Reform clergyman. They even compared Reform to Nazism: "The Germans only attacked Jewish bodies," said one of my fellow students at Ohr Somayach, in what was to become a familiar refrain, "but anti-Orthodox Judaism attacks the Jewish soul."

But a letter from my mother indicating that Rabbi Berkowitz wanted to "talk" to me—received at Ohr Somayach during the winter of my most intense study there—still felt like an attack from behind. I could pretty well picture what had happened. My mother had called Rabbi Berkowitz and told him I'd gone off the deep end. Rabbi Berkowitz, in his ponderous way, would doubtless have expressed his sympathy. Which had prompted my mother to implore him to intercede with me, to explain to me that one could be Jewish without being Orthodox. Naturally (with what suave reasonableness, what mellifluous concern!) he had agreed to make use of his rabbinic knowledge, his Hasidic childhood, and his long acquaintance with me in an effort to save me from fanaticism.

I've said that denunciations of the Reform rabbinate by my Ohr Somayach classmates had become a familiar refrain by then. Well, so had the disapproving comments about my new-found Orthodoxy by most of the non-Orthodox Jews I knew. Mind you, as a product of Reform education, I felt that I had a right to make a few complaints, myself, about all the depths of the Jewish tradition that had never been shared with me until I discovered them for myself. Perhaps Reform Judaism, I thought, ought to be making some apologies. But when non-Orthodox Jews offered their opinions of my religious change, I did not find them the least bit apologetic or defensive. Quite the opposite. Jews with little or no Jewish education were convinced they knew exactly how to critique Orthodoxy, and freely did so to my face, often with ridiculous results.

(Just for instance: no fewer than three acquaintances told me that Orthodox dietary laws were "obviously" rendered obsolete by refrigeration. This is a canard that fifteen minutes with an English translation of *The Code of Jewish Law,* a text published over a century ago, can easily dispel. Much of the detailed dietary legislation in the Torah and Talmud manifestly has nothing to do with health risks. Pork is safe if well cooked. Street vendors in China, following traditions thousands of years old, do not sell crabs or lobsters unless they are still moving. I do not know of any scholar well informed about the Jewish dietary laws, or indeed about the history of any such laws, who confuses them with hygienic regulation. But the notion still makes its rounds in otherwise well-educated Jewish families.)

Of course I didn't expect every Jew to agree with me. But I did expect, at first, some respect for the choice I had made and for the serious educational commitment into which that choice had naturally led. I was wrong.

And what made this hardest to bear was the hypocrisy involved, as I saw it—the way the disapproval seemed so clearly at odds with the principles of the disapprovers themselves. Every liberal-minded, non-Orthodox Jew I knew made it a point of honor to defend the right of Jews to be distinct from other Americans. And they all bristled with indignation about Christian missionaries "preying on" young Jews. Yet from my perch at Ohr Somayach, I couldn't help finding their position curiously inconsistent. I mean, if you're willing to abandon all the traditional strictures that differentiate

Jews from their neighbors, why go on insisting on your right to be distinct? If your children know (and care) so little about their religion that they're attracted to Christmas trees and Easter wreaths, why attack non-Jews (or the public schools) for encouraging them in that direction? If violating the Sabbath, once the most jealously guarded of Jewish holidays, doesn't bother you, why should a missionary? In opposing Orthodoxy, it seemed to me, these liberal Jews were really trying to paper over their own religious contradictions.

Any American Protestant of normal intelligence (I told myself) could easily recognize that most of the Reform Jewish liturgy is based on the structure of Protestant worship; that Reform theology owes at least as much to Göttingen as to the Talmud; that Reform's political activism makes more of the First Amendment than the Torah; and that even Reform's recent turn toward "traditionalism" is driven by a contemporary American Christian movement in the same direction. No less an authority than Irving Howe has lamented that Reform Judaism involves "a religious practice indulged in with lukewarm formalism and little genuine faith." The newly-religious Jews at Ohr Somayach certainly knew all this, and they knew full well that from the traditional Orthodox perspective Reform's version of Judaism was nearly as objectionable as the Protestantism which nourished it. More to the point, Rabbi Berkowitz himself, given his Hasidic upbringing, should know this too.

So who did *he* think he was, instructing *me* in Judaism?

I wish I could say I reached this position dispassionately. I didn't, of course. It had hurt to find myself on the outs with old friends. And it hurt, too, to find myself in opposition to so many Jews…about Judaism. The same Jews who would have been outraged about the Christmas carols sung in my Atlanta high school now looked askance at me for eating *kosher* food. The same Jewish friends who would have condemned any critical remark aimed at a Sikh or a Hindu openly attacked my fledgling Sabbath observance. One B.T. after another has told me similar stories: of "tolerant" friends accusing them of causing anti-Semitism; of relatives suddenly dragging up accusations against Orthodox ancestors, as if a *yarmulke* invited unlimited guilt by association; of parents who winked at intermarriages but complained that their observant children's insistence on Jewish dietary laws "divided" Jewish families.

Then too, behind my bitterness, there lurked a certain perverse pleasure. The liberal Jewish culture in which I was raised was notorious for cherishing a strong sense of collective guilt over the "advantages" we enjoyed. Virtue lay in suffering, or at least in not enjoying good things with an easy conscience. So, in a masochistic sort of way, one charm of Orthodoxy for me was the unfamiliar taste of my own victimization. Running the gauntlet of rejection by liberal friends was exactly what the doctor ordered for an ex-liberal longing to escape, once and for all, the old haunting sense of unearned ease.

Anyway, Rabbi Berkowitz's dislike of his own Hungarian Hasidic roots—a dislike that oozed from his voice as we talked the matter over soon afterward—was hardly, for me, the gentle persuasion my mother had hoped it would be. Just the opposite: it hardened my resolve to be what he disdained. After all, I wanted my Judaism to be *for* something, and it seemed to me he could only talk about what he was against, and had done so for as long as I could remember.

"People I grew up with believed in witches," he told me. "Do you?"

"Of course not," I told him. I don't even remember where, or exactly how, this conversation took place. By phone, it must have been. "But why do you compare me with people you grew up with?"

"Witches are in the Talmud. You know that?"

I didn't answer. He went on: "The Orthodox believe in them. But they don't believe that I'm a Jew. Eh?" His accent struck a vowel for the word "Jew" I could not quite define, somewhere between "ooh" and "ow." He had always said "Jew" like that, and once upon a time, its exotic timbre in his mouth had seemed intriguingly to me like a hint of the dim and circuitous history behind the word.

"I want you to know," he said, "I was born a Jew, I grew up speaking Yiddish, I was in the camps." His voice was rising a little. "And I became a rabbi. I read Jewish books every day and night. I speak

Hebrew. Yiddish, too. If I'm not a Jew, then nobody is a Jew. I don't mind if someone wants to practice Judaism in a traditional way, you understand? The problem with the Orthodox is, they make it the *only* way. No one else counts."

I was ready for that one. "There's one set of rules for playing basketball, isn't there? One set of rules for being elected President of the United States?"

"Hm? And so?" His tone suggested that he had heard this before, and wasn't terribly impressed with the line of argument. But I wasn't going to deny myself the pleasure of telling him off.

"No one complains of tyranny when people who play basketball insist on consistency in the rules. No one screams 'dogma' or 'dictatorship' if someone can't get a place on the ballot because he didn't meet the legal requirements. You say you 'don't mind' if someone wants to observe traditional Judaism the traditional way. I don't mind if someone else wants"—(I was just tactful enough not to say "you want")—"to formulate his own approach to Judaism, either. Only, he should call things by their right names and not pretend he's practicing Judaism when he's really rejected the rules that define it. And he shouldn't complain when people who *are* practicing it object to his sharing the name with them."

He sighed. "You talk as though there were only one set of rules. But how can you know that? Or anybody?"

"Who do I have to be?" I said. And with that the conversation ended.

In the end, I managed to disappoint members of the Orthodox community as surely as I disappointed Rabbi Berkowitz that day, though for different reasons. In fact, the first time I can remember feeling a guilty sense of imposture over my new religion involved the very generous, very Orthodox Laibel Katz, my regular Sabbath host for a year or more. And it involved my decision to quit my job and attend a *yeshiva*, a decision of which Laibel heartily approved.

The trouble was, he approved of it too much. Or maybe I had made the decision too late in life to accept his view of it. I was already thirty, too old for romance, and Laibel's view of it was incurably romantic. One late, sticky Friday night the summer before I left for Ohr Somayach, he walked with me out of his apartment and through a heavy door into the green concrete-and-cinderblock cage of the stairwell—through which I was about to descend seven floors to street level on foot, this being the Sabbath, when elevators were forbidden. But I paused: Laibel obviously had something to say.

"You'll be going to *yeshiva* soon," he began. Laibel was no taller than I, but his added age, I suppose, lent some naturalness to his fatherly tone. "I'm excited for you. I've seen other young men start to learn in *yeshiva*, but you have potential that is extraordinary. Extraordinary." He smiled, and words came out that would have suited someone half his age: "When you come back, I don't think I'll *recognize* you! You'll be changed, totally, a different person."

His rapture expressed itself in more than a smile. He had an urgent way of leaning forward and of wrapping his syllables in his outgoing breath.

"Laibel," I said, instinctively drawing back a bit—"Laibel, don't be disappointed if I don't change as much as you imagine."

"Oh, you'll change! Torah changes a person." With relish, he told me the Talmudic story of how Rabbi Yochanan had persuaded a notorious outlaw named Shimon ben Lakish to study Torah with him, with the eventual result that Shimon became a rabbi himself, married Yochanan's sister and lived a life of exacting piety. "Torah makes you a different person," he said.

"But"—and here the edge of something like panic sliced the outer reaches of my consciousness—"if I *don't* become a different person? You won't be disappointed, will you?"

Laibel brushed the question aside. "I'm not in doubt," he said.

Years later, long since away from *yeshiva*, I had to write Laibel a letter telling him that I was out of a job, living on unemployment insurance, and that my creative energy had focused on writing a screenplay. I never received a reply to the letter and never quite had the nerve to write another one. Maybe Laibel's silence didn't carry the ominous message my own feelings read into it. But I was acutely conscious that Laibel—who wouldn't dream of allowing his children to watch a film (lest they be exposed to "secular influences")—could not possibly understand how I could concentrate my energy on writing for the cinema instead of studying the Talmud. More, I understood that for Laibel, anyone who called himself an Orthodox Jew, and who lost his job while writing for the heretical entertainment media, was probably suffering well-deserved punishment. I could almost hear him asking me, his eyes lowered in the keenness of his disappointment, "You don't have a job, and you can't find anything better to do with your time than working for the *movies*?" Yet I couldn't force myself to lie to him, to tell him that I was sustained in my hard times by immersing myself in the study of Jewish law, though I knew that was what the "different person" he'd so wanted me to be would have written.

Is disappointing people a necessary part of religious growth? Sharing religious convictions with other people forges a special kind of intimacy—almost like falling in love. And as in love, changing one's mind after the intimacy is established entails a certain sort of betrayal. But how can I avoid it? Isn't it odd that so many people one meets, and needs, along the way seem to be frozen at a certain stage of one's own development, so that, in the end, leaving them behind is as hurtful and confusing as the beginning of the journey was? Do we religious types ever learn how to believe without promising, or how to touch someone else's belief without soiling it?

Well, of course, I was a B.T. I'd been told that often enough. Other Orthodox Jews see a B.T. as a different sort of creature from themselves: "Well, that's a B.T. for you."

And they're right, in certain ways. For instance, I see now that turning to an entirely new community as an adult, a community with unfamiliar values and priorities, is like being a child again. And a B.T.'s need for idealization, to make heroes of people in that new world, competes with a child's, if it doesn't actually exceed it. Which means that the disappointments reality brings in its tow can be correspondingly sharp. "By 'the Orthodoxy I believed in,'" writes ex-B.T. Michael Graubart Levin,

> I meant a sort of fantasy-religion world, a place where people somehow could rise above all the faults attendant to being human, a place where people thought of nothing but God and Judaism and each other's feelings all day long.

Levin isn't alone: many religious Jews seem permanently caught in such a childish vision of their faith. But who can blame them, when so much of religion appeals to elemental needs and therefore to the world-view of the child each one of us carries? And if you do happen to outgrow that juvenile vision, what then?

Unlike Levin, I was not disappointed by the meticulous, detailed analysis of the Talmud that made up most of the curriculum at Ohr Somayach. But I was let down by the specifically moral fare, which I studied with an excitable fellow I will call Eliyahu.

Most study in *yeshiva* is carried on outside a formal classroom setting, by pairs of students called *chavrusas*. Eliyahu was my *chavrusa* for the study known as *mussar*. This was a program developed in Russian *yeshivas* in the nineteenth century in order to stress ethical teaching and character development in Jewish education, and to act as a counterweight to what the founders saw as an excessively abstract Talmudic emphasis in other schools.

The ethical emphasis of *mussar* was a relief in some ways, after dry hours of legalism, but its gloomy stringency was more often oppressive than enlightening. Eliyahu and I would read aloud cautionary phrases gleaned from the Talmud, such as: "If one departs from Torah, fire consumes him!" We would repeat these phrases over and over. An old hand, Eliyahu would repeat them with increasing fervor, swaying back and forth from the waist, closing his eyes, grimacing, his voice rising, in a hypnotic way I found unsettling. I tried to imitate him in this sort of rhetorical scare tactic. But I was too self-conscious for the incantations to do their work."You'll get it after a while," Eliyahu assured me. "I've been at it a long time and I'm just starting to get it."

Eliyahu told me a joke intended to make his point: "Two people are studying *mussar* together." He began rapidly swaying back and forth, making the gestures his characters made as he told the joke. "One of them strikes himself in the chest and yells, 'I'm a *gor nisht* [a nothing]!' The other one strikes himself in the chest and yells back, 'I'm a *gor nisht*!' [*Whack*, went Eliyahu's palm against his chest.] The first one whacks himself harder and yells again, 'I'm a *gor nisht*!' [*Whack*.] His partner does the same thing. [Louder and louder.] After a while a third person comes up and sits down. He watches them. Then he hits himself in the chest and yells, 'I'm a *gor nisht*!' [A big *whack*.] Both of the others drop what they're doing. One of them says, 'You just got here, and you think you can be a *gor nisht* already?'"

When I pointed out that the joke might be taken as a satire on his beloved *mussar*, Eliyahu sobered at once. "I don't make jokes about *mussar*," he said.

Eliyahu didn't, in fact, make jokes about many things. Not that he was gloomy. He was a high-strung, pepped-up, fast-talking short kid barely twenty years old, with close-cropped curly hair, an active upper lip, and the excessive (if repressed) sexual energy of late adolescence still oozing from every pious pore. It seemed he had turned this energy against himself, in what may have been the manner of pious young men in earlier generations, but more likely was the manner of modern B.T.s who have tasted license and now yearn to suppress it. Looking at his nervous, over-eager face made me think of Saul Bellow's phrase about the "urgency of dogs with their first erections." Except that with Eliyahu, the urgency was something more chronic and less poignant than what Bellow had in mind. Though still a trifle puppyish.

It had a lot to do, no doubt, with the endless mantras Eliyahu and I recited that thundered about the evil of physical desires.

As dualists, most *mussar* thinkers (to borrow a line from Harold Bloom) picture soul and body locked in a permanent wrestling match. Their teaching crackled with a humorless *agon* I found literally exhausting. Eliyahu found it exhausting too, but he seemed to like the fatigue, almost as though *mussar* tired him enough to deplete the physical tension (sexual tension too, I assume) that would otherwise have absorbed him.

"I used to sell electronics," he said to me during one break in our studying, rocking in his seat and snapping short, surprisingly delicate fingers. "It's a good thing I'm out of that business. Otherwise I might have got addicted: it's like a drug. Full of highs – like sex, almost."

"Really?"

He looked at me as if daring me to doubt him. And as if to drive home the sexual point, he told me about the seductive patter lavished on perfect strangers with a view to gaining their confidence; the sense of triumph over the customer's better judgment when a sale was consummated. He didn't say, "I got a virgin into bed." He did say, "I screwed a lot of towel-heads, doing those sales."

"Towel-heads?"

"Sikhs. From India. A lot of them are in electronics around here, for some reason. They wear towels around their heads." He cocked his own bantam head. "I *screwed* them. I mean, who are they, why should *they* sell to *our women*?" Actually, he had said, "to Americans."

Eliyahu's talk contrasted oddly with our reading. From the Jewish books we studied, it seemed that the last two hundred years had seen a narrowing of the Orthodox perspective on physical pleasure—almost as if in reaction against the great expansion of thought outside the ghettos during the same period.

There was the work of my partner's namesake, Rabbi Eliyahu Lopian, for instance, who died in Israel in 1970. His published writings (very popular in *yeshiva* circles) are permeated with a horror of lust that would have done credit to Jonathan Edwards. Rabbi Lopian threatens young men who masturbate with the loss of eternal life. He even warns his readers that an oversexed *husband*—though his chaste copulation might be safely within the limits of the law—will "become ill and weak" as a penalty for his indulgence.

What I found most extraordinary was Rabbi Lopian's promotion of a view of good and evil that most people, other than the Orthodox, would hardly associate with Judaism at all, since it actually equates pleasure with sin, Christian-fashion:

> An evil person's soul is one whose only desire is for bodily pleasures. That is, he does not commit any sins, rather he satisfies all the desires of his body with passion and relish. He also engages in the service of his Creator, but without desire.…

This is very far from the Talmudic view that virtue consists in the observance of God's law. Yes, rabbinic law imposes a certain discipline on diet and sexual behavior; but it never denies pleasure outright. Under Rabbi Lopian's approach, even one whose observance of the law is so strict that he commits no sins at all—and actually "serves his Creator" to boot—is still "evil," if he also "desires" to satisfy himself! Rabbi Lopian thus assumes a radical opposition between God and ego unknown to the Talmud. According to him, one's physical desires are evil *in themselves*, not only when they deflect the individual from the right path; they are evil simply because they form the seat of "passion and relish," while goodness proceeds exclusively from "the fear of heaven"— conceptualized by Rabbi Lopian as the rejection of pleasure. Rounding out this grim view of human nature is Rabbi Lopian's conviction that the "simple fear of bodily punishment" is the only thing that can fend off "our baser natures which lust after thievery and licentiousness."

Eliyahu's opinion about all this?

"We're soft, you know? We grew up with everyone telling us, 'I'm okay, you're okay.' We need to be slapped in the face even harder than they did in Russia a hundred years ago." To make his point, he raised his face by gripping his cropped pate with the fingers of his left hand, and slapped himself across the face with the right, keeping his smiling stare fixed on me.

Eliyahu was particularly fond of the work of the late Rabbi Yisroel Meir Kagan, author of the single most influential guidebook to contemporary Jewish law in Ashkenazic *yeshiva* circles. I knew Rabbi Kagan to have been a gentle and just man, famed for countless acts of charity. But that only made his harsh language more startling in a passage like this one, denouncing a small concession to mainstream taste in dress:

> Inflation grows daily, and taxes have risen greatly…. The primary reason for this is…an exposed area in a part of a woman's body that should be covered…In our sinful times such exposure has become commonplace. For the Evil Inclination induces women to completely bare their hair and their arms…. This was the wicked Balaam's plan, for he talked the women of Moab into undressing in order to lead the Jews into sin.

The strangest thing in this outburst is the assumption that the women who affect these "disgusting modern fashions," as Rabbi Kagan calls them elsewhere, are actively plotting to "lead the Jews [that is, men] into sin." I suggested to Eliyahu that no woman has ever walked around in short sleeves in the hope of being raped. But he rejected this as a *non sequitur*. It doesn't matter, he said, what the women *intended* when they dressed as they did. The real point was the sinister and ever-present Deceiver, termed the "Evil Inclination" by Rabbi Kagan, working through impressionable females in order to weaken Jewish men's chastity. From the perspective of such people, women can scarcely exist at all, except as temptresses fired by the recesses of male imaginations. Apparently it never occurred to Rabbi Kagan (or to Eliyahu) that women might just get hot in long sleeves and head coverings. Or that this refusal by rabbis to recognize the flesh-and-blood reality of the women they feared might itself feed immorality, in the form of cruelty, misogyny, callousness.

I got a further clue to this sort of thinking in Denver, Colorado, when I happened to meet an Orthodox Jew who, like me, had returned to the tradition as an adult. He had several small children, and surprised me by saying emphatically that he wanted them in single-sex classes even in the earliest grades.

Were there enough Orthodox Jews in Denver who were sufficiently right-wing to make this feasible? I asked him.

"We can make it work," he said, shrugging, then added, "It's so essential."

"But wouldn't a boys-only first grade be going a little far?"

"At one time, it probably would have been," he admitted. "But look around you. This country is absolutely rotten with immorality. Licentiousness is the number-one sin of this culture. I tell you"—he glanced anxiously around at the walls of the synagogue in which we were standing, as if they were stretched-thin tissues through which he could almost see the outlines of lust straining to burst through—"if we don't protect the purity of our children from the very beginning, they're going to be poisoned. And then it will be too late."

Orthodoxy traditionally looks at evil as a contamination from *out there*: an invasion of outsiders and their ways. Which may help to explain Orthodoxy's growing popularity in today's America. Like the Denver Jew who thought he saw lust threatening his children from outside the protective synagogue walls, many Americans now see their culture as a scarce resource. That's nothing new to the Orthodox. As recently as 1985, in a book called *The Renaissance of the Torah Jew*, Rabbi Saul Bernstein could temper his delight at the conversion of so many formerly non-Orthodox Jews with a cautionary note about their world of origin and its presumed power over the converts' children: "The traditional sphere is by no means immune to the dangers that abound.... Its environment is flawed, its composition a makeshift. The process of transmitting Torah commitment to the upcoming generations is yet far from full potency."

Over the years since my conversion, I've grown used to hearing Orthodox Jews talk this way about the "outside world." "I'm there," a diamond-dealing Hasid told me about going to work in the middle of Manhattan, "but I'm not part of it."

He had severe features, a wild tufted beard, a white shirt buttoned to the Adam's apple. Oddly, his dogma seemed all the more firmly rooted in his mind because it was belied (as I knew) by much of his actual conduct. I had once observed him walking down 42nd Street literally arm in arm with a Puerto Rican trader. But his abstract separation from "the world" had sucked the flesh and blood from such memories.

I suspect there's a lot more than bigotry in the appeal to so many people of Judaism's exile-haunted view of things. At a time when anomie seems almost universal, it's intriguing to know that ancient Jewish law codifies rootlessness into a paradoxically secure theological system: for instance, by refusing to put the last touches on a house he builds (a requirement of the *halachah*), the traditional Jew symbolizes not only the temporariness of a dwelling outside the Holy Land but also the deeper incompleteness of the world itself, the imperfect physical world of bricks and mortar, and thus our inherently unstable relationship with that world. Even history is in exile from an Edenic state that is to be revisited only in Messianic times.

The exile motif has the added value of protecting religious idealism. Much of the rabbinic law cannot, by its own terms, be enacted until the Redeemer ushers the Jews into the Promised Land. Therefore, though the law has manifestly not brought about perfection, it cannot be judged a failure. That's why no less hardheaded a thinker than Maimonides could confidently predict that with the full divine law in place, hunger, crime, strife and warfare would be more or less eliminated. These things plagued us, he thought, only because we couldn't yet enforce the Torah—as we were sure to do, after the coming of the Messiah.

So for the Jews, at least, exile has become a way of protecting tradition from its own flaws, a process that keeps the tradition in its vital mediating position between imperfection and ideal.

Now that I think of it, I rather believe that Rabbi Berkowitz (the Reform rabbi for whom I once felt such contempt) turned his own exile into a source of religion, too. In his case, I mean the exile from his own Hasidic background—a sort of home he lost irrevocably to the Nazis, and to which, time after time, he feels himself irresistibly and impossibly called. During one Yom Kippur sermon at his own synagogue, quite unexpectedly, Rabbi Berkowitz began to sing a snatch of a Yiddish song. I had never heard him speak Yiddish. He said he had sung this song in the concentration camps with his friends to keep up their spirits.

"Don't ever say it's the end..."

That was how the song started. He sang only a few words, then stared around at the comfortable, well-fed American faces that filled the sanctuary. Maybe he had never before stumbled upon this particular memory. Maybe the memories of those gray faces and shaved heads (how many of them had been among the boys who had once stolen peeks at the fingers of the priests?) could not flame out to full life in that setting. Rabbi Berkowitz didn't say. But suddenly he was clearly a long way from home. He sat down without singing more of the song. I remember thinking that he was getting old at the time, but at that moment he did not look old.

I may have looked the same way when the crowd recited *kaddish* at a ceremony for the victims of Babi Yar at Constitution Hall.

CHAPTER TWENTY-THREE

Rabbi Noah Weinberg sailed from New York in 1953 ... determined to turn world Jewry away from assimilation and back to Jewish pride... [T]he formula worked... Aish HaTorah students are young men and women who have pursued successful careers in medicine, business, law, education and the arts—and are now discovering their connection to the Jewish people.

— From "About Aish HaTorah," describing one of the world's largest schools for newly-Orthodox Jews

Ohr Somayach ... has stimulated and motivated thousands of people to reconnect with their tradition and heritage.

— From a letter by Prime Minister Benjamin Netanyahu

Mark Twain once ridiculed a missionary by the name of "Brother J.J." who had declared that China would soon be entirely Christianized, inasmuch as hundreds of converts were being made there daily. To which Twain retorted that, on any given day, at least ten times as many new "pagans" were being born in China as the number who turned Christian. So much for Brother J.J.

The logic of missionary enthusiasm dies hard. I've been exposed time and again to the claim that today's Jewish youth is undergoing a "revolution" that is "turning world Jewry away from assimilation and back to Jewish pride," to quote the promotional literature of

one *yeshiva* for the newly-Orthodox. That sort of claim has registered in the mainstream media as well.

But how true is it? For all the unmistakable rightward drift of
American religion, I suspect that any argument that Judaism today
is witnessing a pro-Orthodox revolution invites Twain's retort of
a century ago. Even Rabbi Noah Weinberg, the founder of Aish
HaTorah (one of the largest of the newly-Orthodox *yeshivas*), says
that "we're losing 20,000 Jewish kids each year through assimilation," and he does not say that he (or anyone else) has reclaimed
a similar number annually for the religious fold. One prominent
Orthodox organization sets the estimate higher still, at a "loss" of
50,000 Jews a year, in America alone. These figures sound exaggerated, but a much smaller one would still pack a powerful punch
against the revolutionary claims sometimes made for schools like
Rabbi Weinberg's.

Yes, the fact that a few hundred or even a few thousand Jews pass
through newly-Orthodox schools yearly is certainly significant. But
this has to be judged against the larger pattern of Jewish religious
decline. In a sense, the phenomenon of "return" itself is indebted
to the decline. One successful headline for Aish HaTorah promotional literature was "The Vanishing Jew" (a problem for which it
offered itself, unsurprisingly, as the antidote). Judaism cannot be
vanishing and in full flower at the same time.

Besides, for the Orthodox "revolution" to be real, it must be
fully embraced by Orthodoxy. And that hasn't really happened yet,
notwithstanding many appearances to the contrary. It's true that
the Orthodox community spends a great deal of money to educate
B.T.s like me, and welcomes many of them into its missionary indus-
try once their own proselytism is complete. It's also true that today's
Orthodox community proudly adduces the masses of converts as a
proof of its claim to timeless truth.

But these facts reflect a community status for the returnees that
is much more complicated than it seems to be at first glance. One
reason the Orthodox community encourages missionary zeal in
B.T.s is precisely that the community doesn't trust them: such zeal

functions as a proof of loyalty, a necessary *auto-da-fé*. Nor should one attach the wrong significance to the intensity of such enthusiasm among the B.T.s themselves. The truth is that B.T.s will inevitably tend toward extremes in their devotion, because if the purpose of the devotion is to win full acceptance, then it must, like an addiction, build on itself indefinitely, for nothing B.T.s can do will ever completely win the community over.

If you doubt this, you might want to look at a (typical) tract printed by a prominent Orthodox *yeshiva* in Cleveland, which reveals what B.T.s are up against when they try to impress their new coreligionists. This tract declares that one who "has rejected a materialistic lifestyle [anything outside the Orthodox world is 'materialistic'] ... to devote himself to Torah"—in other words, a B.T.—is bound to be unstable in his religion, permanently subject to "infatuation with his past lifestyle ... so overwhelmingly intense that nothing short of zealousness will protect him from reverting back."

This claim (never denied, to my knowledge, by any Orthodox institution) sheds important light on the well-publicized campaigns of many B.T.s to attract others to Orthodoxy. Their "zealousness" is not disinterested and not a pure expression of faith. It is a part of their own social survival. It results from the skepticism of the religious community, which continually suspects the B.T.s of "reverting back"—a community that must constantly be appeased by B.T.s trying to find their own place in Orthodox institutions. From the Orthodox perspective, B.T.s must "pounce upon anything that might disturb the tranquility of their Torah lives" (to quote the just-mentioned pamphlet again) lest they appear to be returning to their "past lifestyle."

So it is not surprising to learn (from Janet Aviad's *Return to Judaism*) that in Israel, "baalei teshuvah have appeared at the head of demonstrations in two different contexts *mustered by their teachers for the occasions*" [emphasis mine]. Though political demonstrations on Jewish issues are naturally less common in the United States than in Israel, American B.T.s are similarly "mustered" to support missionary causes among other, non-Orthodox Jews. Directly or indirectly, in all these activities they have been responding to community pressure designed to test their allegiance. They are not participating as equals.

True, B.T.s often stress their personal commitment to missionary work, but significantly, even when the words are their own, the language they use often isn't. Some typical comments by B.T.s about proselytizing other Jews, quoted in Aviad's study, include revealing phrases:

> Baalei teshuvah know the language, the claims, the slogans. They know the brainwashing of the media, they passed along the whole way.... Because of the past, *and although they wish to forget it,* baalei teshuvah can show the way to others.

> We can explain ourselves better [than the born Orthodox] because *we know all in life* and have found that the Torah is the true path in life for all Jews.

> We can show...that there is a constant stream from the secular—*which lacks all spiritual challenge*—to the religious camp.

People fascinated by tradition are unlikely to "wish to forget" their own pasts, unless of course their new community finds those pasts unassimilable. No B.T. I know really believes his nonreligious past encompasses "all in life" outside Orthodoxy—but this is the way born-Orthodox Jews tend to view the newcomers, whose backgrounds seem vastly more exotic to the Orthodox community than to the B.T.s themselves. Again, a B.T. could hardly deny a spiritual challenge to the culture in which he first experienced his own religious stirrings. Evidently the B.T.s have learned to describe their own religious lives, even their own religious identities, in terms and phrases coined by their born-Orthodox neighbors. That's a decision that reflects their knowledge of their own tenuous position vis-à-vis their religious community.

Why do B.T.s face such misgivings from the rest of the Orthodox? Partly, no doubt, they face the uncertainty that people born into an isolationist community naturally feel toward anyone entering from the outside. But I think the trouble is sharpened by the double-edged bargain the B.T.s, by their very existence, seem to offer the traditional community. On the one hand, the existence of a school for newly religious Jews—full of former fraternity brothers poring over the Talmud in beards and black hats—offers symbolism dear to traditionalists. On the other hand, the same Orthodox priorities that make the old-timers delight in such images, as images, may actually encourage them to *resist* the influx of "returnees" in the flesh. For generations, Orthodox Jews had to live with the knowledge that most Jews scarcely knew there was such a thing as Orthodoxy. If you believe, as the Orthodox do, that every Jew is bound to a national mission defined by the ancient Law, then you have to envision a way for the Law to reach beyond the confines of Orthodox enclaves or risk condemning the Law to marginal status. That isn't too large a problem so long as the non-Orthodox Jews remain completely alienated from traditional Judaism; then they are easy to ignore, at least for practical purposes. But as more and more non-Orthodox Jews show a real interest in the traditional law, their very interest raises the unsettling thought that in order to embrace so many Jews, scattered so far from the social formations that emerged from the ghettos of Eastern Europe, the established Orthodox may have to reexamine the formations themselves, or the way these structures either accommodate or fail to accommodate the majority of Jews today. It is all very well if the unattached Jews come to *us*, move submissively into the father's house, adopt his ways. But if *we* must go to *them*—aye, there's the rub.

Michael Graubart Levin, who entered Orthodoxy with the help of Ohr Somayach and then left it after finding himself socially isolated, has vividly described the hostility of the established Orthodox. In his 1986 book, *Journey to Tradition*, he writes: "Nothing in *yeshiva* prepared me for the suspicion and lack of acceptance I encountered." A man who had always thrived on community, Levin "could not find that necessary community in New York," and discovered that women he dated, for instance, questioned his religiosity once they learned he was a B.T. "Finally," he writes, "I became so lonely and so fed up that I curtailed my religious observance."

Janet Aviad's study confirms Levin's experience: "The baal teshuva carries a stigma that makes orthodox families hesitate before welcoming him or her as a mate for a daughter or son ... Marriages between orthodox people and baalei teshuva ... [occur] infrequently and exceptionally." Nevertheless, the Orthodox community ignores its responsibility for defections like Levin's with self-serving moralizing: B.T.s "have transgression in their blood," claims one rabbi I know. Sometimes Orthodox Jews take this line to grotesque extremes, such as one Orthodox newspaper's claim that B.T.s were responsible for the spread of AIDS among the Orthodox in Brooklyn.

That's one reason I suspect a small, non-revolutionary B.T. "movement" is really what the Orthodox world prefers, for all the community's protestations to the contrary. The fact is that Orthodox "outreach" is still aimed at a small minority of the potentially available population. The great bulk of Ohr Somayach's students (when I was there, anyway) were drawn from a very narrow slice of the American Jewish public, and it's probably no coincidence that the slice they represented fits rather neatly into the Orthodox social fabric. The B.T.s I knew were middlebrow, middle-class young men, professionals but not intellectuals, and on the whole inclined toward obedience. Acting as host to any number of them for Sabbath meals over a four-year period (after my own year of study there), I was assailed by flights of *déjà vu*: wasn't this one here before? Wasn't *this* one, droning on about the emptiness of the "secular lifestyle," about the course he was taking in business administration and his prospects with an accounting firm—wasn't he here last week, saying the same thing, in more or less the same accents? Considering the unmistakable presence of American Jews in the arts, in literature, in music, in journalism, in science, in the professoriat, the very thin representation of these professions among the B.T.s signals an almost deliberate Orthodox policy of exclusion and neglect.

Yet—note the irony—this very neglect is welded to the local idea of success, that is, the adaptation and socialization of Jews essentially identical to the ones already within the fold. We know the kind of person who will fit in, and we avoid those who probably will not—as artists and reporters and scientists probably will not. In other words, we seek stability, not change. As long as that remains true, any so-called "revolution" in the Jewish world will be more talk than reality.

And this doesn't even take into account another target of the religious community's fear: the B.T.s' non-Orthodox family members. The late Rabbi Avigdor Miller (a Brooklyn authority who once declared it a sin to vote for Walter Mondale) reportedly urged converts to Orthodoxy to break all ties with family: "Change your name and forwarding address. You are in one world; they're in another."

That kind of advice is unusual, fortunately. But even the more tolerant line one encounters in most of the Orthodox community masks deep internal reservations. "Keep in contact with your father," Rabbi Gold once advised me. But, of course, keeping in contact with a father like mine meant creating a contact between the Orthodox community and my father's atheism, or worse. Multiply that contact by several thousand, and you have some measure of the problem B.T.s pose for Orthodoxy—a problem of real significance for a community unused to being challenged from within.

So what happens when the community has to face that sort of challenge? Well-placed voices from within the Orthodox world show that the anxiety it arouses can fuel a good deal of hostility. In 1999, an English translation and "condensation" of an old polemic against the eighteenth-century reformer, Moses Mendelssohn, was circulated by Neve Yerushalayim College, a school for newly-Orthodox women whose promotional literature proclaims it "the largest and most diversified institution of its kind in the world." The point of reproducing the polemic—in English—was clearly to warn Jews newly attached to Orthodoxy away from the philosophical inquiry that was Mendelssohn's *forte*. But the context of the republication also suggests a remarkable assault on its own audience, a warning that the newly-religious (the ones mostly expected to read the essay) can never be religious enough to satisfy the powers that be. (The essay's quasi-official status is buttressed by the fact that its original author, Rabbi Eliyahu Meir Feivelson, was before his death in 1928 the founding secretary of the organization now known as Agudath Israel, one of Orthodoxy's central institutions.)

The sheer nastiness of Feivelson's essay—which the modern editors have, if anything, only intensified in abridgment—is its most striking feature, and this seems all the more objectionable when contrasted with the author's carelessness concerning biographical facts. Feivelson claims, for instance, that Moses Mendelssohn left the study of Talmud "forever" when he moved to Berlin in 1743, at the age of fourteen. In fact, Mendelssohn's specific reason for moving to the capital was to continue his religious studies with the prominent Orthodox Talmudist David Hirsch Frankel, with whom he continued to study for at least six years thereafter. (His famous friendship with Gotthold Lessing did not begin until 1749, when, over a game of chess, Lessing began to introduce his talented acquaintance to German literature.)

Feivelson also claims that Mendelssohn made no contribution to post-Talmudic legal literature. Again, he is wrong. At least two of Mendelssohn's significant opinions are on record concerning specific questions of Jewish law—including a scholarly statement on the proper time of burial for a Jewish epidemic victim—and more would surely survive had Mendelssohn not been anathematized in Orthodox circles after his death. (A rabbi I know in Monsey has been quoted as saying that Mendelssohn's subtle ruling in a controversy concerning certain dietary laws might well have been decisive, had someone other than Mendelssohn rendered it.) This accomplishment is particularly striking since Mendelssohn never aspired to prominence as a Talmudist.

But the real question is not why Feivelson published an unfair essay about Mendelssohn back in 1914. The question is what motivated Neve Yerushalayim to reprint this threadbare slander against a two-hundred-year-old reformer more than eighty-five years after the attack was originally printed. The subject that attracted Neve Yerushalayim could not have been Mendelssohn himself. His work is not widely read today (and almost certainly was not read by the editors). Nowadays Mendelssohn's name is little more than a popular symbol for the Enlightenment-era attempt to reduce Judaism to a rationalist creed—hardly a burning issue in our time. As a matter of fact, as a writer on Jewish subjects, Mendelssohn was for the most part emphatically traditional: he went out of his way to translate Maimonides' completely Orthodox treatise on grammar, even adding an introduction of his own which stressed—of all things—the insufficiency of human intellect to prevail over the assertions of Jewish tradition.

The true appeal of the essay to the Neve Yerushalayim editors, I think, had less to do with Mendelssohn's religious views than with the way he reached those views, Mendelssohn's mode of philosophical inquiry into Jewish faith being necessarily rather similar to the way today's newly-traditional Jews reach Orthodoxy. The comparison is obvious. If you're not raised in a given religion, you can only decide to accept it after having been convinced of its merits. And in that case the conviction will rest largely on the consent of your rational faculties. The editors' real target, in other words, was their newly-religious audience, whose method of reaching Orthodoxy they challenged by way of an attack on Moses Mendelssohn: the editors were warning B.T.s against the habits of their own minds.

Of course, that argument could have been made directly. But that would have been a risky course for the editors to follow. Those who read the pamphlet might have been deeply offended to find themselves singled out as half-heretic in a publication intended for their religious edification. But the message is clear, even if indirect.

No one could miss its double-pronged implication that 1) the newly-religious have necessarily been corrupted by too much thinking, and 2) as a result, they can never really be religious enough.

Why else would the editors preserve a weird passage of Feivelson's essay that concocts a fictitious Yom Kippur Eve, during which Mendelssohn, on his way to synagogue, discusses "Goethe's philosophy of licentiousness" (whatever that is) with Schleiermacher, Fichte and Schlegel—and then, "standing next to the *chazan* [cantor] during *Kol Nidrey* [the emotional chant that begins the service] ... fights back a smile with every ounce of his strength"?

A crusade against latter-day reformers was probably what Rabbi Feivelson was after when he originally penned this crude fantasy. But nearly ninety years later, the fantasy reeks with a fear of Neve Yerushalayim's own audience—B.T.s, that is—and the "licentiousness" of the non-Jewish world, with all its dangerous scholarship (thus the scoffingly-dismissed list of literary and philosophical figures), whence that audience has presumably emerged.

And doubtless it was a similar fear that attracted the editors to Feivelson's replacement of the traditional Jewish definition of religiosity—observance of the Law—with a pietistic standard that can only be intimidating to someone who embraced the law after study in an appropriate adult *yeshiva*:

> A true believer in HaShem [God] and His Torah ... radiates to his family and his disciples and to all who come in contact with him, his love of Torah ... But an equivocating philosopher, despite his performance of mitzvos [commandments], gives off an aura of coldness, of scoffing, of skepticism about all that is holy.

What is this but a thinly veiled put-down of the newly-Orthodox reader, "despite his performance of commandments," and despite the fervor of his belief? As "secular Jews," remember, B.T.s were once encouraged to question their way of life. Now they are told that real membership in Orthodoxy depends on their ability to accept their current status quo, not to "equivocate"; to be "true believers," not "philosophers." Ironically, by learning to question at all, they have lost the right to be accepted by their coreligionists on an equal footing.

The same idea surfaces with astonishing force when the editors summarize Feivelson's condemnation of Mendelssohn's personal faith—the faith he professed *after* he completed his rational progress into Orthodoxy—with these words:

A man whose opinions were for so many years outside the Jewish fold, what impression does Torah make on him? He no longer has the feelings of the true believer, the Jew who has never doubted, the man in whose eyes the Torah has always been the holiest of holies…Doubts and false notions continually assail the "thinking man's" peace of mind…

Again, the intended message is tolerably clear: the modern B.T. (in whose youth the Torah was not "the holiest of holies") is never reliable in his religiosity. After "so many years outside the Jewish fold," he "no longer has the feelings of the true believer" (a remarkable choice of phrases for a religion built on study!) and will be continually beset with "false notions." In a word (rather, in Feivelson's own phrase) a "thinking man" (or woman) does not belong in the first ranks of Orthodoxy. Neve Yerushalayim may call itself an educational institution, but its choice of texts shows that it is really a kind of educational roach motel: intellectual curiosity may enter it, but as far as the school is concerned, it must never be allowed to leave.

The B.T.s are better off letting the powers that be think for them. Accepting their status as semi-exiles. And going meekly to the back of the bus.

And how do B.T.s react to that judgment? For the most part, they seem to accept it, no matter how much the suspicions of the

Orthodox call into question the B.T.s' most cherished ideals about themselves. Most B.T.s humbly describe their entry into Orthodoxy as if they'd stumbled into a paradise of saints and sages. A cento of such narratives has been published by the journalist Richard Greenberg, who—in case anyone missed the point—told the Jewish newspaper *Forward* that many of the stories of religious transformation his book chronicles are "clearly miracles."

Maybe Greenberg has met with a better class of B.T.s than I have. I doubt it, though. Years after our own conversions, while living in the orbit of my *alma mater* Ohr Somayach, my wife and I used to host other B.T.s at our Shabbos table almost every week. The narrators of their own stories (almost all of them new Ohr Somayach students) included a former drug addict and a prison guard, an ex-Buddhist, a pole vaulter, and one former Soviet soldier who claimed his life was saved by a cobra in Afghanistan (when the snake, appearing suddenly near him and threatening to strike, holding its position for over half an hour, forced him to remain motionless away from his base—while, unknown to him, Afghan guerrillas were decimating his camp). Not a dull lot by any means. But I've never been tempted to call their tales of religious conversion examples of modern miracles. In fact, what I've mostly been struck with has been their lack of originality. (All the more remarkable given their colorful backgrounds.) And surely, in all times, the derivative is inconsistent with the truly miraculous.

I don't mean to be unfair. Of course I understand how young men and women, in the first flush of religious enthusiasm, may explain even the most intimate discoveries in the broad strokes of pious jargon. Religious conversion is uprooting; one grasps at the language of the only community that seems to sympathize. "It was lonely groping alone," one B.T. has written of her early experience, and I've shared that feeling far too often to sneer at it—or at its consequences. Still, I can't believe that so many different B.T.s, with so many different histories, could all go on describing their discoveries of Orthodoxy in almost exactly the same way, years after their conversions—unless someone else were writing the script.

And of course, someone else is—though even journalists like Greenberg seem not to have noticed it. The earnest returnees Greenberg met and talked to weren't only speaking to him. Through him and his book, they were addressing an Orthodox community whose acceptance they desperately need. And they know full well that acceptance isn't going to be won by originality. Like the bean-grain-and-beef stews most Orthodox Jews eat on the Sabbath, Orthodox culture is a blend in which distinctiveness is not supposed to show. Yaakov Jacobs, former editor of the Orthodox *Jewish Observer* and *Jewish Life*, told me once of hearing a speech from a newly-Orthodox Jew who was honored at a religious function.

"He was a young man who was said to have been in professional broadcasting," said Jacobs. "And when he started peppering his talk with [Yiddish expressions like] '*takeh*' and '*mamesh*,' I confess I felt very uncomfortable." Jacobs was right to be uncomfortable—but I'll bet most of his coreligionists were simply charmed. "*Frum* [Orthodox] people want a pat on the back," a sour B.T. once told me. "So that's what we give them."

Here are excerpts of recent accounts written by B.T.s about their own experiences, published in a leading Orthodox journal, edited (by me) to spotlight that "pat on the back":

We heard classes that literally opened up the mind.... He [the rabbi] showed one example after another of major prophecies that had materialized throughout the centuries up till the present day. Prophecies that defied logic and nature but nevertheless came true.... [T]he Torah is the source for the spiritual truths I was so drawn to in the New Age ideas.

I had always felt a twinge of envy coming across a Jew who seemed to know what Judaism was about... "There is a God who created the world and wrote the Torah and gave it to the Jewish people." These simple facts were proven and hammered home with such cogency, it was breathtaking....

They [the rabbis] established the divinity of the Torah so
that even a hardened cynic couldn't dispute it.

As if a complete and irrefutable understanding of God weren't
enough, Orthodox Jews could also shame the newcomers with
exemplary family lives:

Religious families spend more quality and quantity time
together with the children than do their secular counter-
parts . . . . All the self-destructive behaviors typical of modern
teenagers—drug use, promiscuity, eating disorders—are
far less common in [Orthodox] families.

We [B.T.s] are concerned over how our [non-religious] past
affects our children . . . Most of all, we look with longing at
our [Orthodox] neighbors' network of family – who provide
support, advice, role models . . .

What I find hardest to believe in all this (and there is a good
deal to wonder about) is that the questing minds of earnest doubters—surely most B.T.s begin as earnest doubters—could have had
all their doubting stopped in its tracks just by joining an Orthodox
community and enrolling in a *yeshiva*. This contradicts everything I
know, or think I know, about the sort of people willing to ask themselves hard questions. B.T.s must still have doubts. They must still
wonder about God and righteousness, and about whether anyone
really has the last word on either subject.

But where are the questions? Why aren't B.T.s questioning
Orthodoxy as they once questioned secular culture? Again and
again, I've heard B.T.s say they came to Judaism looking for "the
truth." But the Talmudic method, relentlessly applied, is a battering
ram to certainties. The lawyerly subtleties that pervade the *yeshivas*
are poor grist for dogma, and mysticism is an even more slippery
slope, leading out of Judaism as easily as it leads into it. Nor does
Jewish tradition, a palimpsest of shifting and clashing principles,

look much like the simple "moral values" preached in popular back-to-basics sermonizing on the religious right.

Hence my suspicion that many of the *real* stories of religious return aren't being told openly. If they were, the Greenbergs of the world would be hearing a richer variety of religious narrative, tales that would not end conveniently with a conversion to Orthodoxy, the way romantic comedies used to end with marriage, but would take into account that religion is *lived* (not just sought after), and that the religious life of a truth-seeker subjects religion to constant tests.

Yet most of the stories I actually hear are void of such challenges. "I was raised in a typical liberal environment and finally saw through it," one B.T. told me. Of course, he was saying what he assumed I wanted to hear. But I knew this fellow, and I wanted to tell him I had actually liked him better two years earlier—when he was half-Orthodox, with a headful of questions and a breakneck intellectual pace that left no time for complacency. Why had he changed?

And the funny thing was, I didn't have to ask. I knew why. He'd done his share of self-doubting, of personal and social transformation. Now he wanted acceptance. He had found his precarious perch, and he'd come to prefer a degree of security to perpetual motion. He was due for a rest.

He was an earnest, committed person, to be sure. Certainly there's nothing disgraceful in settling down. But if this sort of left-over life is the best Orthodoxy can do with its most intellectually committed members, then, I think, we have a long way to go before we have a right to crow about an Orthodox "revolution."

CHAPTER TWENTY-FOUR

I was both moved and unsettled when I asked a learned, middle-aged rabbi what he thought about developments in the Middle East and he answered, hardly raising his head from his Talmud (his black-and-white beard grazed the black and white columns of text), "Why do I have to think about that, when the Prophets and *chazal* [the Talmudic sages] have already explained it all?"

I suppose I shouldn't have been so surprised. The traditional Jew clings to the Bible and Talmud on his path through history the way a mariner used to clutch his compass. And that's probably inevitable. The comforting rhythms of Jewish life, with all their logically unfolding optimism, are certainly not found in the madness of actual events, at least not the way events form themselves to the naked eye. It is text, not history, that reveals the hand of divine providence. Or less grandly, it is the collection of distinctive Jewish texts that imposes a little order on the chaos of time. "Without our traditions," says good old Tevye, "our life would be as shaky as a fiddler on the roof."

That's why the Talmud, for an Orthodox Jew, can very nearly swallow the modern world. Without it we'd be at the mercy of senseless change. With it, we can see—or think we see—how change, even the change of fifteen centuries, is not only understandable but (at least in a sense) largely an illusion. For in the timeless space of Talmudic debate, nothing much really changes: time means little more than repetition and renewal, development taking the backward-looking form of commentary.

I have learned both to admire and to distrust this way of thinking. On balance, my admiration outweighs my distrust, for I know that even my distrust of the Talmud owes something to Talmud study. That is, the relentless reinterpretations that are the stuff of Talmudism have introduced me to the central method of my own style of reform: my habit of looking at a thing, including my own life, problems and all, as a point balanced on the accumulated heap of centuries' worth of questions and answers, a position in which novelty is forced on me by the very tottering hugeness of the foundation I stand on. In other words, I owe even my desire to unsettle the Orthodox Talmud to the turbulence of the Talmud.

But what is this remarkable text? And what is someone living in modern times to do with it?

I'm not really equipped to give a scholarly answer, though there are quite a few good books that do: I found Rabbi Adin Steinsaltz's *The Essential Talmud* an excellent place for a beginner to start. But I'm not a scholar. And maybe the answer that matters most, here and now, has to do with how the Talmud actually entered my life. And how it has changed it.

The introduction came about through the unlikely offices of Shmuel Lehrman—nervous, rude, persistent—the co-worker who first led me into a half-darkened room and began to read from a faded page of text, the contents of which were almost a millennium and a half old. Soon we were tracing the questions asked of this line of text by an array of medieval and post-medieval commentators. After that we began, inevitably, to raise questions of our own. And suddenly I found I had entered a species of living conversation that defies the boundaries of time.

That was the Talmud. That was pacing back and forth in a room with dimensions that opened out on a view of centuries, that intersected with the play of countless other minds glancing over the same ground. That was the Talmud; and I soon fell completely under its spell.

Or almost completely. I still wanted to know a little more about it.

Jewish tradition is surprisingly equivocal in its treatment of the origin of this monumental work. Indeed, tradition speaks somewhat sadly of the writing down of the rabbinic teachings that form the kernel of the Talmud. The process is described as a sort of concession to the stormy history during which the Mishnah, as it is called, was compiled during the 2nd century C.E. The rabbinic tradition was meant to be oral, we are told, passed along from teacher to student, refined in freewheeling debates—in other words, a product of a sort of pedagogical turbulence. Maybe the rabbis grasped instinctively that turbulence was a necessary ingredient of the sort of inquiry they wanted, so that only an external turbulence could justify the resort to the solider medium of writing in the first place. And even then, the written version had to mirror much of the shifting, inconstant shape of oral debate.

Shmuel may or may not have understood that, but he knew enough to explain that the Talmud's origins were anything but static and peaceful. Historians confirm that over roughly five centuries after the Mishnah, the hard core of rabbinic teaching, was set down in writing—while the Jews struggled to adapt to changes wrought by two disastrous Roman wars and the development of the Diaspora in earnest—scholars in the two great Babylonian academies tried to adapt Jewish law and custom to radically altered circumstances. And in so doing they fretted over, expanded on, analyzed, questioned, integrated, reconciled, chopped up and reinterpreted the laconic text of the Mishnah. The minutes of this debate, combined with all sorts of folk wisdom, sayings, legends, stories, advice, even political commentary, probably edited into final form between 500 and 600 C.E., eventually became the Babylonian Talmud, the ultimate source text for nearly all traditional Jewish law down to the present day.

And by the time they were finished, they had not simply adapted the Mishnah to a new time and place. In a sense, they had said goodbye to time and place forever. They had made the law not merely a thing, but a process.

So when Shmuel started swaying from the waist over his open Talmud, and invited me to join in his discussion of the text he read, he was inviting me into a paradox in print, a dialogue that never really began and that cannot possibly be contained by an ending. For one thing, as I quickly found, the Talmud isn't really a text at all. True, at first glance it looks like one. It is divided into tractates, each with its own topic heading, and each tractate is further divided into chapters. Each chapter consists of several passages, each beginning with a quotation from the Mishnah, and following that, with a discussion of the text quoted.

But the orderly superstructure conceals a maddeningly spontaneous and digressive technique—both a product of and a goad to intellectual instability. Discussions in the Talmud begin more or less where one might expect, but rarely remain there for long. One law will remind a sage of another law that may be similar in language but very different in subject matter. Or a law will be brought into the discussion because it clashes with or sheds light upon a law already under consideration, and then the interlocutors will decide to pursue the new law for a while, like hounds on the hunt leaving one trail for another, and then the discussion may peter out in one place, spiral into digressions, and then suddenly erupt again, without warning, somewhere quite distant.

All of this represents only the first problem for the beginner. The underlying fact it suggests—that the Talmud's structure is that of oral discussion rather than written analysis—points to the second difficulty: the bareness or incompleteness of most passages. One cannot reach legal conclusions simply by reading the Talmud's discussion of an issue in one particular location. The Talmud may take up the same issue in a dozen different places, as intellectual battle lines ebb and flow over a similar point, and the Talmud may even appear to reach different conclusions in different locations. One of the major purposes of the medieval Talmud commentaries is to refer the reader to the loci of these related discussions, and to reconcile the differences that crop up in the various discussions and the conclusions reached there. In fact, the mere positioning of these commentaries—they are inserted around the inner and outer margins of the larger Talmud text like a sea of print around an island—tells an important story in itself: the commentaries do not merely amplify the text but support, embrace and locate it in the larger sweep of argument. And this first level of commentary is only the beginning. Layer after layer has been added on top of it, until an intelligible reading of any given Talmudic passage—if it is to be relevant to contemporary decision-making—requires post-Talmudic reading of texts whose composition may span many centuries.

All of which means that the style and method of Talmud study are also those a thoughtful person is likely to apply to life itself—circling back to early experiences, to principles and assumptions, challenging them, supporting them, questioning them, adding to them, laying down new layers of conclusions, reactions and discoveries on the residues of years and decades past.

It's really too bad the Talmud is pretty much inaccessible to anyone who hasn't devoted a lot of serious effort to the mechanics of studying it. Too bad not only because it deprives many people of a unique intellectual experience, but because the Talmud's inaccessibility contributes to the wide rift between Orthodox Jews and nearly everybody else, and because Orthodox Jews probably aren't using the text or its implications to anything like their full capacity. The Orthodox know the Talmud well but guard it jealously; many other people would surely give it more creative expression if they could only penetrate its difficulties.

The difficulties...

I readily admit that my own introduction to the Talmud was tough going. To begin with, no one ever actually told me of the greatest thrill I've found in the Talmud: its way of reproducing in legal argument the methods by which we reinterpret (and therefore define) our own selves. I had to discover that for myself: wading through a narrative of legal discussion to uncover the hidden assumptions behind it all, to unravel the tangled skeins of meaning, to answer one question and then, necessarily, turn back to examine two more. Learning, slowly, that Talmud study involved such an arduous and precarious process cost me much frustrating time. Finding in it a potent metaphor for self-discovery took even longer.

For another thing, the Talmud is not—repeat, *not*—the consistently elevating text many starry-eyed Jews eager for "spirituality" would like it to be. Its basic material is too prosaic, too legalistic, for that. Michael Graubart Levin, chronicling his career through Orthodoxy, has commented that "learning what was inside the Talmud was…something of a disappointment…. I had expected the Talmud to explain *why* I should believe in God and Judaism; instead, I was only learning *how* to do so." Which, in fact, is an important clue to the Talmud's method, and to the difficulties the student is bound to encounter in its grip. The Talmud explains very little. It expounds, lays out a problem, sets up seemingly simple propositions—and then attacks them. This process can be fascinating, and to the extent one tries to embrace religious truth along the lines of behavior laid down by these methods, it can be highly practical too. But one thing it isn't is a direct path to spiritual wisdom. You might as well study law books to stimulate a mystical experience.

And it can be exhausting. My first weeks at Ohr Somayach felt like training sessions at Grossinger's. I was expected to remember varied nuances contained in almost innumerable commentaries and super-commentaries on every phrase of Talmud we studied. More, I was expected to understand them, and to apply each author's logic to a baffling assortment of problems raised by the medieval and modern codifiers. A long day of this pushed me to my limits, so much so that I felt physically worn out as well as intellectually overtaxed by the end of each day. Naturally, not everyone is prepared to master a text studded with such demands.

But why should I detail the problems of one more callow newcomer, cracking the medieval world of the Talmud? Any moderately experienced reader, even if he's never studied a word of the Talmud, has almost certainly encountered some criticism of it. Perhaps no comparable text in history (if there is a comparable text) has absorbed so much bashing.

Of course, many of the commonplace critics don't know the Talmud's virtues because they simply can't read it. And in fact just reading it isn't enough: one must know how to study it, to ask the right questions, to note parallel texts, to leap from commentary to commentary. To do that effectively requires an educational process that can take years. As a result, most comments on the Talmud available in the general literature are made, alas, after only a superficial survey.

Also, the Talmud is still associated in many people's minds with an overscrupulous, hair-splitting Judaism, an unfair stereotype but a powerful one, so that many people who might be fascinated by it never even make the effort of making its acquaintance. "Talmudistic," says language critic William Safire, has come to mean "over-precise," "tediously academic," even among Jews.

Yet the Talmud has a way of getting the last laugh on its critics. Emma Lazarus, the Jewish poet who gave the Statue of Liberty its inscription, regarded herself as an enlightened woman and campaigned fervently against the Talmud among the Jewish immigrants of New York. She called it a "repository of superstitions," urging Jews to escape from its "darkness." Yet today, Lazarus' own politics seem, if anything, rather more musty than the Talmud's timelessness. The most modern of biblical critics continue to mine Talmudic literature for insights. Lazarus is remembered only for the statue.

Similar things happened to earlier critics. Before technological progress stretched the horizons of possibility, the Talmud was ridiculed for its hypothetical references to a "tower that flies in the air" and other supposed absurdities. Today, as technology approaches wizardry, modern students are glad of the Talmud's imaginative excursions into the significance of air and space travel. The point is not that the Talmud predicted these things—that would certainly be going too far—but that the Talmud was prepared, in the early Middle Ages, to imagine the unimagined.

Guy de Maupassant claims in one of his short stories that no one emerges from the Talmud completely sane. I suppose the great writer was entitled to an opinion on the subject. Still, those who have actually studied the Talmud nearly always hold a different view. Any number of students have found its disciplines nourishing and stimulating.

That said, I quickly acknowledge that some of the criticism is valid. Even the purely legal and logical discussions of religious issues in the Talmud (I'm not speaking of its wide-eyed repetition of folklore and folk medicine) are not entirely satisfactory.

Most troublesome, to my taste, is the Talmud's difficulty with the essentials of theology. All in all, the Talmud offers very little in the way of apologetics or even explanation. As Michael Levin found, it simply assumes that the Law is binding and worthwhile and proceeds to expound its application.

Regarding a work so committed to the application of logic to religion, it is disturbing to have to second Levin's point that the Talmud makes no attempt to penetrate the "why" of the biblical commandments. True, there is a certain nobility in this refusal to question the express will of God. How could any "explanation" of what God has commanded supplant the plain certainty that God has in fact willed it? Still, the refusal to look *inside* the commandments entails a large cost, because it underscores the fact that at the very root of Judaism there must come a point where logical analysis fails. If biblical law is to be accepted without question, it cannot be made fully available to reason. Which means, inevitably, that the upshot of the Talmud's attempt to rationalize the Law, however noble, was bound to fall short of its own implicit standards.

Then there are the other modern complaints. Masses of superstition and more or less useless arcana are lodged throughout the text. The Talmud contains prescriptions for avoiding demons and warns about eating or drinking things in pairs. It claims to describe sea monsters, talks about jewels the size of houses, names birds that grow large enough to darken the sun, and insists that snakes can leave their poison in cheese or in uncovered water bowls. In one notorious passage the Talmud purports to enumerate the dimensions of different parts of God's "body." Even in more down-to-earth matters there are many passages that can embarrass a sensitive reader. Modern scholars assure us that the Talmud's treatment of history is partial and legend-ridden at best; that its medicine is nonsense; and that its natural science, though occasionally prophetic, is more often extremely crude. It can also be sexist. Compounding my own difficulties, as I began to study it, was the fact that the older men to whom I turned either couldn't understand what bothered me, or answered with rationalizations I found worse than my original problems. "Just think of germs," one fellow told me when I pointed to a passage about malignant demons that lurk in the night air.

Still, like so many other students before me, I've come to love the Talmud. I wouldn't want to tamper with it, not even to remove passages that irritate me. If the Talmud's science and history are no better (though no worse) than one would expect of a sixth-century compilation, its intellectual accomplishment is still unique. In its way, the Talmud is a work of really radical inquiry. In pursuing the right answer the Talmudic method tramples relentlessly on certainties, sometimes even biblical ones. "A scholar who cannot prove from the Torah that pork is *kosher* is no scholar," says the Talmud. Here—standing alongside the humble acceptance of revealed religion—is a wonderful confession of intellectual fearlessness, of the almost limitless possibilities of inquiry.

The Talmud abounds in such moments. What boldness, to assert that "there is only one statement in Scripture that is beyond questioning"—and then to question it! What profound self-awareness lies behind the Talmudic rabbis' name for their own way of attaching obscure Scriptural proofs to accepted practices: "a mountain hanging by a hair"! And what heroic faith in the ultimate reasonableness of God's world, against all odds, resonates in the Talmud's method, its obsessively digressive attack, which constantly relates one issue to another—so unlike the manner of Western treatises—and which defies all attempts at a merely imposed consistency.

And this only touches the legal side of the Talmud, the hard ridge that first confronts the student. The Talmud can also be mined for folklore, mysticism, parables and homiletics, to name a few things. Its accounts of some of the great sages bring them so vividly to life that young *yeshiva* students have wept as they read the description of Rab's funeral, or of Rabbi Akiba comforting his colleagues at the ruins of the Temple. Perhaps even more important for life in general, the Talmud forces its students into dialogues with sages who lived centuries ago, and centuries apart even from one another. In other words, the Talmud attacks linear time, that most restrictive of Western constructs. The intellectual patterns demanded of the Talmud student involve a more flexible approach to time, an approach that recognizes that reality circles at least as much as it progresses, that the questions that matter don't change very much, despite the different dress in which they appear in subsequent generations. And this alone is worth all the effort.

Is the accomplishment without dangers? Alas, no. From my perch in the insular world of the Orthodox community, I am aware that the Talmud's great treasure can be abused. Too subservient an apprenticeship can spoil the questing spirit that is the Talmud's greatest legacy. Rabbi Chaim Soloveitchik, in a remarkable essay, has already pointed out that modern times present unforeseen challenges to the Talmud's political vocabulary: the internal combustion engine may not change anything fundamental in the Talmud's approach to forbidden labors on the Sabbath, but the dynamics of democracy (particularly in a secular State of Israel) change all sorts of social and legal realities the rabbis assumed were timeless. So do the social conditions of postwar American Jews, who no longer live in ghettos (or their early-medieval equivalents in ancient Babylonia). Even among the Orthodox, transience has largely eroded the traditional power of communal authorities, rendering the old enforcement procedures worthless. Today, a man who leaves his wife but refuses to give her a *get*—the divorce certificate required by Jewish law—cannot be forced to do his duty, as was the common procedure as recently as the 1930s. Many women suffer as a result. Meanwhile, Orthodox rabbis search in vain for a legal answer drawn from the courts of third-century Pumbeditha.

I suppose this means that, in the end, the Talmud demands of its disciples services beyond those of mere obedience. And this goes for conventional pieties, too: I cannot say, as the old rabbi once said to me, that all modern history was written down in the Bible and explained in the Talmud. To say that is ultimately cowardly, for it refuses to accept the burdens the Talmud's editors themselves freely embraced. They were willing to reinterpret their past; so must the rest of us.

But I'd hate to think that this implies the failure of the Talmud. Maybe the truth is that Orthodox Jews today are failing their heritage. For centuries the Talmud has nourished us. Maybe more is expected of this generation than of previous ones? Maybe now, in this turbulent time, we (I) need to reciprocate—to feed the Talmud with our creativity and uncertainty, as the ancient rabbis did. Certainly we cannot allow today's imperfect status to be the last word. Nor can we afford to wait for more radical problems to appear before we take up the challenge and begin to reinterpret, reassess, reintegrate—that is, to live Talmudically. As the early reformer and poet Judah Leib Gordon wrote in the nineteenth century, "Woe to the tenant of a house where the ceiling is cracked, and the builder does not repair it, because it will eventually collapse, and thereby cease to be a danger!"

CHAPTER TWENTY-FIVE

I am in Denver, Colorado, in the early fall of 1991. I am eating a *kosher* hamburger with my wife, both of us sitting across from my wife's brother, Jon, who has been engaging me in animated conversation about his forays into "spirituality."

I like Jon. He is a powerfully-built, black-mustachioed six-footer who has climbed Mount Kilimanjaro carrying a seventy-pound backpack. Jon has studied *tai chi*, and immersed himself (between bouts of earning money as a lawyer and trying to write a science fiction novel) in Zen. Denver is his most recent home, but Jon's restlessness will soon draw him from city to city, just as it pulled him into Denver, where he moved largely (so he says) to put room between himself and his mother, with whom he is "in conflict." His restlessness has not made Jon self-centered. I have often been touched by his spontaneous generosity: shortly after my son was born, for instance, Jon suddenly arrived in Monsey and, singlehanded, built a crib for him from a kit I had bought at Sears and left helplessly, in notched and bracketed pieces, all around the bedroom floor. I have often wished I could see more of Jon than I do.

So the encounter in Denver ought to be a pleasant one. But tension ripples the air. Throughout my trip to Denver, and even with Jon, the personal side of my visit keeps slipping behind my unsought persona as The Orthodox Jew. Changing planes in Minneapolis on the way out to Denver, I was suddenly accosted by a stranger who, addressing me as "rabbi," questioned me about a riot that had taken place in Crown Heights, Brooklyn just a few weeks earlier, in which dozens of police had been injured and one Hasidic Jew had been killed by a mob of black men sometimes described in the press as "protesters."

The trouble had started after a car in a motorcade that included the Lubavitcher Rebbe had run a red light and spun out of control onto a sidewalk, killing a young black boy named Gavin Cato.

"Why is there this trouble between blacks and the Jews?" the stranger wanted to know. (And dark clouds rose inside me, bringing with them the sense of futility familiar since childhood: "Why do you Jews have such problems with other people?" the Pakistani on the bus had wanted to know... And I can still see his smiling face and the pale upturned palms of his hands, as my own palms moisten and anger locks a vise on my heart.)

And now Jon, to my surprise, is addressing the same question.

Sitting in East Denver's one *kosher* hamburger spot, Jon begins to talk about the riot. It was terrible, he says, the way people attacked Jews. Anti-Semitism was a germ that would not die. But it was also the Jews' fault this time, he is saying. These Jews, indefensibly, had "invited" the attack by dressing the way they do in that "ghetto." By standing out so needlessly.

Most of the inhabitants of the surrounding neighborhood in that part of Brooklyn are black, aren't they? he asks. Well, the Hasidim should realize how blacks react to traditional Jewish dress. The Orthodox are too different for their own good, too blind to realities. They insist too much on living as if no one else noticed them. That's why they have such trouble with outsiders. (Because of clothing? I wonder. After all, wouldn't their skin color alone have set them apart? But I say nothing.)

"Look at me," says Jon, his handsome face darkening as he gestures toward his own well-muscled chest, his sweeping mustache an aggressive statement all its own. His biceps tense under his striped knit shirt. Now it's as if *I* were the gentile, the schoolyard bully facing his defiance: "I'm a Jew," he says. "But I'm normal. And people can see that. I can do the things they do. Now, if those fellows in Crown Heights had looked like me, no one would have attacked them."

Maybe. Uneasy memories haunt me of a Georgia gas station where my family stopped on our first trip to Atlanta (where we would soon live) to ask for directions. It was a relentless Southern afternoon, soggy but rainless under the oppressive weight of the heat. My father had gone inside to ask about directions, since we were on our way to a new house in that new city, and my brothers and I had got out of the car to buy Cokes from a vending machine. I don't know who told the young attendant there that we were Jewish. I only know how he came slowly out of the station to stare at me (I was the one nearest to him), literally slack-jawed with astonishment. He sidled around to see me from all angles. He was a gangly, pimpled kid with a crew cut. Sweat popped out along his forehead as he stared at me, but he seemed too absorbed to notice the heat. I held my Coke bottle against my front teeth. Around my upper lip a sweet steam rose into the heat, and as I twisted my head to stare at the stranger from behind the mist he stared back at me, full of wonder at some weirdness he saw in me, but that I couldn't even guess at.

And then I understood. I was a Jew. He was examining me, staring at my head for the expected abnormalities he'd learned about on some grandmother's knee, I suppose. Horns? He couldn't find so much as a *yarmulke* on me. In fact, he couldn't find anything at all unusual. And that kept his eyes locked on my body as he circled and gawked. He couldn't get over it. It was my very ordinariness that made me grotesque. The Jew who looked like Anybody.

I never met Yankel Rosenbaum, the Crown Heights riot's Jewish casualty, and never saw his face, except in the black-and-white pictures that appeared in newspapers after his murder on the night of August 19, 1991. And of course those snapshots weren't taken in the knowledge that people like me would remember the murdered man solely on the strength of them. What are they now, really, those photos, but arbitrary images of a lean, bearded youth wearing a black skullcap, his genial face fringed in a dark beard? (Who took them? A mother? Thinking of what? A trip he was about to make off to college? Certainly not of death on a city street that hot, late night in August.)

I stare at the photos again and again, thinking how easily I might have changed places with this young Orthodox Jew. That is, if I, and not he, had happened to be spending a night in Crown Heights and had decided to drive a few blocks to get a haircut—as Rosenbaum did just before he was murdered.

What would *my* photos have looked like in the newspapers the next day? Would the newspaper readers have noticed only the *yarmulke*, as Jon apparently did in Yankel Rosenbaum's picture? Would they have noticed anything else: *my* face, *my* name? Would the readers identify with me or immediately find reasons for believing (again like Jon) that *they* could never have been in my place? Would my death have frightened or embarrassed other Jews? And which group would deny the truth more deeply, those who made me a stand-in for their nightmares, or those who turned me into a whipping boy for a cultural past they wished they could outgrow?

Though I never saw him, it's possible that I once crossed paths with Yankel Rosenbaum, without knowing it. I had gone to Crown Heights, myself, early in my pursuit of Orthodoxy.

In a way, it would have been hard not to. Lubavitch Hasidim thronged the front ranks of the Orthodox missionary movement, or *kiruv*, as they called it, from the Hebrew word meaning "to bring close." The Lubavitchers' goal was to bring other Jews "close" to their own religious way of life. And Crown Heights held the world's largest community of Lubavitchers. I had met Lubavitch Hasidim as far back as 1973 where, in a dreary Los Angeles suburb, a bearded rabbi and his son had herded me along with the rest of a Jewish Sunday School class into a tiny storefront office where the two of them wound phylacteries around the arms and foreheads of all the male students.

When my turn came the rabbi's son asked me if I knew how to say "*sh'ma, yisrael*," or "Hear, O Israel." I told him I did, whereupon with amazing speed he wound the soft leather straps seven times around my left forearm and slipped a box bound with more leather over my forehead. I recited the Biblical words then, which were familiar, and wondered much at the straps, which were not. The room was shot through with an exotic odor: leather, old books, stale air, and from somewhere the faint trace of Eastern European cooking, something fried, something boiled. And then the straps came off, and the world returned to normal, except that afterwards I realized I had been given a pamphlet that explained that the daily wearing of phylacteries would guarantee Israel's military victories in the Mideast. The pair also gave me a large round button to wear, with blue letters that read, "I PUT ON TEFILLIN TODAY, DID YOU?"

I never wore the button. But I kept it for years. I remember thinking, at times, that it was about the funniest thing I had ever seen. And then a sadness would swiftly replace the thought. Was this what Judaism was, was this *all* it was, I wondered, this Judaism that had helped to make me who I was, that had dogged the steps of my family's history just a hundred years or so behind me? Was this crude fundamentalism and stale humor all there was to it? Straps that bind the arm, a slogan boasting of imaginary power?

Today I know that the phylacteries used by the Hasidim are different from the ones I wear now, wrapped around the arm in the opposite direction from the ones used by other Jews from Eastern European countries. The differences were meaningless to me then, as were the differences I now see between the Hasidim and other Orthodox Jews. Sameness lies in distance. Now an accent, a hat style, a way of pronouncing this or that Hebrew vowel allow me to distinguish one very pious Jew from another. To Jon—who asked at my wedding how many Hasidim were present and was astonished when I answered "Two or three"—they are all a mass of black suits, *yarmulkes* and beards.

As they were to me, in my early days in New York. When I first saw them, the Lubavitchers in Crown Heights looked like all other religious Jews: I was startled at the apparition of so many such people. It was their differentness from me that loomed over everything. The Lubavitchers' part of Brooklyn was a short subway ride from mine, but at first, going there was like going to the moon. I should stress that their differentness was stronger to me than dress alone could make it, because, unlike Jon, I was interested in their life. I listened to them talk to each other. I looked at them and remembered that button, those straps. But the close-up view burned the quaintness out of the memory.

For all their cheerfulness, the Lubavitchers I saw did not match the confidence of the slogan on the button they had given me years before. They radiated struggle, a sense of siege. Maybe they themselves were unaware of it. Maybe the sense of pressure from outside was so much a part of their religious identity that they could not have separated it from the consolations of their religion, even if they had wanted to.

But there it was. Because they were Jews? New Yorkers? Because I was one? Or wasn't?

Did it matter?

The more I learned, the more complicated it all became. A streak of tension ran through the neighborhood's history. The immigration of Hasidim into Crown Heights after World War II had touched off a destabilizing chain reaction. Established middle-class Jews mostly moved out, leaving the neighborhood a smoldering brew of opposites: cash-poor Hasidim, in beards and black hats, underclass blacks and Latinos, all of them competing for the same space.

Unscrupulous businessmen deliberately set the fears of the old and new communities against one another. As blacks moved in, nervous whites were urged to leave by real estate brokers—"blockbusters"—who then sold their homes at a premium to black families who were led to believe they were buying places in a thriving white neighborhood. After that, drawn by low prices, large numbers of the Hasidim began to filter back in, building a Hasidic concentration inside what had become a heavily black slum, a ghetto inside a ghetto. Today's Crown Heights was built on a rubble of broken promises.

(I think of sitting in Constitution Hall, as the *kaddish* commemorated millions of Hitler's victims, under the dark verbal shadow of the Bible's most famous broken promise: "Your seed shall be as the sands of the seashore." And if it had been true? I wondered. What would it mean? Safety in numbers? Or more potential victims?)

Talking with Jon, in Denver, about the Crown Heights riot three thousand miles to the east stirs uneasy associations. Jon does not even consider the possibility that the riot was provoked by anything other than the obvious Jewish identity of Crown Heights' Jews. And I know what he is thinking, though I'm not entirely sure I want to know.

The mix of feelings is too personal, too complicated. In the comfortable and artificial atmosphere of the Denver burger joint I find it difficult to recapture the sense of isolation I've sometimes felt wearing my *yarmulke* on a city street. Isolation—but pride, too. Part of me wants to convey that feeling to Jon; part of me wants to disown it.

Jewish dress isn't just an invitation to attack, I want to tell him. You want to think it is because it embarrasses you. But think of the pride that can come with shedding such embarrassment. With openly dressing as the Jew you've been so afraid to acknowledge in yourself.

But is it only pride?

I remember.

Now, I thought, the first time I wore the skullcap outside my own Brooklyn apartment. *Now I'm not anonymous any more. I'm a Jew.* I could feel eyes fasten on me from behind, eyes noticing and boring into that *thing* over my scalp. Almost unbearable the first time, it was something I knew I had no right to shake off—much as I wanted to—just by taking off that one small object, stuffing it my pocket. Why complain about the stares? They only proved, I said to myself, that yesterday's comfort was an illusion, the product of my own disguise. *This* is how they look at a Jew. This is reality. Nothing has changed, except that yesterday I was under cover. Today I *know*. I told myself this was something I should take in stride. Yet I felt my chest tighten every time I entered the street, felt the skin prickle along the back of my neck.

Reality?

Is truth supposed to feel like terror?

It's not exactly that I reveled in victimization. After that first step, it was just that pride insisted there was no going back. I couldn't do it by halves. To take off the skullcap once I had started to wear it would have felt cowardly. Dishonest too, now that the main reason for *not* wearing it would have been the desire not to know the differentness I could never, honestly, deny again.

In such a situation, you keep on. After a while you do it out of habit, or just out of the momentum you've established with the first step. But by then, it doesn't matter anyway. Even if you did take off the *yarmulke*, you couldn't hide if you wanted to. Now the attempt to look like everyone else would only call more attention to yourself. You've lost your anonymity forever.

A sense of shame washes through me at the complexity of the feelings I recall, none of them, strictly speaking, religious at all.

I find I cannot tell Jon any of this.

I try a different approach. I start to tell him that dress style demonstrably has little or nothing to do with anti-Semitism. I don't get very far. Even the truth—for it is the truth—feels dreadfully thin in my mouth, remembering as I do that first step into the open, that first day with a *yarmulke*. If I put on the skullcap in order to stand out as a Jew, how can I deny that the Hasidim, too, stand out? Or that they want to? And didn't I feel danger, as well as pride, in taking my Jewishness out of the shadows that first time?

And if I resist conceptualizing Jewishness as a danger—because, after all, that is only defining Jewishness from the point of view of those who hate us (and who ought to be the worst possible authorities)—am I guilty of minimizing its costs, or of pretending that the costs are irrelevant to the shape of the whole?

Why must so many details come back to the same irrelevant question, the question of danger, when religion is meant to supply and answer so many others?

"In 1978," reported the *Daily News*, "a black youth was beaten by a group 'in Hasidic garb'; Mayor Edward Koch said the incident threatened 'the fragile thread of intergroup harmony and tolerance.' ... There was an outbreak of incidents in 1987 and 1988, when a snowball fight between blacks and Jews led to a rock, bottle and knife confrontation."

"In 1987, after the firebombing of a house owned by blacks, about 30 blacks and 30 Hasidim enlisted in the first black-Hasidic patrol in the community," said the *New York Times*.

To this tale of ethnic cooperation, the *Times* added an ominous postscript:

"It lasted a few days."

Memories.

The deceit of photo albums?

Right now I'm looking at a round, little-boy face smiling at me from a newspaper photo. This one is of Gavin Cato, the seven-year-old black boy whose death under the wheels of an out-of-control car driven by a Hasid sparked three days of rioting in August 1991.

It also caused Yankel Rosenbaum's murder. So now I'm haunted by Gavin Cato. I'm repeatedly assailed by the odd, numb feeling that something in the boy's picture—the only one I've ever seen—ought to spell the first signs of tragedy.

But nothing does, of course.

The face is simply that of a cheerful little boy.

Or is it? Time has written other things over those innocent features. Seeing Gavin Cato's face now, a black-and-white image boxed out of yellowing newsprint, my first feeling is sorrow—sorrow that his short life will always be tied to memories of blood and anger. And then I can only think how frail a young life is, compared with the power of newspapers and politicians to efface living details under the sinister dyes of a tragic death. Now that he is dead he is a perpetual symbol of victimhood. A strange fate for a boy who looks so carefree in his obituary photo.

I want to protest. Memory ought to be a living thing, shouldn't it? An organism like any other, with its own cycle of growth and decay. But our obsession with explanations, with "facts," keeps getting in the way of a naturally experienced past. Memory is arrested like a broken clock; the living child is snapped off from his newspaper image and fades away; the image, a fiction, a *manqué* built out of superficial details, lives on, and so do the narratives that purport to explain it.

Images like these are inherently false, but they are as indestructible as the plastic bottles that clog our landfills. They build themselves into the psyche, then into legends, then into our collective memories.

How infuriating it can be to find yourself set against them, on the wrong side of a fiction-building lens. I remember riding a subway home from Brooklyn on another summer night, stifled in a black suit (I had been on a date), almost alone in the car because it was after midnight, when a youngish black man, well dressed, boarded the same car together with a woman. He took one look at me, and walking past me with the woman, said to her, "See? *That's* the reason for our problems."

❖   ❖   ❖

Jews are haunted by stories as by ghosts.

This is how the *New York Times* described the spark that ignited the powder keg on the night of August 19, 1991.

> The Lubavitcher Grand Rebbe Menachem Schneersohn was returning from his regular weekly visit to the grave of his wife at Montefiore Cemetery, accompanied by the unmarked police car normally sent along with him as both a courtesy and a security measure.

> Accompanying the Rebbe was a dark blue station wagon driven by one of the Rebbe's followers, Yoseph Lisef, 22 years old. In the car, too, were twin brothers, Yakov and Levi Spielman, who were training Mr. Lisef in escort duty. The station wagon fell behind the convoy and, according to witnesses, ran a red light at the corner of President Street and Utica Avenue and struck another car, sending it skidding onto the sidewalk about 8:20 P.M ....

(This is the ghost's vague shape, you see. A series of coincidences. Death grabbing his chance.)

That station wagon jumped the curb, sped over the sidewalk. It pinned Gavin Cato, who was fixing the chain on his bike, and his cousin, Angela, into window grates. Gavin was probably killed instantly. Angela was critically injured.

Now the *Times* again:

> Both a city Emergency Medical Service ambulance and a private ambulance operated by the Hasidim arrived on the scene as an angry crowd of blacks gathered from the busy intersection and nearby West Indian restaurants and pizza stands.... Youths in the crowd attacked the driver of the station wagon and the crew of the Hasidic ambulance....

Police Commissioner [Lee] Brown...said that the police
had told the Hasidic ambulance to get out "in the interests
of preserving the peace there..."

So the Jewish ambulance drove off. Without Gavin or Angela
Cato.

Anger spread like a lethal infection through Crown Heights. So
did wild rumors among the blacks: the Jews had been driving recklessly; the driver was drunk; they had run down the black children
and sped along. Or, if not that, they had made no effort to move
the car off the child pinned underneath; or the driver (incorrectly
named Lisef in the *Times*' first story, later called Yosef Lifsh) had been
removed to safety by the Hasidic-run ambulance, while the two dead
or critically injured black children were left there dying, ignored.

Soon the crowds were out of control. The rioting began.

"Racing along President Street," reported the *Times*,

> a group of black youths surrounded Mr. [Yankel] Rosenbaum,
> a visiting rabbinical students [sic], and stabbed him at about
> 11:25 P.M., the police said. He died about an hour and half
> later at Kings County Hospital. Commissioner Brown told
> reporters the death appeared to be in retaliation for the
> rumors on the street that the Hasidic ambulance had not
> tended the injured black children.

As vividly recalled as the events of that muggy evening may sound,
there is something ghostlike about the newspaper account of it.
Some details are missing, others invented. Reality appears as a shat-
tered prism, bits of the truth falling every which way.

For instance:

Yankel Rosenbaum was not a "rabbinical student"; he never had
been one. The black youth who fatally stabbed him probably knew
nothing at all about the auto accident, let alone the rumors about

the behavior of the ambulance crew. He did not live in Crown Heights and would later claim he had no idea why the crowd was attacking the young Jew. If so, his act could not have been "in retaliation" for anything.

Even the background facts involved here are surprisingly murky. What was the reason for the motorcade that caused little Gavin Cato's death in the first place? Everyone agrees that the Lubavitcher Rebbe was on his way back from Montefiore Cemetery, when a station wagon in his motorcade ran the red light and caused the deadly accident by jumping a curb and slamming into a building. But after this, the accounts begin to conflict, even as to simple details.

The *Times* claimed that the Rebbe was returning from a weekly visit to his wife's grave. But *New York Newsday* gave a different explanation for those weekly cemetery trips:

> Followers say he [the Rebbe] converses with his dead father-in-law, who preceded him as leader of the rabbinic dynasty that traces its roots back to 18th Century Russia...Upon returning from the cemetery, Schneerson often recounts those conversations to thousands of his followers—some here in Brooklyn, some linked to him through worldwide closed-circuit broadcasts—in hours-long talks, called farbrengens, which are then analyzed for nuance and meaning in much same way Talmudic scholars wrestle with centuries-old tracts.

Visits to the grave of a departed wife suggest isolated moments of personal grief. But visits meant for conversation with the ghost of a religious leader (and, please note, meant for subsequent publication) are events of communal, and more festive, significance.

Can the mind's eye hold both visions at once?

Surely every motive that leads to the extinction of a young life, of *two* lives really (Cato's and Rosenbaum's) ought to be important. But what were the details here?

And in this case the details may have had practical significance, for there have been persistent rumors that the driver of the fatal car had been drinking before he ran the red light at President Street and barreled into the Cato children. (Police deny that the driver was intoxicated, but their reports are sketchy as to details.) Now, if the driver had been in attendance at a grieving husband's visit to his wife's grave, it is logical to assume that he hadn't had a chance for a drink. But a regular meeting between the Rebbe and his predecessor's spirit would have been both a public and a cheerful event, the kind of event, in fact, at which Hasidim typically celebrate with cake and "*schnapps*," or whiskey. So if *Newsday* was right, it was entirely possible that the driver had been drinking shortly before the fatal accident.

And if so .... If so...

Matters like these weren't on my mind the morning of August 20, when I woke up to word on the radio that a pogrom had begun in Brooklyn the night before.

Just as I did after the Lebanon massacres in 1982, I reacted to the news as if it were a transplantation from a collective past.

A pogrom.

Shrieks, clubs. Polish Jews cowering in their hovels. Peasants burning houses, smashing skulls...

Crown Heights. 1991.

A pogrom? That was the word I had learned to use for such things. A product of old grievances, I found its use vaguely satisfying in a way. "Every Jew carries within him some old, or recent, scar from an inflicted humiliation," wrote Jacobo Timerman in a book-length denunciation of Israel's 1982 Lebanon invasion—the invasion that brought about the tragedy of Sabra and Shatila and thus launched, among other things, my own search for Jewish tradition. We carry those humiliations with us, says Timerman. So we also carry the words for them. And, of course, there's a cost attached to that kind of memory. "Heroism," Timerman writes, "is a daily need."

But heroism against what? Against the old scars or the new? Is it courageous to fight valiantly in a battle that ended long ago? Or to start one that nobody wants? Could it actually be more heroic—to forget?

What do we know about Gavin Cato? I mean, except for the fact that his death started a riot and caused a murder?

New York Newsday claimed that according to "family members," Gavin and Angela Cato (who was also injured by the Hasidic car that killed Gavin) "had always played with neighborhood Jewish children."

A poignant reflection, and obviously meant to be.

It would be nice to look at what happened to Gavin as merely ironic and, therefore, as ultimately accidental. Then the tragedy of his death would be that it *was* an accident, keeping the story clear of more complicated regions of act and motive.

But that cannot be. I have never yet met a Lubavitcher, in Crown Heights or out of it, who has told me of seeing Lubavitch children playing with black youngsters. Quite the opposite, in fact.

"Do I send my children to school with them? No. Do I invite them in my house? No. We're just different," a Lubavitcher named Yeshaya ben-Abraham told *The Daily News* after the rioting. "We have different diets, different habits, different music…. We don't want it, a 'coming together.'"

I'm sure ben-Abraham was telling the truth. As far as I know, all the Lubavitchers of Crown Heights embrace pretty much that line with respect to "outsiders." So why was such a vastly different story quoted without comment in *Newsday*? Did someone lie to the paper? Did the reporter do his homework? Did *he* lie?

And why didn't anybody write in to the newspaper to point out the error? For surely many people connected to the neighborhood where all this happened knew that the picture it painted was a false one. Was everyone afraid to dispel the peaceful impression it suggested, even if everything else about the story belied it? Did the sentimental appeal of that one detail of the story outweigh its unreliability? What sort of service were we rendering the dead—or ourselves—in keeping quiet?

Says the Talmud: "While a heathen cuts your hair, you should watch him in a mirror." ... "Do not bend over before a heathen, lest he crush your skull."..."A heathen may not circumcise a Jewish infant, even if others are watching, since he may take an opportunity to let his knife slip and sterilize the child." A born-Orthodox scholar I met in *yeshiva*, a plump, hirsute fellow with stubby fingers and a good-humored mouth that played hide-and-seek behind the black tangle of his beard, told me once how a teacher of his, seeing him about to board an elevator along with two gentiles, grabbed his shoulder from behind and pulled him back.

"Most of us forget the laws about Jews keeping away from gentiles," he said to me. "But my *rebbe* never forgot. He told me not to get on that elevator until I could ride together with someone."

It's the word *someone* that sticks in my craw. That's how Orthodox Jews talk. A Jew is "someone." We Jews all know—it's a truism with us—that the seeds of the Holocaust were sown when Jews were dehumanized in the discourse of medieval European Christians. But we haven't yet explored the consequences of our own exclusion of non-Jews from the scope of the simple, ordinary words for human beings. I have no doubt that oppressed European Jews learned to tune out others defensively, literally in order to survive. Still, the anonymity of the non-Jew can't be rationalized as altogether innocent.

Not when one of those non-Jews, a young child, disappears under the wheels of one of our cars.

❧ ❧ ❧

If we know nothing of Gavin Cato, what do we know about the other victim, about Yankel Rosenbaum?

Well, first of all, we know that he was *not* the caricature implied in the *Times*' description of him—a description that was, in its own way, another sort of dehumanization. Rosenbaum was *not* a "rabbinical student": that error, deliberately or not, made him sound quaint and alien, a pale youth hunched over ancient tomes.

In fact, Rosenbaum was not even a "Hasidic scholar," another phrase that proved popular with the press, and which clearly implied a *yeshiva* student with a black coat brushing his knees and side curls to his shoulders. Rosenbaum was not studying at a *yeshiva*; he never wore long coats; he did not have side curls. The imputation of exotic Jewishness to Rosenbaum was a persistent mistake in virtually all newspaper accounts (and the point that resonated most immediately with my brother-in-law Jon). *New York Newsday* claimed (like Jon) that "Rosenbaum was a target because he was wearing the traditional garb of Hasidic Jews—a black hat, black coat, white shirt and tie." Except that this is *not* traditional Hasidic garb. And, more to the point, it wasn't Rosenbaum's: the only pictures I have seen of Rosenbaum, one of which was taken just after he was stabbed and appeared in several newspapers, depict him as both hatless and tieless.

I cannot believe this much-repeated error was completely inadvertent. The real Yankel Rosenbaum was something much more disturbing to the readers of these misstatements than the anachronism the texts implied. For the unpleasant truth was that in most respects, he could easily have *been* one of those readers.

Rosenbaum was a graduate student in history—at an Australian university (not a *yeshiva*, not a Hasidic *shtetl*). He was researching a dissertation on the Holocaust when he was killed. Except on the Sabbath, he often wore black denim jeans. Apart from the skullcap and the dense beard, Yankel Rosenbaum walking around Crown Heights might have been almost any graduate-level university student on a study break.

He was twenty-nine years old at the time of his murder—tall, thin, gregarious, a popular man. Maybe the most poignant story about Rosenbaum accentuates how little of the fringe figure there was about him. A friend of his, another Orthodox Jew, happened to be gay, something completely unacceptable in Orthodox circles. Shortly before Rosenbaum's death, his friend told him the truth about himself. He remembers that Rosenbaum said simply and gently, "We have to talk about this." No theatrics, no lectures, no expressions of horror.

I think *this* was what really terrified so many newspaper readers, Jewish and non-Jewish, about Rosenbaum: his ordinariness. Like the gas station attendant outside Atlanta (upset because he couldn't find anything bizarre about me) the newspaper writers were frustrated that this Jewish casualty of an anti-Jewish riot was—well, *normal*. He was not exotic; not "the Jew."

He was "someone."

Over ten years before Crown Heights, Philip Roth, in his novel *The Ghost Writer*, had stressed how Anne Frank's diary brought the nightmare of the Holocaust alive by presenting its effects on a family barely distinguishable from its gentile neighbors:

To expect the great callous and indifferent world to care about the child of a pious, bearded father living under the sway of the rabbis and the rituals—that was pure folly. To the ordinary person with no great gift for tolerating even the smallest of differences the plight of that family wouldn't mean a thing. To ordinary people it probably would seem that they had invited disaster by stubbornly repudiating everything modern and European—not to say Christian. But the family of Otto Frank, that would be another matter! How could even the most obtuse of the ordinary ignore what had been done to the Jews just for being Jews, how could even the most benighted of the Gentiles fail to get the idea when they read in Het Achterhuis that once a year the Franks sang a harmless Chanukah song, said some Hebrew words, lighted some candles, exchanged some presents—a ceremony lasting about ten minutes—and that was all it took to make them the enemy. It did not even take that much. It took nothing—that was the horror. And that was the truth.

Writing about Yankel Rosenbaum, the newspapers consistently reversed that truth. For them, the point was not to arouse the world's outrage at what was being done to Jews, but to reassure themselves that the only likely victims were those who, in Roth's words, had "invited disaster" by being stubbornly different—who had done it to themselves. Now the object was not to circumvent or shame the intolerance of a world that persecuted those who would not admit (and who could blame them?) that the Christian West was enlightened humanity's highest hope. Instead, the goal was to invoke that very intolerance against the distinctive few as if it meant safety for all the rest of us. Of course, the effort was futile: we all knew that no Jew, however assimilated, was safe from identification as a Jew, immune from persecution. But the desire to escape that knowledge could be overwhelming. Hadn't Mayor Dinkins himself praised New York City, that bottleneck of racial paranoia, where Yusuf Hawkins had been chased to his death just two years earlier for the crime of being black, as a "glorious mosaic"? And didn't even Jews desperately want to believe the mayor and not what they saw on the streets of Crown Heights?

Yet Rosenbaum was not killed for dressing or acting eccentrically, not for repudiating modern norms, not for rejecting the "world." He was killed for nothing more blamable than being a Jew. And then, to add bitterness to the injury, he was caricatured in the press—for the same reason.

Rosenbaum was killed on his way to an acquaintance's apartment. He had wanted to get his hair trimmed before leaving New York on his way to London, to do more research. He knew nothing about the accident that had killed Gavin Cato. He did not know about angry people in the streets. Apparently he got out of his car on President Street, intending to walk the remaining block or so. It was shortly after 11:00 at night. A large crowd of black youths ran at him, shouting angry words he probably did not understand. There was a riot taking shape at the time, though he could not have known that.

One of the "youths"—like him, a stranger to Crown Heights— was a sixteen-year-old named Lemrick Nelson. The crowd around him was yelling: *Kill him! Kill the Jew!* Nelson didn't know a riot had begun, let alone why. He knew nothing about the Lubavitcher Rebbe, about Gavin Cato, or about the Jews. He probably had no idea what sort of provocation the crowd around him thought it had. But for some reason he understood the crowd's blood lust, its hypnotic rage. Carried away by the shouting, he opened up a four-inch folding knife and plunged the blade into Rosenbaum's chest.[4]

Mortally wounded, Rosenbaum spat blood at his murderer and the mob that had egged him on. "Cowards! Cowards!" he shouted at them, in his still strong, Australian-accented voice. "It was twenty to one. Unfair! Unfair!"

"Unfair" is the last recorded word of Yankel Rosenbaum.

I find myself drawn into this chaos of facts, if only in search of answers to the sort of questions my brother-in-law Jon asks. Or doesn't ask.

For if Jon is wrong about the causes of Yankel Rosenbaum's murder—and I am sure he is—I cannot say that the Jews of Crown Heights, as a body, were right in portraying themselves after the riot merely as victims.

---

4   This is based on news accounts published at the time. Later, testimony would suggest that Nelson did not stab Rosenbaum until police had arrived at the scene, when Rosenbaum prevented him from running away by grabbing his shirt. Nelson did join the others in beating Rosenbaum before the arrival of police, and did stab him.

No, the Jews did not invite attack by standing out.

But they had something to do with the miasma of bitterness that drove the riot. Too many facts stand between reality and the Jews' preferred posture of innocent detachment.

For instance: why did the twin brothers who accompanied the driver of the car that killed Gavin Cato, young Lubavitchers named Yakov and Levi Spielman—sons of Rabbi Joseph Spielman, an important spokesman for the Lubavitch community—why did those boys refuse to identify the driver to the policemen who arrived at the scene? Press accounts were perfectly clear about the fact, if not the motive. (One of the twins claimed afterward not even to remember the accident, and both were conveniently out of the country while the grand jury heard testimony about it.) What were they covering up for? Fear? Tribal solidarity? Reflex?

Why did no Orthodox Jew, as far as I can remember, criticize this conduct on the part of two people who were supposed to be supervising a driver, and who instead apparently tried to shield him from the police after he ran over two small children? The Spielman twins were young, yes. But they were not exactly children. Not small children like the Catos. They held a position in that car of some responsibility. And they were the sons of a prominent rabbi. Where was their father's voice? Where was the community's sense of justice? Does its implicit toleration of the Spielmans' conduct imply a repudiation of at least some norms of civilized law—the same norms, incidentally, we Orthodox Jews invoked when we condemned Rosenbaum's murder?

And if not, why not?

What does it mean for *me* to be identified—by religion, by history, by ethnicity—with things like this? Or with the Talmud's warnings about the dangers of all non-Jews? Must I accept these things the way one accepts one's family, with its quirks and sometimes disagreeable relations? If so, is it a religion I really share with my fellow Jews? Or is my belief formed *in spite of* them?

It's August 21, 1991. It's 7:30 in the morning, with a smoldering sun already well risen into a grayish sky. On the streets of Crown Heights, black mobs are shifting, shifting on the cluttered asphalt, hurling bottles and rocks at Jews, Jewish-owned homes and the policemen who protect them, the whole air a stuttering *bam-bam-bam* of concussions.

The second day of a riot.

And where am I?

Not there. Along with the Hasidim who commute daily from Monsey to New York City's diamond district, I am prosaically on a bus, on my way to work.

"They're killing us, and nobody cares!"

It's a shout from somewhere behind me, while vague shapes roll along the green chintz curtain stretched across the center aisle as middle-aged women make their ponderous way to seats on their side.

"The newspapers are calling it 'protests'!" the voice goes on. Shrilly: "*Protests*? 'Protests' when they're yelling 'Kill the Jews!'?"

Twisting around, wanting to see him but not to meet his eyes, I make out an outraged Jewish profile. The man is standing up at his seat. Around me the other men are sitting down, wrapped in prayer shawls and the leather straps of their *t'fillin*—morning prayers are under way. The passenger is clean-shaven, an Orthodox Jew but not a Hasid, and he is not praying. He's got a copy of the *Times* gripped in two tight fists. His head's pivoting back and forth, his black hair down on his forehead (the Hasidim are sternly critical of hair worn this way), scowling at the droning Hasidim around him. He seems almost at the boiling point. I realize suddenly that his anger is directed at least as much against *them* as against the *Times*.

The Hasidim take his meaning, I think, for they avoid his eyes just as I do, though they seem to do it much more easily. I suppose this sort of thing is old hat to them. They know they're different. And to be different, after all, is to be disliked. They're used to being misunderstood, even by other religious Jews, so much so that they don't even react when their antagonist reaches the next level of outrage, making his target explicit:

"People like you let them kill millions in Eastern Europe!"

Still no answer. Some of the older ones among them may carry tattoos on their forearms. Their families were among those the Nazis drove to slaughter. We all know that; the Hasidim know we know it. They don't even pause in their prayers. The other man, non-Hasid as he is, hardly exists for them.

"And now you want to do the same thing in America? Well, I say, never again! We will not abandon Jews in America they way you people did in Poland and Germany!"

He's throwing down the gauntlet, but even now, the Hasidim go on praying. One of them near me shrugs. Their patience, or passivity, seems almost incredible. And yet, on second thought, it makes sense. After all, what is this to them, out of two thousand years of pain and longing? What more can the world add to their indignities? To the Hasidim the future, as well as the past, is contained in the mind of the Almighty. They believe they have access to a truth that transcends politics and street fights. What does it matter if no one else understands?

The angry passenger sits down, and rubs a forearm across his eyes. "I just can't believe it," he says, not speechmaking any more, just talking. I see now that his pain is real, even if there is a formula in his anger.

"That kid Rosenbaum is dead," he says. "And what are we doing about it? Do the blacks just sit back when one of theirs is killed? You see what they do. But we do nothing."

And now, finally, one of the Hasidim does respond: "Listen," he says to the man at his elbow in this crowded, swaying bus, its aisle choked with praying men. (He is an impatient man. I have seen him snap at a woman who took a long time to walk past his seat one morning, causing him to suspend his prayers.) He says: "We're

davening now. *Bist du a Yid? Fashtayst?* [Are you a Jew? Understand?]
Let us *daven*." And he goes back to his prayers.

To this day, few people in the Orthodox community seem to know
(any more than the angry passenger did) that the Hasidim did not
"do nothing." Actually, many of the bottle-throwing hooligans on
the streets of Crown Heights that August were Hasidim: Jewish
rioters.

According to Police Commissioner Lee Brown, the night of the
two deaths in Crown Heights saw a "standoff" between two hundred
Hasidim and an equal number of blacks at the scene of the fatal
accident, at about two o'clock that (Tuesday) morning. More than
two hundred cops were needed to separate the factions. And the
Daily News reported that "by 6 p.m. [the following evening], rival
mobs of black and Hasidic protesters—perhaps 250—had gathered
outside the Empire Blvd. stationhouse, hurling rocks, bottles and
insults at each other and police."

So the Jews in Crown Heights were not, or at least not entirely,
the passive victims of aggression that many other Orthodox Jews
assumed they were (for our reasons), or that assimilated Jews like
my brother-in-law Jon apparently wanted to believe (for their different ones).

What were they, then? Fighters in self-defense? Thugs? Bigots?
Hurt and angry people trying to make sense of a senseless murder?

Does it matter?

Fully a thousand cops in riot gear filled the gray-black mesh of
Brooklyn streets on Thursday. They were there to contain the rioting, but apparently were under instructions not to take any overt
aggressive action. Their job was not easy: forty-three of them would
be hurt by day's end. Another eighteen civilians were injured too.

The police could not be everywhere. Many Jewish families in Crown Heights were virtual prisoners in their homes for three days, afraid to enter the street, afraid even to stand near a window. One woman later described calling 911 in terror because rioters outside had smashed her windows with rocks. "Would you like to make a complaint for broken glass?" she says the duty sergeant asked her.

"This is fucking insane," snapped one cop on the streets outside (according to newspaper accounts). "They don't want us to do anything. I'm not going to be out here getting shot at for nothing."

Meanwhile a *Post* photographer captured one of the most disturbing pictures from Crown Heights: it showed a terrified Jewish boy, twelve years old, crouching over the body of his unconscious father. The boy is shielding his face with one arm, his knuckles pressed against his forehead. The man lies twisted up on the weedy edge of a sidewalk littered with bricks (thrown?), his head away from the camera, invisible behind the black-suited torso, his black hat lying upside-down at his feet. He had been knocked out cold.

At the same time, self-styled black "activist" Sonny Carson was enjoying it all. He visited Crown Heights just long enough to ridicule mayor David Dinkins' warnings of mass arrests. "This is our turf, and if anybody doesn't like it, let them try and do something about it," Carson told a cheering crowd of blacks. "So all you young people out there, do what you got to do and keep on doing it."

Then Carson promptly did what *he* had to do—took to his heels. Soon he was well out of range of the rioting, or of the police.

Herbert Daughtry, Protestant minister and black spokesman, showed real courage: he stayed with protesters on the streets, resisting violence. They would protest, he said. They would not riot. The group led by Daughtry marched to Lubavitch headquarters chanting, "Yosef, Yosef, Yosef!"—a taunt aimed at Yosef Lifsh, the driver of the car that killed Cato.

Ironically, it sounded like "Yusuf, Yusuf, Yusuf!"—which would have named Yusuf Hawkins, the black victim of racial violence in Bensonhurst almost exactly two years earlier, killed by a car while running across a highway to escape a crowd of white tormentors.

During those three days of riots, I kept looking, without success, for a way to get into Crown Heights. I wanted to be there. I wanted to see things for myself, though not because I thought (as I do now) that the truth, whatever it was, lay hidden behind fogs of prejudice.

At the time, I wanted to get there for the opposite reason: I wanted to see it because my Jewish past and Orthodox beliefs had already shaped in my imagination a version of events I preferred to believe. And I wanted to confirm that version, and thereby thrust my Jewishness through the door of proof once and for all.

What did I expect to see—what did I think I had seen already, somewhere in the realm where imagination meets history?

I thought that, there in Crown Heights, I would see a drama illustrating how people's emptiness goads them to persecute the very images that tantalize them. The television wars. I thought that the rioting in Crown Heights was the raw exposed edge of American materialism (looting as the caricature of runaway capitalism, enacted by people maddened by the ethic of money while unable to get their hands on it), and that the tantalized poor had turned all the hate behind their anguished mimicry on the Jews— simply because the Jews seemed to have beaten the vicious materialist cycle, finding the happiness that had always eluded the rioters.

That's what I thought.

I can see now how neatly this would have satisfied my own needs. Maybe it's a good thing that no one would lead me around that neighborhood back then, and that I bowed to the commonsense realization that I had no business risking my safety by going there alone. If I had seen the hurled stones and heard the curses, I probably would have stuck to my prejudices, assuring myself that the evidence of one's own eyes and ears is too strong to doubt. Now I realize what a trap such certainty would have been. "I *know* what *goyim* are like," a Holocaust survivor said to me once. Facts mean nothing to one who *knows*. He carries his own reality around with him, all the more specious for being so bound up with what is undeniably true, his own memories and pain. Experience can be every bit as meretricious as faith.

Rabbi Abba Paltiel, president of the Jewish Community Council of Crown Heights, told the press, "From the first moment, it was obvious that [the rioters] were looking for an excuse...These are people who base their freedom on hatred."

Isn't that just the sort of assumption the smiling Pakistani on a bus had in mind when he asked me, years ago, if I ever thought about "the other side" of the Arab-Israeli conflict? *Do* we see the other side? Or is it precisely seeing the other side's fury directed at our life and limb that makes it impossible for us to see it clearly?

Lubavitchers avoided talking publicly about what was happening. It wasn't only Gavin Cato and the accident that killed him they clammed up about. Their natural suspicion of the "secular" press, sharpened by alarm as the riots worsened, led them to be silent even about subjects that might have won them public sympathy.

They would not, for instance, discuss the slain Yankel Rosenbaum. Not one friend of his interviewed by the *Times* would so much as give his last name. Every one of them told reporters he was afraid of being somehow drawn into the trouble if he said too much—even though, at the same time, Crown Heights' Jews were complaining that they had all been drawn into it already, and that their story wasn't being told. The old reflexes, the traditional recoil into themselves, held sway over the Hasidim. An Australian Lubavitcher, calling himself a friend of Rosenbaum's, gave an interview to columnist Ray Kerrison, but insisted on a pseudonym even when describing the streets he'd lived in for ten years.

"Go away from here!" a Lubavitcher shouted at a black reporter during the riot, as if sending away the reporter would silence the black critics, reverse political history. This was not stupidity. It was fear. Even when a grand jury cleared Yosef Lifsh, reputedly the driver of the car that killed Cato, of any criminal wrongdoing, and Brooklyn D.A. Charles "Joe" Hynes asked the presiding judge to release the minutes of the hearing in order to dispel fears that the case had been deliberately soft-pedaled—even then, all ten of the government's own witnesses refused to allow the disclosure of their testimony. In all, more than three quarters of the witnesses (presumably Jews) insisted on "secrecy."

From whom? The newspapers did not say.

Behind the silence, or near-silence, was a festering grievance. One Lubavitch woman who did speak to a reporter said: "I am hurt mainly that the media is saying it's a two-way street instead of saying they [the blacks] are here trying to do a pogrom. They're trying to kill us."

"From the start," wrote columnist Jimmy Breslin, who was attacked by blacks while covering the riots, "it was foolish and dangerous to believe that this rage involved only Jews and African-Americans. It is so much more deeply disturbing to stare hard at the situation and see that the rage of poor blacks is not against any specific group of whites, but is against all whites." Well, if against all whites, then certainly, at the very least, against all *Jews*. But it was clear from the newspapers that few besides the Hasidim themselves (and Breslin) were prepared to see it that way.

Yet that, too, was far from being the whole story. Other grievances were abroad in Crown Heights.

"We warned that the seeds of discord, [if ignored, would] reap a bitter harvest," lamented Herbert Daughtry at Gavin Cato's funeral. "I warned that there was going to come an eruption … that people were not going to continue to take this."

"When Mayor David N. Dinkins went to … Crown Heights to appeal for calm Thursday," reported *Newsday*, "he climbed onto the stoop of a building with bricked-up windows on Eastern Parkway. Until recently, the building was home to minority families.

"The landlord stopped all the services so he could rent it to Jews," said David Rodriguez, a Crown Heights resident, minutes after Dinkins left [continued the article]. "I used to live in that building." … Black leaders say they also suffer from an official double standard that has favored the Hasidim in the distribution of a dwindling supply of city-owned apartments.

It is hard to quantify humiliation or rage. Not all statistics support the story told by blacks of systematic favoritism. In fact, there are some indications that the political power of the Lubavitchers in Crown Heights was on the wane by 1991. But bitter memories die hard. Ten years earlier, flush with the rewards of political patronage for having delivered crucial votes to Abraham Beame's successful mayoral campaign four years before that, "several Hasidic developers in Crown Heights engineered the often brutal displacement of black and Hispanic tenants," *Newsday* wrote. In 1979, "City Council President Carol Bellamy … found financial irregularities, discrimination in job training and 'allegations of harassment and racial discrimination' in buildings owned by … Rabbi David Fischer," who directed the Lubavitchers' leading social service and housing agency.

Yet when the city later awarded three buildings to the Reverend Heron Sam to develop low and middle-income housing, Lubavitch spokesman Rabbi Joseph Spielman screeched that "the official position of the city is to drive the Jewish community out of Crown Heights."

One's sense of grievance has a way of driving other people's complaints out of mind. Could this be why we do so much complaining? Are we afraid that, in these complex days of Jewish statehood and Jewish-American prosperity and political power, releasing our own sense of victimhood would bring too many unpleasant complaints—complaints about *us*—to menace our ears like an evil drum-roll?

A local Lubavitcher named Reuvain Brenenson brought flowers to the Catos' home before the boy's funeral. The Rebbe himself, however, never contacted the family. He never even made a public statement deploring the boy's death. Mourners, nearly all of them black, walked from the wake to Gavin's home on President Street carrying candles. According to the *New York Post*, "they were flanked by police in riot gear."

Meanwhile, no black leader or politician attended the funeral of Yankel Rosenbaum, held Wednesday outside Lubavitch headquarters. Al Sharpton and Alton Maddox were holding news conferences that day demanding the arrest of Yosef Lifsh, allegedly the driver of the fatal car. Dinkins, who spoke at Cato's funeral, reportedly met with "youth leaders" on the day Rosenbaum was interred. He told the *Post,* "I was told by my people that it was not going to be a funeral per se, and I did not want to intrude"—whatever that meant.

Certainly the event looked like "a funeral per se." "Close to 2,000 Hasidic Jews marched behind Rosenbaum's casket yesterday for his funeral," Said the New York *Post.*

> Rosenbaum "came here to study about anti-Semitism and the Holocaust," said Rabbi Shmuel Butman, head of the Lubavitch Youth Organization. "Too bad he found the Holocaust here." Rabbi Jacob Goldstein, chairman of Community Board 9, compared the night of terror that followed to atrocities committed by Nazis against Jews during World War II. He said gangs "targeted homes that had mezuzahs..."

Considering words like these, maybe Dinkins was wise not to attend. But when he did visit Crown Heights' bereaved Jews, six days after the deaths of Gavin Cato and Yankel Rosenbaum, it was to stand stiffly in line in a dusty room at 770 Eastern Parkway, the headquarters of the Lubavitch Hasidim, waiting his turn to receive a blessing from the Lubavitcher Rebbe.

What might have been a painful political drama, had he attended Rosenbaum's funeral, was replaced by something painfully like political farce.

When the mayor's turn came to stand directly in front of the holy man, the Rebbe handed Dinkins two dollar bills, doubling the gift he usually handed out to visiting supplicants—meaning, as he explained to the mayor, a double blessing for "double the success." Under the circumstances, the gesture looked more condescending than generous, as if meant to remind Dinkins, as everyone in New York already knew, that the mayor would *need* a double helping of divine assistance in his upcoming bid for re-election. Dinkins' popularity was at an all-time low among Orthodox Jews, who represented a significant voting bloc. Nor were many blacks happy with his handling of the Crown Heights riot.

In a newspaper photo taken of the scene, Dinkins stands awkwardly before the Rebbe (who is seated), a *yarmulke* clumsily plastered to the top of his head, his white suit standing out nakedly in a sea of black jackets and hats. The impression of abjectness wasn't only from Dinkins' posture: he sounded almost sheepish when he asked for a blessing.

"You blessed me once before [before the previous election] and it worked well," he said.

Meanwhile, somewhere else in New York City, the black lawyer and activist C. Vernon Mason was saying spitefully of Dinkins, "He has become politically and racially castrated. He has lost all credibility with the people."

While the Reverends Al Sharpton and Herbert Daughtry crossed the street to the Crown Heights church to stop in at Gavin

Cato's wake, a man ran alongside them carrying a sign reading: "The white man is the devil."

No one contradicted him.

"I am convinced it's not curiosity that has brought me here," wrote Jacobo Timerman of his journey to the home of an Israeli colonel who had resigned his post rather than carry out his assigned part in Israel's invasion of Lebanon in 1982. "It could be a need to confirm, to perceive the material forms, those that endow specific existence to an event I regard as historic."

That noble formula almost amounts to a definition of certain aspects of religion—or, at least, it seems to explain how religion keeps us from forgetting the "historic." I can't say glibly what the Crown Heights riot "meant." But I know that it had meaning for me, meaning that attacked some of my tenderest points, and I know that "material forms" must keep it alive for me against the natural inertia of time and psychological self-protection.

"If we let events drift and drift and drift, we'll be back here again," said the Reverend Daughtry over Gavin Cato's dead body. "Do something now. Don't wait until it explodes."

Do something now. But what?

Maybe this plea (even with the unanswered question it contains) embodies a lesson that religion teaches about time. History moves us along without asking our permission. Its grip can be either an embrace or a stranglehold. It can wrap lives cut too short in a commentary, written by time, that is prophetic (a reminder of the aimlessness of evil) or cold and callous, depending on all sorts of things.

I like to imagine a spiraling of time that would pin me to experience even as it stimulates me with its own motion—surely much religious ritual enacts a similar impulse. But I'm afraid the ideal belongs to fantasy, and religion needs to distinguish fantasy from imperative.

Religion cannot dare to be fantasy.

I must learn.

The effects of the Crown Heights riots are not exceptions to life's inexorable movement, the emptying of facts into memory and myth. Even the immediate aftermath of those events was read as part of a narrative already shaping in collective imaginations, a filter for collective memory. On August 26, 1991, when all the fighting and the arrests were over, the riots claimed another victim when 68-year-old Brokha Estrin, a Holocaust survivor, jumped from her third-floor apartment on President Street and died on the pavement below.

Why?

Friends said she had been traumatized by the violence outside her windows earlier that month. "For the last few days, she would tell her neighbors and family in a variety of different expressions that she couldn't take living here any more," said Rabbi Shea Hecht. "She said this whole thing brought back bad memories of the Holocaust... She couldn't fathom why people couldn't get along with each other."

The accounts of her death stunned me, because they showed the terrible interarching power the present and the past can exert over each other.

On one hand, a memory of rioting calls up other memories until the ghosts are arrayed so thickly they suffocate the present and make life a nightmare, intolerable to the dreamer who cannot awaken. Yet at the same time, narratives triggered by one woman's suicide reach back into the past, revising, editing, probably cheapening the anguish that had erupted outside her window just weeks earlier. Was that riot really another "Holocaust"? Is it decent to put things that way?

For that matter, isn't it an offense to the recent dead, to Yankel Rosenbaum as much as to Gavin Cato, to slip their deaths into a preexisting story sprouted from events in other countries, events that ended before either of these two lives had even begun?

I think it is. And as a religious man I feel I have an obligation to resist the affront, the reduction of human lives to a fragment of an abstract legend.

But religion is part of the problem, too.

Religious people are spinning the legends.

Can anything stop this process, these interlacing fingers over the eyes I would like history to have? I am struggling to keep the images of death and violence vivid for me, if only so as not to betray the victims by letting them shrink to the dimensions of sermons.

I will probably fail.

Even if I don't, can the terrors of these deaths awaken a civilizing impulse, somewhere? I must hope so.

But where?

And how is it to be stimulated? Is religion right in teaching that suffering saves civilization from arrogance?

Or does such pain just sharpen the hates that go on doing the damage, thus proving religion right and futile at the same time?

Chapter Twenty-Six

I n some ways, I suspect I'm different from many others who have entered Orthodoxy. My enthusiasm—which in the early days of my religious development was taken for piety—was really closer to curiosity, or to a drive to find a reality of faith as deeply felt and lived as the everyday reality that had always dogged me.

The key to the foregoing phrase is *drive*. On my way to Far Rockaway for my first Orthodox Day of Atonement, my suitcase was stolen at the bus stop and, along with it, my one pair of shoes that did not contain leather (leather shoes being forbidden during the fast). So I walked until after the fast without any shoes at all, through gravel, mud and rain puddles on a bleary, drizzly day—not so much from pious rectitude as from a sort of gung-ho determination to have the details right.

Case in point: out of worry that I would be overcome by thirst during the fast (with its lengthy prayers), I drank so much water just before sundown that during the climax of the prayers that night I was seized by a ferocious need to urinate.

Services were in an auditorium in what had once been a public school building. Like most such rooms, it echoed with every sound. At that moment the only sound was from the massed voices of the worshipers around me crying aloud (I have never completely got over the uninhibited *volume* of traditional Jewish prayers) for God's forgiveness. Up front was old Rabbi Shlomo Freifeld, a monument of a man, now ailing with spinal cancer but still massive in his knee-length black caftan and full white beard, a man regarded with awe by his congregation and extremely exacting in matters

284

of religious observance. He had been known to shout down congregants who talked during the service. And there *I* was, slipping through crowded rows of devout Jews preoccupied with prayer, at precisely the moment when I should have been absorbing the words as intently as they were.

I don't know how much noise I made. I am sure my race for the exit could not have gone unnoticed, but I was past caring. The need in the bladder was so intense that as the noise of fervent prayer faded in my ears, I was hustling and sliding down the halls of the converted school building—I had no shoes, remember, only slippery socks, and the floors were made of polished tile, recently waxed—almost knocking down a boy (who was on a similar errand, I suppose) on my way into a low-ceilinged bathroom to relieve myself. The final note of the comedy was the discovery that I was disappointed, but not really distressed, when I got back to the sanctuary and confirmed that I had entirely missed the most important part of the prayers.

So even then, it seemed, my attitude toward what I was doing differed from the attitude of most of those around me. The coldly lit auditorium in that school building, so bare that the movement of a chair echoed from every wall, and so crowded that each time I stood up for a part of the prayers I had to wait for an opportunity to move my folding chair without colliding with one beside or behind me, was not congenial to subtleties of feeling. The worshipers around me prayed loudly, with exaggerated gestures, sometimes bursting into tears, sometimes slapping their chests with their right hands, as though to beat away a sinful thought. Evidently the language and rituals of the penitential prayers were exactly to their taste. (So were the furious speeches delivered by Rabbi Freifeld, as I later learned when I heard him thunder to a packed auditorium: "You live in filth! Television is filth! You *watch* it!"—and with infinite contempt pantomime the act of spitting on the floor.) Impressed but not won over, I muttered along in uncomfortable near-silence. Gung-ho participation didn't solve everything. Going without shoes was one thing; dipping wholly into the old prayers, their rhythm and vocabulary, their assumptions about my own deepest feelings—well, that was something else again.

A few days later I was celebrating Sukkos, the Jewish holiday that deliberately mirrors exile, during which Jews eat their meals in temporary huts with rickety, incomplete roofs to symbolize our vulnerability and absolute dependence on God. I sat in a crowd, in a folding metal chair at a long table in a flimsy hut on a chilly fall night with a wind whipping around us all, and I tried to eat my chicken soup amid the noise and the smells of things that had fallen to the concrete floor the previous night.

And I felt alone—utterly lost in that crowd. Cast away from my old life, dragged into a new one like a pebble rushed along in a river. And I thought: maybe this is how Sukkos, with its exile motif, is *supposed* to feel. But at the same time, I was sure it didn't feel that way to the people around me. *They* knew, or thought they knew, where the undertow of religious life was drawing them. I didn't know.

I do know that my attitude toward Orthodoxy isn't the conventional Orthodox one. That I've committed myself to living within the parameters of traditional Judaism, to defining myself partly by its standards, only enriches the irony. It means, I suppose, that I've become a sort of exile within an exile—an exile inside Orthodoxy (which is itself built out of the consciousness of exile), trying to build a vocabulary of my own from an assortment of symbols that are part of me without exactly being mine. I've come full circle: from an aspiring writer, struggling to bring together my personal history and my culture's language, to an aspiring Jew trying to find my own identity in the rubble of ancient legacy.

Of course, every religion has its special vocabulary. I worry sometimes about the religious language I've chosen, or that chose me, burdened as it is with so many layers of interpretation. I worry that it may numb me to the direct view of things. Oddly enough, it's exactly those things at the source of religious feeling—passion, charity, moral ardor—that may suffer most. It's well known that rabbinic methods can deracinate the Bible's plain storytelling. Of course, such a method can serve religious ends: the sufferings of its characters can be abstracted into tidy moral lessons. But if their pain isn't felt, what is the lesson? The rape of Dinah becomes a tale of comeuppance for the girl's forward behavior; a massacre of thousands of Israelites in the wilderness is rationalized as a fitting punishment for faithlessness. Even the prophetess Deborah's gorgeous brutality is sanitized in the Talmud to the point that her shriek of triumph in the fifth chapter of Judges (so like Clytemnestra's in the *Agamemnon*) is actually said to contain a lesson in *humility*!

I wonder if all this has any effect on the way we Jews, especially Orthodox Jews, internalize our ideas of justice. Do we worry more about the violation of rabbinic rules than about the wounding of a human spirit? And if so, could this have to do with the way rabbinic moralizing sterilizes the Biblical characters? With the way we've been taught to abstract morals from vivid narratives? For that matter, does the bigotry of the irredentist zealots who make up Gush Emunim, for instance, with their land-over-people policies, owe anything to the rabbinic whitewashing of Joshua's bloody career? Or Deborah's victory lust?

I also wonder if there's anything we can do about such things. Doesn't it happen because religious people always have to impute to God some of our own mental mechanics—language, reason, rules—with all their built-in limitations? Isn't that why the Bible is always so chopped and pruned precisely by its most pious readers? Why God is the most imperfectly realized of all ideas—because whatever the imagination can't see clearly, it swathes in false but familiar clothing, the way they bandaged the head of The Invisible Man?

I can accept all this as inevitable, I guess. Religion can have no more courage for facing the unknowable than we ourselves have. But surely there's a particular violence inherent in turning some words into flesh. How can we avoid cheapening our own deepest concepts when we insist on *explaining* them, as religion necessarily does?

Does the selective blindness that may be necessary in the moral interpretation of the Bible, just for instance, make any sense as a way of judging real people? (Was Dinah really responsible for her rape because she was proud of her clothing? Does a just God endorse Samson's indiscriminate murder?) It seems that a religious use of the Bible leads us toward just these difficulties. If so, does religious study predispose us to prejudices, to psychological hamstringing in our judgments about just those most essential and delicate points of human nature?

I worry, too, that the rightward drift I see among Jews today is happening largely for the wrong reasons. Much of it arises from a search for community. But this says more about the loneliness of our times than about the suitability of Orthodox Judaism to fill the void. The Orthodox community does not readily absorb newcomers, as I have found. And even without the newcomers, it's strained almost to bursting by its own internal pressures. Many B.T.s, reacting against modernism, are seeking clearly defined moral standards. But rabbinic legalism is hardly the royal road to certainties. The modern, fundamentalist taste for bashing modernism by positing a set of unchallengeable dogmas not only doesn't produce anything very convincing; it makes a coarse patch-work of Jewish tradition, which is long on questions and debates, short on catechisms.

Nor will B.T.s in search of an idealized past change matters by building a sort of *shtetl* in the air of their imaginations. If they try to imitate prewar culture by mythologizing the past, they'll only parody it. And even the parody might not be so much worse than the original. Shmarya Levin, a talented Russian Jew who knew well the prevailing standards in the ghettos of prewar Eastern Europe, wrote about them bitterly:

I would not be wrong in saying that one-third of the heder [schoolroom] hours were taken up by the stupid, ugly squabbles between Rebbe [the teacher] and the pupils; the remaining two-thirds poisoned by the first.... The heder, the narrow one-roomed school, lightless, unclean, laid its stamp on the Jewish child and brought ruin and misery on its tenderest years. In my time the Jewish heder was already an institution rotten in every corner.... Only the very few, the chosen ones of fortune, escaped from those years of oppression more or less unharmed, with minds and bodies unruined.

From *Fiddler on the Roof* to the modern B.T. movement is a long leap, but both have in common a sentimental sanitizing of the roots of today's Orthodoxy. The religious path that sensitive souls now would like to see as a way of escaping from the gray concrete of the modern world (a world "founded in inhumanity," as Albert Schweitzer said) once exercised its own sort of oppression over human beings. According to historian Howard Sachar:

In defending themselves against despotism from without... Jews frequently created despotisms of their own. Even during the "quasi-emancipation" period of the 1860's the lives of most Jews in the Pale were dominated by an inflexible traditionalism. A short jacket or a trimmed beard were viewed as symptoms of dangerous free-thinking.... Until late in the nineteenth century, those who ventured to protest against the usages and customs of the Pale were crushed back into conformity by the massive weight of tradition.

This is not the sort of life-giving tradition people like me have hungered for. And yet it's a real part of our history. We glorify it at our peril, for whatever history is, it cannot be rewritten and it does not stand still. However much we turn from a culture we dislike, we can never go back to what was never there in the first place.

❧ ❧ ❧

As for misguided traditionalism, we've had a bellyful of that too, haven't we?

The world was shocked when Baruch Goldstein, a quiet young Jewish doctor from Brooklyn, gunned down twenty-nine Muslims in a Hebron mosque before being beaten to death himself by other worshipers. (Israeli soldiers killed a number of other Palestinians outside the mosque that day.) An aberration, some said. But I had other suspicions, especially when a young man wrapped in his *tallis* on a Sabbath morning yelled at the rabbi from the back of my own synagogue, "Baruch Goldstein is a hero! He stopped the peace process. Kill them all!"

The rabbi had just delivered a sermon containing a rather tepid appeal for calm as Israel began to implement the Oslo accords. I knew that the rabbi, like most of the congregants there, was adamantly opposed to even this much compromise with the Palestinians, and that his plea for quiet had been reluctantly made. Still, when you hear the words "Kill them all!" in a synagogue, you expect some kind of reaction.

But there was none. The rabbi ignored him, and proceeded (a little sheepishly, I thought) with the service. People went on with their prayers as if there were no heckler in the back row, who went on applauding a mass murder in one breath and in the next calling out, with unconscious comedy, "I threw an egg at Shimon Peres. And I'm glad I did!"

Not long afterward, in November 1995, came the assassination of Israel's Prime Minister, Yitzhak Rabin. Now the Jews had turned their guns on themselves. Rabin's killer was a young Orthodox Jew named Yigal Amir, who (like Baruch Goldstein) saw Israel's Palestinian problem in terms of holy war and who took Goldstein's rationale one step further: if war with Palestinians was a religious law, then Rabin's acceptance of some sort of peaceful resolution was a crime against God.

The assassination made Henry Kissinger, of all people, break down publicly in tears. But among the Orthodox? No one seemed surprised; few were even saddened. In synagogue Saturday night, just after the Sabbath, where I first heard the news, it was being chatted about almost casually. Among many of my coreligionists the discussion was gleeful. The Arab-lover had paid the price. Theodicies seemed to ripen on every tree; some of my neighbors reminded me that Rabin had commanded the detachment of Israeli soldiers who had sunk the Irgun ship, the *Altalena*, after the 1948 war. "He killed Jews," said one acquaintance, meaning, evidently, that his murder was comeuppance for that old grievance, still kept alive by some Begin enthusiasts. (Never mind that the order to attack the ship wasn't his, and that he didn't fire the shots.) Jews interviewed on radio in Brooklyn's heavily Orthodox Borough Park were gruesomely optimistic; reminded by a reporter that Amir had not murdered Shimon Peres, the architect of the Oslo accords who had temporarily taken the slain leader's place as Prime Minister, one Hasid remarked about the killer, "Maybe this guy has a brother."

Perhaps the scariest thing about all this was the curiously passionless way it was said, as if it were a lesson written on a blackboard, a moralizing anecdote from the Talmud. Rabin might have been a cardboard cutout for all the emotion his death stirred among the ultra-Orthodox. The morning after the assassination I called a couple my wife and I had planned to meet for lunch that day and canceled the appointment, saying that on such a day Jews would not be going out to restaurants.

They were astonished. "Everyone else is," the woman said. "What's so special? Rabin wasn't one of us."

Well, was *I* one of "us"? I was like a man on a tightrope who suddenly sees that the rope is fraying at both ends. I couldn't go back. And I couldn't stay where I was. Between secularism and religion, I had cast my lot with the only side that seemed to hold out any promise of a future for what fuddy-duddies like me used to call "the human condition." And certainly the post-modernist world wasn't getting any warmer. But between reason and bigotry, or between peace and brutality, I started to wonder whether I'd ended up on the wrong side of a great divide.

After all this, what is my Judaism about? Why am I still so deeply engaged by it?

Maybe it's enough to say that I don't regret the decision to turn back on everything that makes up my life, to examine and re-examine, to widen the context of identity by locating myself within an older history and tradition. I admit that this choice hasn't been made cheaply. Digging deeper into a past that is only partly personal has meant sacrificing a certain breadth of freedom. Judaism's tendency to cloak its world in layers of significance and symbolism leaves even simple actions burdened by religious meaning. That has consequences. I cannot decide to take a Saturday off and enjoy, let's say, a good film. I can't write on Saturday, no matter how deeply the desire stings. Saturday is the Sabbath and films are off-limits; so is writing. As long as I continue in my own particular, traditional orbit, they will have to remain so.

I find I am more conscious of these demands, rather than less, as time goes on. Sometimes I chafe under them. I'm no longer confident that they reflect divine revelations of right and wrong—I see their human origins and human limitations much more clearly, and as a result, I have a harder time obeying them under pressure. And then I find myself ambivalent about whichever choice I can make: it's unsatisfying to fall back on a rule out of mere habit, but then it's equally unsatisfying to break a rule, to abandon part of an interwoven system of symbolic action, out of mere impatience or fatigue. Sometimes I miss the simplicity of my old non-religious days. And then again, sometimes I miss the naïvete of my early religious ones.

Yet I still think the demands have been worth the trip. Without taking me far physically, my journey has introduced me to a world that contains as rich an experience of life as any I've ever heard of. I would never have met the Peruvian priest, the brilliant Rabbi Sirkin, the drifter I call The Creature (who read my short stories), or any of the other troubled or driven souls I've described here if I had stayed where I was—in middle-class suburbia—or gone into the heady groves of an academic Arcadia. Orthodoxy has sometimes been confining. It has never been dull.

Most of all, in the years I've been traveling back into my religious heritage, I've experienced the most tantalizing of discoveries: I've experienced a part, a very deep part, of *myself*—a part I would never have known if I hadn't taken a step back from me as I am now to consider my moral and cultural antecedents.

One way of describing the way I've tried to live is to paraphrase the familiar story of the creative movement of the nineteen-sixties (my first complete decade), and the idea it offered of "finding" oneself: one of its most popular phrases. As a matter of fact, the first stirrings of the B.T. movement in America were discernible about that time. I know I was influenced by the youth movement of those days, which spoke of escaping from contemporary conditions and discovering eternal truths.

But I'm also conscious of having turned the metaphor of self-discovery on its head. And that's something for which a specifically religious life must take at least some of the credit (or blame). The quest for oneself was allowed to take many forms in the heady days of the Sixties. But under the seldom-questioned influence of progressivism, most people assumed back then that it was to be at least a movement *forward*—the encounter with perfection to take place in a world of the future, when all our contemporary dross had been purged.

But I, with others like me, ended up taking the trip in a very different way. I had watched the progressives shy off in every conceivable direction, and I was unable to bring myself to label any of their sidelong responses a way "forward." I had lived with international do-goodism and My Lai; with the national security as defined by Richard Nixon; with medicine and psychology (America's two most respected expert professions) tainted with suspicions of institutional megalomania. Even good old liberal humanism could be caricatured in the "realistic" creed of a Democratic governor of Colorado, Richard Lamm, who declared that old people "have a duty to die" to make room for more productive citizens. Progress itself, I had begun to suspect, was an exercise in self-definition, a surrender to ideologically grounded claims of what "progress" ought to be. Was it good? Who was it good *for*? How were the new principles supposed to answer those old questions?

That may sound like an arrogant way of thinking. Maybe it was. But whatever it was, it pushed many of us to look behind "progress" for an older ideal. In one obvious sense, this was the ordained movement in reverse—a movement *backward*. But of course it wasn't only that. Turning back is never the same as not moving from the past at all. The question I started by asking—and it's the question I am still asking, many years later, though its object changes as often and as thoroughly as I do—was how the world I knew, so clearly an incomplete and imperfect world, had got that way: where it had taken the wrong turn on the road toward self-discovery. History can be flight as well as advance. Had the last two hundred years (during which traditional Judaism had fallen out of fashion) produced a better machinery for apprehending truth? Wasn't it possible that the recipe for reality I had been handed at birth was not really "the future" (meaning the full possibilities of the future) but, by a paradox of fate, a movement off course? That the keys to the real future lay somewhere in the past, forgotten or discarded?

Arrogant or not, these seemed like real questions to me. They still do. The knowledge of the past can't simply be shrugged off. Even the most modern wisdom has to cohere somehow with what can only be called truth. And if wisdom may be sought in the future, truth cannot be: whatever it is, it already exists, already *has* existed.

And the harder I looked for that moment at which my life seemed to have turned onto the wrong road, the more convinced I became that the moment had passed long ago. Long before I, or my parents, had ever lived.

Epilogue

I am on the Monsey bus again, this time heading back from a long day of work in Manhattan. The bus is crowded as usual. Because it's springtime, and daylight lasts until after six o'clock or so, I've just recited afternoon prayers (which must be said before sunset) with the Hasidim on the bus: gripping the overhead racks while standing and praying, swaying back and forth with the movements of the aluminum shell, rocking into the heavy green curtain, dusty and stale-smelling, down the middle of the aisle. Now I'm resting in my seat and watching Monsey draw nearer.

The timelessness! Next to me, a Hasid is studying his Talmud. I happen to know the passage he is reading and as I glance at the book in his lap my mind rapidly makes connections, hopping from commentary to commentary, remembering the questions and challenges posed by the text.

Then I think of the age of the chain of commentary my own thoughts have just joined. And of the endless daily cycles, eerily like those of this commuting bus, back and forth, home to work to home again, that make up a life.

And I recall some beautiful lines from Yeats:

When you are old and gray and full of sleep,
And nodding by the fire, take down this book,
And slowly read, and dream of the soft look
Your eyes had once, and of their shadows deep;

How many loved your moments of glad grace,

And loved your beauty with love false or true,
But one man loved the pilgrim soul in you,
And loved the sorrows of your changing face;

And bending down beside the glowing bars,
Murmur, a little sadly, how Love fled
And paced upon the mountains overhead
And hid his face amid a crowd of stars.

Curiously, living with so much attention to the past means that I'm constantly thinking about the future—about a time when *this* time will be the past. I think about the time when *my* loves may have fled and hidden. How will people see me then, denuded of the passions that drove me? How will my children feel about the path I set them on, by deliberately turning back from the one set for me?

I think Yeats would have understood. I mean, does it seem like an accident that his love poem hints at the terms of the divine love described by the biblical Jeremiah? I'm thinking especially of this passage:

I remember thee, the kindness of thy youth, the love of thine espousals, when thou wentest after me in the wilderness...

Or this one, from Hosea:

When Israel was a child, then I loved him, and called my son out of Egypt... I taught Ephraim also to go, taking them by their arms; but they knew not that I healed them. I drew them with bands of love; and I was to them as they that take off the yoke on their jaws...

For the "pilgrim soul," substitute the literal pilgrimage out of Egypt. For the sorrows of the "changing face," substitute the vicissitudes of the wilderness and the beloved nation's failure to follow God's love through those "changes." And remember that both prophets, like Moses before them, tell us that when God's ardor was sufficiently frustrated, he eventually did hide himself in the heavens, like the lover in the poem. I suppose Yeats, writing of love that "hid his face amid a crowd of stars" was no different from anyone in the West, haunted by images of longing and exile like these, images that shape not only our ideas of love but our hopes for redemption.

The images may last forever, but do they really belong here? Do I? More than ever, it seems to me, I keep asking myself—even sitting here wearily on a familiar bus—*What am I doing here?* I asked myself that same question years ago, lying inches from Janet in a dark apartment in Bloomfield, New Jersey, and at the time I was naïve enough to believe I'd answer it finally and forever and get over all the anguish of it, just by traditionalizing my religious observance.

No such luck.

But what is *anybody* doing here? Where does anybody stand in all of this? Since the pervasive disillusion of the moment has extended to what we used to call, with touching optimism, "human nature" (not to mention the religious and moral ideas built on the idea of such a "nature") I know all too well that religion isn't a panacea amid so much dislocation.

But does that prevent looking back—looking back even harder, maybe, more longingly, because we look back from a less naïve perspective? Wasn't it Adam and Eve's new knowledge, which spoiled Eden for them, that sharpened their desire for it? Isn't the Promised Land even more precious if we know we need to improve it before we can truly return to it? If we go back to old shrines chastened by experience—more hesitant, less zealous, less secure—isn't the overall gain in wisdom worth the ambiguous loss in faith?

The Hasid next to me doesn't give me much time to think about any of this. He wants to talk. He chuckles loudly and points at the green road sign indicating our approach to Monsey.

"Did you know Monsey is a big city?" he asks me, in his nasal accent.

"Is it?" After all, Monsey is barely a small town.

"There's a map in heaven," he explains buoyantly. "In heaven the important things are big and the unimportant things are small. The big *goyishe* cities, they're nothings. You might hardly find Manhattan at all. Monsey, with so many religious Jews, where they study the Torah—that's a *metropolis*."

I like looking at his curly, uneven beard as he talks animatedly. "Maybe any place is big," I suggest, "if seen from deep enough inside."

He regards me with some puzzlement, half certain I am agreeing with him but not quite understanding my lingo. Then an idea strikes him.

"You're, how you say, a B.T., aren't you? You weren't always religious?"

No, I wasn't, I admit.

"Ah, I thought so."

A smile.

"*Nu*, a B.T. may be raised with strange ideas, but you can come out of it. Just keep learning."

Our bus has reached Monsey. We get out and go our separate ways.

Made in the USA
Columbia, SC
15 September 2020

20746928R00173